The Great Indian
WEDDING
PLANNER

Sonam Poddar Hissaria

wisdom
tree

ISBN 978-81-8328-457-8

Published by
Wisdom Tree
4779/23, Ansari Road
Darya Ganj, New Delhi-110 002
Ph.: 011-23247966/67/68
wisdomtreebooks@gmail.com

Printed in India

Contents

To my grandfather, my idol,
and my son, my strength.

Preface

As a young girl growing up in a Marwari family, I was fascinated by weddings from an early age. Replete with colourful rituals, elaborate arrangements, entertaining games, song and dance, laughter and tears and family bonding—weddings have always had a special magic for me. As I grew up, I had many opportunities to plan small events for my family and learnt that organising an event can be a lot of fun. While I went on to qualify as a software engineer, and became a mother, my passion for wedding planning continued. It developed from a childhood interest, became a hobby and has now become my profession.

I run a wedding planning website www.shaadietyadi.com where I offer brides-to-be professional help with all aspects of organising a wedding. This book emerged out of the same passion to help brides have fun while planning their wedding, create a joyful occasion on the happiest day of their lives and conjure up wonderful memories that will last for a lifetime. Having said this, I will not claim any credit for the ideas presented in the book. While some of the ideas have emerged out of my experience of organising weddings, many others are the result of extensive online research, which are listed as sources in the Bibliography. I hope this book helps many brides plan the perfect wedding of their dreams.

Introduction

Matches are made in heaven...but weddings have to be planned here, on earth...and wedding planning is known to have turned many a pretty bride into a bridezilla!

Doesn't every girl dream of a perfect wedding? This book is for every bride wanting to celebrate this momentous event in a befitting manner and within her budget.

Indian weddings are renowned the world over their joy and exuberance. An event so grand however, demands a lot of work—more than you think! And this book can be your guide.

Once you decide on the number of events you wish to include and the number of days you plan to spread them over, this book can help you plan all that follows. From setting the budget to choosing the theme, there are tips to help you all the way.

Having an event manager is beneficial as a professional with good knowledge of your customs can help you plan your wedding better. This book can help you choose someone who fits both your budget and your personality.

Let me help you get organised with my idea of a wedding binder. Trust me, it will prove to be your saviour in a number of ways.

The wedding invite is the preview to the wedding and it will be received by an audience bigger than that attends the wedding. Designing of wedding cards should thus be inculcated in the planning stage, only then will it reflect the theme of the wedding perfectly.

Shortlisting and selecting the venue is one of the most important decisions you'll make in the event planning process. The process of shortlisting the perfect venue has been dealt with in detail.

Wedding albums are treasured memories and the perfect picture instantly takes you back to the happiest day of your life. Choosing the wedding photographer may well be the most important wedding-related decision you take. Following the details listed here can help you select the best photographer to record your Big Day.

Food plays a very important role in Indian weddings and maximum care is taken to serve the choicest delicacies to the guests. Ensuring that the food served at different events is liked by all is a complex task. I will help you choose the right caterer and prepare the menus.

This book serves as a guide on how simple dietary changes and some age-old beauty regimes included in a bride's daily routine would work wonders. It also includes tips on bridal attire, jewellery, choosing the right hairdo and make-up stylists. The book also contains a small guide so that the bride can do her own make-up for smaller functions.

The book provides a number of checklists, which act like a planning monitor, ensuring timely completion of various tasks.

And yes, the most important of all—budget! I have detailed all that you would need to plan and maintain your wedding budget along with some very simple but powerful money saving tips.

There is also a little guide to help you plan your honeymoon.

Beautifully dressed ladies, fun mehendi celebrations, a grand *baraat* accompanied by dhol beats, dance, music and a lavish buffet… Sounds like a perfect wedding, we say!

But, beneath all these celebrations, there are the jitters of preparations, which keep both the families on their toes all the time. So let's make things easier for you! Just read on and follow the tips to make sure that your D-day is absolutely perfect!

This book is a simple guide to planning your big day…the perfect way!

Chapter 1

Manage Time, Don't Race It

It's a busy weekday morning and a mountain of paperwork awaits you, yet you go googling for that perfect caterer for your wedding reception. It's consuming you now that the big day is drawing near and so much remains undone. Are you panicking? It's okay; this pre-wedding time is difficult for all.

Brace Yourself for the Crunch

The heaviest wedding-planning activity takes place right after you get engaged—when you set your budget and zero in onto your reception venue and then again towards the end—when you attend to details like the wedding outfit trials and shopping favours for guests. So you need to get organised, right from the get-go. Remember that as days get busier, every free moment of yours will go in planning.

CREATE FREE TIME

- Get to the office early and start emailing your vendors to get the ball rolling.
- Make a couple of follow-up calls during your coffee break.
- If possible, use your commuting time to pore over the contracts. Update your to-do list.

- As you lunch at your desk, file research in your binders or update your wedding budget.
- Other doable lunch-hour tasks—update your wedding website. Research honeymoon destinations.
- If you get a longer lunch break and can step out of office, shop for favours. And if it's a pleasant day, head outside with your cell phone and call vendors.
- Have a doctor's appointment? Take along the wedding photographer's work samples. Examine them while you wait.

Just make sure you're prepared. List down questions beforehand to help you interview each vendor quickly but thoroughly. Asking vendors to email you samples of their work can speed up the appointment process.

HI-TECH BRIDES STAND TO WIN

Busy brides must go hi-tech to save time. Besides smartphones, use special wedding-related software and apps like www.weddingplanning.in or www.planningpod.com to track your expenses, update guest lists and set deadline reminders.

COMPENSATE FOR UNEXPECTED PROBLEMS

Even with the best-laid plans, things come up. You find that your chosen reception venue isn't available, and you need to take a couple of extra mornings off to visit more sites. The friend who was going to help out with the wedding invitations may come down with flu. Tackle it calmly. Tell your boss upfront that at times, you'll need to step out during office hours. Ask if you can work some Saturdays instead to compensate. This way you will not sound out-of-control or irresponsible. Arrange to work late, if you're scheduling early morning vendor appointments. Reassure your boss that you will meet all your project deadlines.

As you've no doubt discovered, the pre-wedding period can be very challenging for you are juggling million new tasks along with the demands of normal life! Time management helps you assert greater control over your use of time and energy rather than allowing tasks and demands to control you. It's a given that you'll never be able to do everything that you think you should. Time management techniques ensure that the activities you don't do are those of your choice—your lowest priorities.

Primary Tools of Time Management:
- Lists of activities and tasks
- Schedules

These tools let you analyse, understand, organise and prioritise your use of time. They make you not a schedule and task slave but the master of your own time.

MAKE LISTS, DON'T TAX YOUR MEMORY

Lists are a key tool in effective time and task management. People without lists keep worrying if they've remembered every task that's important. You can't possibly hold everything in your head and you'll drive yourself crazy if you try.

So make lists for everything you need to get done. Wedding planning checklists are also available on bridal resource sites and this book. Have multiple lists for work tasks, wedding tasks, social activities, today, tomorrow, next week, for someday...you get the idea.

Prioritise the tasks and activities on your lists. Mark items H, M, and L for high, medium and low priority. Increase your motivation and get a sense of accomplishment by ticking off items as you get things done. Your lists help you decide what to do at the moment, what to schedule for later, what to handle yourself and what to allot to another.

If a particular task puts you off, tackle it later. Shift temporarily to another priority item. You can get two or three other items done in the time you spend fighting yourself over the difficult item.

Schedule to Work with a Smile

Schedules allow you to understand and plan your use of time. You do not have to stick to any particular schedule, vary and alter it as you see fit.

WHY MUST YOU SCHEDULE?

- Written plans make responsibilities seem more manageable and less overwhelming.
- Scheduled tasks are more likely to be completed.

- If you are current on important tasks, you will avoid worry and last-minute rushing.

Schedule Effectively

- Use a daily or weekly planner on paper or your smartphone app.
- Write down appointments, activities and meetings in an appointment book. Always know what's ahead for the day. Go to sleep knowing you're prepared for tomorrow.
- You also need a long-term planner. Use a monthly chart to plan ahead.
- Allow sufficient time for sleep, a well-balanced diet and leisure activities.
- Prioritise your activities
- Prepare for activities and tasks ahead of time.
- Plan to use 'dead time'.
- Schedule a weekly review.
- Avoid becoming a slave to your schedule. Remember to stay in charge.
- When substituting a scheduled activity, ensure you reschedule it to a new time.
- Be realistic about how much time you spend on each activity.

If there is very little or no blank, uncommitted time in your schedule grid, you will need to re-evaluate how you are allocating your time. You need uncommitted time to allow flexibility, accommodate unanticipated events, tasks and activities.

Array of Schedules Facilitating Time Management

Consider using the following array of schedules to organise your time:

MEDIUM-TERM CALENDAR

This is the overview, don't include too much detail. Enter important dates such as important events, projects, meetings, holidays and breaks. Post this schedule in your office area for referral and review and to chart your progress.

GENERAL WEEKLY SCHEDULE GRID

Plan your activities in blocks of hours throughout the week. Fill in all on-going activities.

ACTUAL WEEKLY SCHEDULE

Modify and detail, working from your general weekly schedule.

DAILY SCHEDULE OR 'TO DO LIST'

Complete the night before or the first thing each morning.
Include things you intend to accomplish that day including tasks, appointments and errands.

Tick off items you have completed.

Periodically evaluate your time usage, then modify according to your priorities:

- Are you using your time to best achieve your goals?
- Are you doing what you planned when you said you would?
- Can you identify areas when you can use your time more efficiently?

All this time management may seem like a lot of work, but you'll end up working even more without these techniques. Investing in time management pays off, beginning the very first week. Spend the time you save thus with your partner instead. And relax enough to enjoy your wedding!

Chapter 2

Hiring an Event Manager

You have found your perfect life partner and are all set to tie the knot. But when you sit down to plan the biggest day of your life, hundreds of questions arise: Size of budget, type of theme, the vendors to book and more. All the work that goes into planning your wedding can get overwhelming. Well, did you know, hiring a wedding planner can be cheaper and more convenient than self-planning a wedding? People tend to think professional planners are a waste of time and money. Interestingly, the truth is exactly the opposite.

Consider hiring a wedding planner to help with the preparations so you can relax and enjoy your big day. You can choose from planners who handle last-minute tasks leading up to the wedding or those who take charge of every event detail, from the engagement to the honeymoon and everything in between. The right planner not only keeps things organised and on schedule but also guides you when you look for the perfect venue, dress, cake and bouquet. Wedding planners have become so crucial to the event's success that couples often book the best planners over a year in advance.

Why Hire a Wedding Planner?

FOR ROBUST PLANNING

You will get a first-hand experience of professional planning for they start from scratch, keeping your budget in consideration while preparing their plan. They help select the theme that will extend to decorations, gifts and invitations, advice on venue, transportation and catering. They offer a customised wedding that meets your requirements and budget.

VAST VENDOR NETWORK

Professional marriage planners have a network of vendors who can make your dream wedding possible. Access to this wide network of decorators, caterers, printers and transport providers multiplies your options. Moreover, planners can negotiate discounts and get price reductions, which are unavailable in regular course. You save on costs and get assurance on service quality.

CREATIVITY THAT IMPRESSES

Most wedding planners are creative individuals who come up with interesting ideas that add to the decor and entertainment and make your event more memorable. A professional planner instinctively knows what lighting combination goes best with your theme. Also, they can advise on impressive venue and menu choices to make your wedding stand out.

ACCESS PACKAGE DEALS

Wedding planners can help you get package deals from hotels and marriage hall owners. They know where the best deals reside and help you avail such opportunities. Professional planners, also, fully understand all the 'conditions apply' and hidden costs embedded in vendor contracts which you might find difficult to decode.

ACTS AS DELIMITER

You may have lavish plans about the upcoming wedding and want to do so many things. If left on your own, your extravagance might make you overshoot your budget. A wedding planner can help you find a middle ground that does away with unnecessary expenses.

REDUCE YOUR PLANNING STRESS

Don't you want to be free to enjoy your biggest occasion? A wedding planner lets you do just that by taking away the stress involved in meticulous planning and budgeting of a big event. Why lose the glow on your face and look all tired and messed up, running after vendors and checking hundred minute details. These days, professional wedding planners efficiently carry out all tasks from venue booking to picking flowers, buying dresses to arranging guest pick-ups. Leave it to a professional to book, follow-up and oversee all services and also keep costs within budget. With them managing everything, all you need to do is look absolutely stunning and smile beside your sweetheart.

A competent wedding planner can ensure you have a beautiful wedding where everybody enjoys themselves without making it cost a fortune.

And no, if you are thinking that only the affluent ones can afford it, then you are wrong.

How to Select the Best Planner for Your Wedding?

Hiring a wedding planner is one of the first decisions you are likely to make in the process leading up to your wedding, so let me guide you.

DIG DEEP

From newspaper articles and advertisements to wedding websites, search widely to get hold of the right planner. However, word of mouth is the best thing to trust—married friends and family can not only provide you contact details of wedding planners they have worked with but also vouch for the professional's knowledge and ability to understand your requirements. Before appointing a planner, do your own homework—check her credentials for work experience and service quality.

Also, search for the planner who can be accommodated in your wedding budget. Make a rough estimate as to how much you are ready to spend on the wedding and therefore the planner. You cannot spend more on the planner compared to the wedding.

DEFINE THE PLANNER'S ROLE

Your venue may come with a coordinator but this person usually cannot provide all the services you'd like. A wedding planner will take care of all details, so take the time to find someone who can meet your planning needs.

Some wedding planners offer comprehensive wedding packages while others oversee specific tasks. If you prefer, you can even choose a wedding planner to help out just during the week of the wedding. This way, you can enjoy the process of wedding preparations but leave last-minute tasks to someone else which can alleviate a lot of stress.

For comprehensive planning packages, find out what services are included.

- Does the contract only cover the wedding or will the planner help prepare for the bridal shower, sangeet, other wedding functions and honeymoon?
- Will she help you with creative aspects of the wedding like developing a theme or will the planner just handle vendors, set up and scheduling?
- A complete range of wedding planning services includes everything from venue selection, decor, entertainment, logistics, trousseau shopping and packing, hair and make-up, photography, videography and more. Some planners take care of certain areas and some may handle all.

It is important for you to know if your planner would be able to handle all those areas where you might require their help. Don't be shy asking for services that may not be part of the normal wedding package such as coordinating a catered lunch for the bridal room on your wedding day. Most planners are willing to do whatever it takes to make your event a success!

EXPERIENCE COUNTS

While you might be carried away by someone offering to do things for you cheaper, wedding planning is one area where experience counts.

Find out how long the planner has been in business and whether he or she works alone or with a larger company. Affiliation with wedding professionals is a sign of experience. Somebody who has been in the field for long would have a stronger and wider vendor network that can be tapped to source talent and services aligned closely to your budget and vision.

Has the planner described how she handled previous weddings, particularly those similar to yours in terms of size, theme or location? View your planner's portfolio to get a feel of her work across different looks, themes and budgets. A good wedding planner would have a diverse portfolio, which means he or she can work towards almost any requirement.

Smoothening the bumps and soothing a few ruffled feathers is necessary before a successful wedding is organised, and you wouldn't want your wedding to be the testing ground for someone.

SINGLE PLAYER OR A TEAM OF EXPERTS?

Both have their advantages and drawbacks. If your planner works alone, determine whether she will be able to handle all the wedding details, especially on your wedding day. Ask the planner what happens if there's an emergency that keeps her from making it to the wedding—is there someone qualified to fill in?

If the planner works with a larger team or company, find out whether you'll work directly with her or with a group of assistants. Make sure you understand exactly which tasks the planner is going to handle and what all will get delegated to others (read: those with less experience). While a group effort can make for a successful wedding, it's best to find out ahead of time exactly who your point person is for certain tasks.

YOUR BUDGET SHALL CALL THE SHOTS

Your wedding planner plays a major role in keeping your budget in check. In fact, a good planner may even secure enough vendor discounts to offset the cost of her services. Find planners who bring steady business to vendors you like. These are the ones who will be able to save you money. Ask about their experience in negotiating vendor contracts and have them describe any great deals they've secured for previous clients. While you shouldn't expect enough deals and freebies to substantially slash the bottom line, the right planner can help stretch your wedding budget further.

Discuss your budget with your planners and make sure they're willing to work within these financial parameters. Beware of planners who try to gloss over this topic or seem unwilling to talk about potential discounts; find a planner who will.

Look for a wedding planner who fits your budget category. If your budget is tight, look for ones who can avail discounts from vendors through long-standing relationships. If you are inclined to spend lavishly, opt for planners who work with designer vendors.

GET REFERENCES

Ask for referrals or testimonials from previous clients. Calling up old clients will reassure you on the working style, reliability and efficiency of the planner. Also, try speaking to some of the planner's regular wedding vendors. They often provide good insight—comparing the work of one planner with others in the area. Request copies of any certificates or degrees the planner has secured relating to event planning.

Reach out to your married friends for their recommendations. Try attending a wedding organised by the planner you wish to hire.

MATCH YOUR VISION

To pull off your dream wedding, you need a planner who shares your vision.

Consider planner work portfolios that feature weddings similar to what you want.

- Someone who primarily oversees traditional weddings may have fewer choices to offer if you're planning something different, like a beach wedding.
- If you're planning a grand affair with hundreds of guests, a local planner accustomed to handling small, informal gatherings probably won't have the skill to pull off your big day.
- Planners used to handling high profile weddings with big budgets may lack enthusiasm and enterprise to stretch your small wedding budget. Most wedding planners rely extensively on their vendor connections and contacts and may not have the clout to score discounts or locate vendors beyond their regular network.
- If you have unique considerations for your event, make sure your planner can handle the challenge. For instance, flying 200

guests to your destination wedding in the Caribbean requires a lot of coordination. Locate a planner experienced in planning destination-weddings.

Personality Match is Equally Important

Wedding planning is time consuming and can be incredibly stressful. If you choose a wedding planner you don't get along with, it can make things even more difficult. Personality counts just as much as experience and reputation.

Look for someone who will listen to your ideas and work closely to implement them. In a meeting or two, you will come to know if the planner can visualise what you seek.

Many wedding planners offer a free consultation to allow both parties to test the waters before the contract is signed. Even if the planner charges a small fee for this initial meeting, it's worth it. Before taking a call, meet up with at least two planners to get an idea of what works best.

Get a Contract First Up

Often, there are a lot of arguments and conflicts around what was and what wasn't a part of the package. Get a signed contract upfront, to avoid hassles later. If you want some extra arrangements or benefits outside the listed packages, mention them to your planner beforehand. All this will ensure a smooth and healthy working relationship.

Discuss Attendance and Duties

One of the perks of having a wedding planner is that she will coordinate all tasks and events leading up to your wedding day and handle any emergencies so you can relax and have fun. Unfortunately, not all wedding planners are present at the venue on the day of the wedding. Some do not attend events scheduled before and after the wedding. So, before you sign any contracts, ask planners how long they intend to stay through the ceremony and reception.

If a planner won't be there for the live show, find out exactly what tasks she will handle that day in terms of set-up, scheduling or meeting exigencies; for example, running out for more spirits if the bar runs dry. Be sure to get the name of your point person for any other incidentals.

When the wedding's over, the planner's work isn't done. Enquire if the planner will stay back after the ceremony to supervise clean-up and collect and deliver wedding gifts to your home. Finally, ask if she will handle post-wedding tasks such as collecting your deposits from vendors and returning rented items.

DECIDE ON COMMUNICATION

With all the decisions involved in planning a wedding, you'll need to constantly be in close contact with your wedding planner. Before you select a planner, check how they'll communicate with you leading up to the wedding—email, phone calls or meetings? You may like to work on email or you may prefer meetings for a more personal touch.

It's also important to understand how often your wedding planner will get in touch with you. Some brides prefer weekly updates, while others want the planner to handle as much as possible without consulting them. Check the contract for any limits on the number of daily or weekly calls, and find out about extra charges for more frequent contact. Finally, if your planner works part-time, make sure she will be available at times that work with your schedule.

CLARITY ON SERVICE FEE

Looking for peace of mind on your wedding day? That's priceless. While you may not be able to put a price tag on that feeling, it will cost you. That cost is the amount your wedding planner charges for her services.

- Ask how the planner calculates service costs. For some, it's a simple flat fee or hourly rate, while for others it's calculated as a percentage of your total wedding costs.
- Enquire if there's a deposit and when that, as well as balance and final payments are due.
- Most importantly, get a list of all included services in writing so there's no confusion or disagreement after the contract is signed.

- Request that the contract includes a list of any potential extra charges along with an explanation of each.
- Finally, ask your wedding planner how she handles refunds if your wedding has to be postponed or cancelled. Some planners will return a portion of your deposit while others have a strict no-refund policy.

Don't hold back on asking if the planner can work on your budget, especially if you have a tight budget. A planner will actually be happy with this question as then the budget is being discussed upfront and there are no surprises later. This way you will also get a clear insight as to why hiring a professional can be great for your wedding. Budget planning is something that professionals can handle best.

A Wedding Planner's Laundry List of Responsibilities
- Find and rent ceremony and reception venues
- Plan a wedding budget
- Draw a wedding day timeline
- Recommend wedding professionals that match the couple's style and budget
- Review and negotiate vendor contracts
- Oversee quality control
- Manage guest list and RSVP
- Suggest/secure accommodation for out-of-town wedding guests
- Plan pre-wedding parties—engagement party, bridal shower, bachelor party, etc.
- Purchase wedding favours
- Accompany couple on wedding vendor appointments
- Design wedding look/theme
- Oversee all wedding-day activities
- Many more miscellaneous tasks
- Plan the honeymoon
- Set up events so that the client can relax and enjoy the special occasion

These are, by no means, the only tasks a wedding planner is expected to perform. People generally hire a professional to do all the things they are unable or unwilling to do themselves, it's likely you will come up with duties that aren't listed here. But that's normal. When you are busy ensuring every bit of your wedding is perfect, you would want someone more experienced and tactful to guide and supervise all along. Relying on family members can help only partially—they may fail to give you a clear picture of everything or even suggest many things at once. Hiring a wedding planner can relax you enough to let you bond with your partner's family.

Chapter 3

Figuring Your Wedding Budget

Marriages may be made in heaven, but they have to be paid for, right here, on earth. Suits, saris, jewellery, beauty regimen, sweets, feasts… weddings are the quickest way to spend a lot of money.

While the Mittals and the Chatwals have taken wedding grandeur to a new level, even the middle class often ends up spending far too much on a wedding, sometimes taking loans for the same.

Do not get trapped in excesses for 'marriage is not the end but the beginning of the shared life of two people. You do not want to start it on a note of debt'.

Indian weddings are known to be elaborate affairs, where families spend a lot of money to entertain their guests and celebrate. No matter how big an amount you are spending on the wedding, there is always a budget.

Plan Your Budget
START IMMEDIATELY
Your wedding is almost fixed. Congratulatory messages start pouring in. The most important thing to do now is to set the wedding budget.

Yes, all decisions thereafter will be easy. Setting the right budget is one mammoth task.

If only your pockets were as deep as your love for one another. Let's face it: Weddings can be expensive. Creating a reasonable wedding budget means knowing what you can afford to spend, deciding what matters to you most and then allocating your money appropriately. You can have a great wedding day, whatever the size of your budget. Making some smart decisions upfront can help keep costs under control.

Setting a wedding budget is the best way to manage spending. Knowing exactly what you can afford will help you better communicate with vendors and each other as you prepare for your dream wedding day.

Write down your priorities, stick to your budget, don't spend too much time getting distracted by images on social media.

Preparing the budget should be your first step. People planning a wedding for the first time are particularly susceptible to under-budgeting. So keep room for some unforeseen extras. Once you have fixed the location of the wedding, immediately start scouting for the venue. Your venue will determine the cost of many other services.

Envision It Right

Have you always wanted a lavish wedding with over 2,000 guests? Well then, the budget has to be grand. Or do you want an intimate one with just around 300 guests? A budget cannot be fixed until you envision the event in your mind. Talk it out with your fiancé and set your priorities straight.

Split the Wedding Expense

Lack of clarity in the wedding expense has led to misunderstandings between many a bride and groom and their families. To make the wedding a truly happy occasion, it is important for the two parties to openly discuss their financial positions early on. In traditional weddings, often the bride's family pays for the entire wedding. In a more contemporary approach, sometimes, the two families share the expenses.

Take a Realistic Look at Your Finances

Based on who pays for what, a budget can be drawn up. Figure out how you can each comfortably contribute to the budget without going into the red. Money is a touchy subject and being honest and upfront about how much you have to spend on your wedding will not only squash confusion but also set the precedent on how you resolve money issues once you're married.

Research Available Vendors

Most people do not have a clue what a wedding will cost, so first do an overview of all expected expenses. Set separate budgets for the wedding, reception, clothes, gifts, honeymoon, etc. Most wedding professionals will be happy to give cost estimates on phone. Consider major expenses like clothes and jewellery first, only then think about things like stationery and music.

Follow the Guest List

An important step in setting your wedding essentials budget is to determine how many people you want to invite to your ceremony and reception. The guest list dictates key budgetary considerations, starting from the size of your venue to the number of plates to be catered, the transport, gifts and more.

Open a 'Wedding Account' to Track Spending

Once you've pulled your wedding funds together, place them in a separate bank account for operational ease.

Set Budget Priorities

Resist the impulse to rent a Rolls Royce or limo. Begin with a realistic overall budget. Make a list of 'must-haves' to ensure you spend primarily on things that matter the most to you. Pick your top three priorities—attire, jewellery, food, invitations, cake, champagne, music, guest gifts, venue, decor, printed items, photography, videography, reception, transportation, drinks or honeymoon? Must you consider expectations of some important family members? If yes, that's the fourth priority.

Once your top priorities are set, everything else can be skimped on because it's a waste to go all out on things that don't matter much to you. Some wedding items and services automatically come with a hefty price tag. But knowing where to shell out the big bucks and where to cut costs can make all the difference in your planning. For example, you might want to splurge on a top-bracket wedding photographer who is famous for perfectly capturing all those special moments. To balance costs, you may then opt for a 'beer and wine only' reception instead of an open bar.

Resist the Urge to Splurge

It's easy to get swept off by all things opulent when planning for your wedding day. Resist it. While it's okay to pay a little more for big-ticket items—food and beverage, photography and floral design, you need to spend judiciously on gifts and miscellaneous items, lest they guzzle up your budget. Much as you'd love to give each close relative a Swarovski crystal picture frame as a 'thank you gift', why not shop smarter for less-expensive options.

Track Your Budget

If you somehow go over budget in one category, you will need to cut the budget in another area. It is important to stay aware of your budget and realise the ramifications of all your actions. Tuck a little away: Sticking to a set budget can prove tricky at times. Track your budget on spreadsheets to ensure actual expenses do not overshoot projected figures. Over-estimate a bit while making the blueprint and set aside contingency funds to take care of any sudden and unforeseen expenses.

Budget as a Team

It is important for both the wedding parties to manage the marriage budget prudently. At no stage must they let budget issues cause any emotional strain. Both the bride and groom should take the initiative to maintain a cordial relationship between the two families. This way, wedding planning will be fun for everyone and make for a happy start to the bride and groom's new life together.

No matter what your budget, knowing where you are spending and how, will help you think about the bigger picture. Which expenses are fixed and which depend upon the number of guests? Where can you reduce negotiable items to make room for non-negotiables? Budgeting can provide these answers.

Wedding registries and gift ideas are yet to catch on in India but it does make sense to state upfront what you prefer as a wedding gift when close relatives and friends enquire. You would not be stuck with three microwaves and no washing machine then.

Wedding Must-haves

Every wedding comes with a set of requirements whether dictated by religion, tradition, culture or society. The choreographer who teaches you the latest moves for the sangeet ceremony and the sushi chef specially flown in to make the starters may be optional. But certain elements are mandatory, irrespective of the kind of wedding you have. The first decision you will have to make concerns the venue.

VENUE

When selecting your wedding venue, both convenience and cost are key. If you are getting married locally, look for a place close to your residence, even if it means paying a little extra. You will be saving much on transport costs like hiring cars and buses.

You must book a hall six to eight months in advance. Ensure the contract says the price is fixed and there are no hidden charges. As the wedding season approaches, vendors tend to hike the price or levy extras.

You'll find the hotels and banquet halls relatively hassle-free as a professional banquet manager is in charge to coordinate things. In South India, *kalyana* mandapams are popular venues. These come bundled with a couple of rooms for the bride, groom and their families.

TIP

Always negotiate a combined rate for the venue and the food. Certain halls and hotels charge only for the food and the venue comes free.

TREND

After the Aishwarya Rai–Abhishek Bachchan wedding, getting married at home has become trendy. While this may be difficult in large cities where people live in small flats, it could be a viable option in smaller towns. In case you decide to hold a home wedding, add the costs of sprucing up your house to your budget.

Food

There's no easy way around this; your guests would be talking about the food served at your wedding for days after. And if the food turns out to be bad, they would be talking about it for months. So, this is certainly not the area to be lax.

Pick a caterer who comes highly recommended. Sit with the banquet manager well in advance, discuss the menu options and always insist on tasting. Even if the food seems good at the tasting, fall back on recommendations when you finally make your decision— food cooked in small quantities for the tasting may not taste the same when cooked for a big gathering.

If you plan to serve alcohol at the wedding, try and work out a deal where you can bring your own booze. Sourcing liquor from the hotel is expensive. Most hotels are happy to let you bring your own alcohol for a small concierge charge.

TIP

Negotiate a two-tier food rate: One rate for a plate of starters and another for the main course and dessert. Choose some excellent starter options and serve them. Lots of guests end up eating only the starters and do not venture to the main course. You save on a lot of unwanted costs this way.

TREND

The days of noodles nudging their way into the pasta, past the dal on your plate are over. Stick to one kind of cuisine. If you do want to have a multicuisine spread, you could perhaps choose an oriental cuisine for starters—serving sushi, spring rolls, wontons and others; Indian food for the main course and western desserts like mousse and crème brûlée.

Decor

This is an area where you can really go extravagant if you want to send out the message—I am having a 'big, splashy wedding'. Or you can choose to keep it simple, elegant and low-key. The venue you choose also determines your decor costs. If the wedding is in a hotel that is well-lit and maintained, you save on lighting and need not spend much on decor. Wedding mandaps and halls however, may not always be freshly painted, requiring extra attention and money for decoration.

TIP

State your budget to the florist or the decorator upfront and then ask them what they can do within that amount. If the decorator shows you his portfolio and you pick your options off it, you are likely to overshoot your budget. Also, do not decorate around a flaw like chipped paint on the walls; unless you can completely hide it, it's better not to draw attention to that area. It may work out cheaper if the venue has a tie-up with a decorator. But this is a must—supervise, supervise, supervise!

TREND

The trend is to keep it simple—elegant flowers, fairy lights and a nice colour scheme. Also, it would be nice to have an eco-friendly decor. Try and reduce the plastic content in your decorations.

CLOTHES AND JEWELLERY

Brides-to-be lavish maximum time, attention and money on this. It's also the area where you can make the most of your creativity. While certain colours and items of jewellery are governed by traditions, you still have enough scope to express your unique personality.

To get the best deal on your wedding dress, buy it from a store that has a very high turnover. If you want to get it tailored, then skip the designer and try going straight to his tailor. Designers outsource most of the work to embroiderers and tailors and these people have the experience and expertise to make your dream outfit at a fraction of the cost. Also, avoid exclusive boutiques that offer a limited collection of very expensive clothes.

TIP

Keep reusability in mind while buying clothes and jewellery. Most cities see wedding exhibitions every year, just before the wedding season begins. Visit these to understand trends. Do not buy from the stores there as they could be rather expensive. Once you get an understanding of what you want, go ahead and explain it to your tailor. You can also hire outfits for some pre-wedding events.

TREND

Check out the latest Bollywood movies to spot what's in on the wedding couture front. In jewellery, short-term trends should not influence your purchases, stick to the classics. Avoid buying overtly 'blingy' jewellery.

INVITATIONS

The first notice of your impending nuptials, invitations run from single page announcements to long-drawn-out versions that can double up as books. Ideally, have one invite, and small cards for different functions. This way, you can choose your guest list for each function. If you have friends, who are graphic designers, take their help to design unique personalised invitations.

TIP

Get two different sets of cards made—one for those who will certainly not be coming for the wedding but have to be invited nevertheless. These can be simple wedding announcements. The fancy, full edition can be given to guests who are special and sure to turn up. Instead of simply scanning the card and emailing it, use e-cards—they are far more personal and creative. Spend a couple of hours in the market that specialises in wedding invitations. You will definitely find better designs and cost-effective options.

TREND

Wedding invitations are contemporary Indian now. They have also moved from being a roster of family names to one that focuses on the bride and groom.

TRANSPORT/ACCOMMODATION

Accommodating outstation guests and transporting them to and fro can be very expensive, so budget accordingly. Try and find service apartments in your area. These work out far cheaper than hotels. Also, insist that the wedding venue provides you with a few rooms—use them as changing rooms and for guests to rest, if needed.

Hire a bus rather than several cars for the wedding day. Also, remember you would need additional transport for a couple of days prior to and after the wedding—to pick up and drop guests to airports and railway stations. Most people do not remember to budget for this.

TIP

Negotiate a daily rate instead of a per kilometre one. You will not be able to anticipate how many trips the car would have to make. Always set up a control room or desk at the hotel or the service apartments where your guests are lodged. All requests for soft drinks and snacks should go to the control room. This will ensure your guests don't run up huge room service bills.

TREND

Write a courteous letter to the guests detailing the facilities available to them. Your guests will get the hint what all are included and what they have to pay for themselves. Long distance phone calls made by guests is always an unpleasant surprise.

Break Up Your Budget

This budget checklist has been designed to help you determine major expenses that may come into play. Once you complete this checklist, you'll have a better understanding of what your wedding will cost.

Start by compiling a list of your finance sources which could be you (the bride), the groom, both sets of parents, grandparents, maternal uncles as well as other generous family members or friends.

In this worksheet, we will go through all the steps to decide how to plan your wedding budget. So start by coming up with a realistic figure.

Enter Total Budget

Once you have a realistic figure for your budget, we will divide that amount into various categories and what those categories should include.

Engagement Ceremony

The major expenses involved in this pre-wedding ceremony include:
- Rent for the venue

- Decor of the venue including arrangements like the stage where rings will be exchanged
- Invitations and postage
- Food and beverages
- Bride's/groom's attire
- Jewellery
- Engagement rings for the bride and the groom
- Photographer and/or videographer
- Gifts for the groom and his family
- Gifts for the bride and her family
- Sweets boxes and other favours for the guests
- Transportation

WEDDING AND RECEPTION EXPENSE (Assuming it's at different venues and different timings):

Wedding Ceremony: The ceremony involving *jaimala, pheras* and other rituals includes:

- Rent for the venue
- Event rentals—chairs, tables, flatware, glassware, china
- Catering and servers (including taxes and tips)
- Catering equipment
- Valet parking, if applicable
- All transportation like horse carriage for *baraat*, limos/bus for guests, family and bridal party that takes them to and from the hotel/house of the bride and groom to the ceremony site.

Reception: Your wedding reception will take up the bulk of your wedding budget. The budget for your reception will include:

- Rent for the venue
- Event rentals—chairs, tables, flatware, glassware, china
- Catering and servers (including taxes and tips)
- Bar and non-alcoholic beverages
- Catering equipment
- Valet parking, if applicable
- All transportation like shuttle service, limos—for guests, family

and bridal party to and from the ceremony site to the reception venue.

Music and Entertainment: These include:
- *Baraat* and ceremony music—dhol, DJ
- Cocktail hour—DJ, live performers
- Reception entertainment and music—DJ, dancers, live performers
- Equipment rental

Decor: In an Indian wedding, decor takes up a good chunk of your budget, especially because there are so many elements that go into it. These include:
- Mandap and ceremony decoration
- Chair covers/sashes
- Overlays/table linen
- Lighting effects
- Balloons
- Fireworks
- Bar arrangement
- Restroom arrangement
- Reception centrepieces and decorations
- Reception stage
- *Jaimala* stage
- Overall decor of the venue with flowers and drapes

Wedding Attire and Jewellery: These include the attire of the bride and groom at the two main events and all associated accessories:
- Bridal saris/lehengas/suits for the ceremony and reception
- Bride's lingerie
- Bride's jewellery for ceremony and reception
- Bride's shoes
- Hair and make-up (including mehendi) for the bride and the groom
- Spa (manicure, pedicure, massage) for the bride and the groom
- Groom's sherwani/tuxedo for the ceremony and reception
- Groom's shoes, *safa, kalangi* and other traditional accessories

Gifts: In Indian weddings, this eats up a big chunk of the budget. There is no list for this but it usually includes the following:

- Gifts for the groom
- Gifts for the bride
- Bridal trousseau
- Silverware and jewellery
- Gifts for the groom's family
- Gifts for *baraat* guests

Photography: Well, this has a long list—depending on your budget and requirements, you can trim it. It includes:

- Photography—candid photographer and/or studio photographers
- Videography—number of videographers and the hours of coverage
- CDs or other digital media with all the photos
- DVD of the wedding video
- Cinematography (a new video concept)
- Engagement portraits
- Pre-wedding shoot
- Couple portraits
- Ceremony and reception album package
- Additional albums/photographs for gifts

Stationery: This includes:

- Invitations and enclosures—RSVP cards and envelopes, maps, etc.
- Announcements
- Postage
- Wedding programmes
- Welcome notes
- Thank you notes

HONEYMOON

You should always plan for this in your wedding budget, lest it become a burden to pay later on, and you end up compromising. This should at least include:

- Airline tickets
- Accommodations
- Car rental
- Food
- Daily allowance
- Passports and all necessary documents required for travel to the chosen destination

MISCELLANEOUS

This is where all those random 'little items' add up. Make sure you have an extra cushion for all those extra expenses.

- Wedding gifts for each other (if you choose to do so)
- Favours for the guests
- Welcome baskets for outstation guests
- Hotel room/Honeymoon suite for the wedding night
- Accommodation for guests
- Wedding planner's fee
- *Dakshina*—fee for the priest
- Marriage and other licences

Use It Right!

As couples often find, your dreams may be far bigger than your pocketbook and you may need to cut back on your expectations. Although it's tough to accept you can't have everything, there are several creative ways of saving money—some of them are sneaky and simple, like selecting a natural wedding reception site, a place which won't require an expensive decor. A wedding hall properly decorated or open-air garden sites are best suited for low budget receptions.

An Indian Wedding Budget—What to Splurge on and Where to Save

This momentous occasion will undoubtedly be the biggest celebration of your life. It's your chance to make lasting memories and impress your guests in your own inimitable style.

Here is a list of items where you do not want to compromise on aesthetics or quality.

Food: It is the first thing that comes to mind when we think of an Indian wedding. You'll want to make sure that your guests get to feast on the best spread possible.

Photography and Videography: A good photo album will be a memoir that will evoke, each time you open it, the same emotions you experienced on your wedding day. Is there a better way to relive your special day with your loved ones? Future generations will see it as their legacy, so it is extremely important that you appoint a good team of photographers and videographers to cover every detail of your wedding.

Hosting Your Guests: In a country where guests are treated like god—*Atithi Devo Bhava*, hospitality acquires an even greater significance during a wedding. It's not only expected but also seen as an expression of our culture and values. How far would you go to woo your guests is completely your choice. Do you want to pay for their travel, stay, entertainment and provide gifts too? That's one of the things you need to ask yourself, keeping your budget in mind.

Jewellery That's Timeless: Jewels enhance the beauty of the blushing bride, more so when it has been handed down by the bride's mother or grandmother. A marriage is thus the perfect time for you to make something special that can later be passed on to future generations. Given that jewellery has long been considered not just for the purpose of adornation but also as security in times of contingency, makes it a value investment.

Wedding Planners: Being a new concept in India, wedding planners are wrongly labelled as a luxury expense. But planning a wedding is stressful—the pressure on a family to have the perfect wedding is immense. Wedding planners, with all their industry know-how can help couples determine the best venue and vendors and creatively package events within the specific budgets.

Honeymoon: This is one occasion in life that warrants spending more than you usually do. After months of planning, stressing and the hectic wedding celebrations, it is nice to have some together-time to look forward to. Soon you will be thinking of life ahead in terms of buying a new house, starting a family, so this is probably one of those times when you can justify the cost.

Don't forget that you are celebrating the union of not just two people but also two families. All that matters is that you enjoy your day. Lavish weddings are an Indian trademark. Everyone wants their wedding to be the talk of the town. Even after all the meticulous planning and brainstorming, wedding budgets often go haywire. So here are tips to make your wedding unique and special without having to go overboard financially.

SAVE ON

Prune Your Guest List: If you have already made one, recheck to cross out names of casual acquaintances. This pruning may be painful but the truth is that limiting the size of the event is the fastest and easiest way to control your budget. Again, your single biggest cost will be the reception food and alcohol, so you can reduce that expenditure by paring down the number of mouths. Make your wedding a small one, inviting only the closest friends and relatives to give it a more personal, intimate and memorable touch.

Pre-book a Venue Well in Advance: Early birds can clinch good deals. Booking eight-nine months in advance could fetch you a good discount. Invite several quotations to negotiate tightly.

Get the Venue Right: Select a venue that has a lot of character and inherent beauty as you won't need to spend much on creating an ambience then. Check for special offers on certain hall or venue bookings. Some venues offer props and decorations free of cost. Some offer waiters and hostesses. Also, many venues come with a pre-decorated area. If you are really tight on budget, choose a venue that already has a set-up in place and you can save on decor. A public lawn or community hall may be available for a surprisingly low fee. But be careful: A home wedding won't cut costs if you have to bring in additional restroom facilities, seating, lighting, etc.

Avoid the High Season: Industry experts say nearly 70 per cent of weddings take place between December and February when venue costs peak due to high demand. Even in matters of the heart, the laws of supply and demand apply. You are likely to get better deals on virtually every wedding service if you schedule your wedding in one of the 'off season months'. An off-season theme wedding can cut costs and at the same time put a veil on things you are cutting down on.

Save on Invites: Though they set the tone of your wedding by being the first thing your guests will see, with a bit of creativity and personalisation, you can come up with beautiful invitations that don't cost much. Just by making an invitation that is not oversized or letter pressed, you can save a lot of money. Reducing the number of inserts also helps. Large and heavily customised wedding invites chew up your wedding budget. Many volunteer organisations make handmade wedding invitations at a far lower rate—contributing to charity makes your invite special.

If you're looking for raised print, thermography is almost half the price of engraving. Engraving does impart a more formal look to the invitation, as unlike thermography, the raised print is pressed through the back. For larger wedding parties, buy at bulk party stores or wedding warehouses to get the best deals. Also, avoid separate cards from the bride and the groom's side. If you are creative, you can design your own invitations. Factor in postage, including stamps for the response card envelopes. Email scanned copies of the card to those living abroad.

Save on Return Gifts: You may overspend on return gifts simply out of generosity. Therefore, set a budget and think of ways to get value for money. Remember, your guests are there to celebrate your big day with you and that's what really matters to them. Traditionally, South Indians present coconut, blouse pieces and betel leaves to their guests whereas Marwaris tend to give sweets and money. If you have to follow these rituals, find ways to make them cost-effective.

Candid Photography vs Studio Photography: While candid photography is gaining popularity, studios are doing their job well too and the price difference is huge. A reputed candid photographer can charge anywhere between one-four lakh rupees for a three-four day wedding shoot, video charges being extra, whereas, at the same cost, studio photographers can provide you two still photographers and one videographer. For around twenty thousand more, you get an amateur candid photographer as well. So think over it! Photography is one area where it is difficult to cut costs. But there are ways to get a great deal.

Serve Themed Food: Theme the event to hide what's not included. You can save on the spread for the smaller functions by having a theme that's extended to the cuisine. So if it's a Rajasthani sangeet, you need only Rajasthani dishes. Stick to one type of menu—that's classy as well as cost-effective. Go for different cuisines for different functions. To save more, avoid serving expensive out-of-season items, and give the caterer some elbowroom with the menu. Continue your theme and budget-management by limiting the bar to theme-related cocktails and beverages.

Favour Local Fragrance: Select flowers that are in season and locally available. Availability and price vary from one city to another. But stay away from white blossoms. As they bruise easily, florists must go through larger quantities to find good ones that match the shade, thus the cost is higher. In India, options include native flowers such as marigolds, roses, rajanigandhas and jasmines, which are very fragrant and add immensely to the mood and traditional festivity. Reserve the imported flowers like orchids, lilies and heliconias for the more formal and western functions like reception and cocktail evenings.

Experiment with Decor: Decorate strategically. Spend your money on things people will see the most throughout the event—not things they'll glimpse momentarily. Instead of covering the entire venue with flowers, use adornments that are more unique, personalised and less expensive like fruits, balloons and ice sculptures. Use fewer flowers, but display them creatively. Additionally, try candles/diyas, ribbons and other materials. Using drapes and lighting with flowers can reduce your decor budget significantly. Add chair covers with beautiful bows to make your venue look dramatically different. Flowers and drapes can be seen and appreciated in the daylight. For evening functions, play a lot with the lighting. Place lamps and lanterns instead of spending too much on flowers and drapes. Instead of having flowers as centrepieces, place a bunch of grapes, a pear and an apple in a bowl, and spray them with gold paint. Ice can be sculpted beautifully and it doesn't melt even in scorching summers. Balloons are another alternative, especially for a Christian wedding. Lighting can be used to elegantly highlight balloons and other decorations. Get an art designer friend to design your mandap.

Look Beyond Designer Labels: Even though donning the perfectly gorgeous bridal trousseau is every girl's dream, see if you can give the highly over-priced typical bridal lehenga a miss. After all, you will probably wear your reception outfit only once. Emphasise less on designer labels and more on comfort, colours, patterns, fabric and cuts that look good on you. There is a plethora of options available at online stores as well as consignment stores where you can get equally beautiful outfits that bear a designer look. You could even have them custom-made by an upcoming designer, this way you get an original designer outfit at a fraction of the cost. There are stores renting out wedding dresses too. A groom's dress worth around ₹40,000 can be rented for a few thousand rupees. Remember, you don't have to spend a million to look like a million.

Hunt for Value-buys at Sales: Shop during sales, visit exhibitions and promotional events for value deals, you can get huge discounts on bridal wear during off-season, which falls right after the wedding season. Most sari and shoe stores hold annual sales offering up to 50 per cent off. Shop smart by choosing trends that are evergreen so that your trousseau looks classy and never outdated. Buy saris from wholesale markets as wedding giveaways to relatives. You get great suit pieces, shirt pieces and trouser lengths from mill stores—at almost 40 per cent less than what they are priced in the shops.

Don't Buy on Impulse: Plan all your spending needs and make lists. If you need crockery, durables or household goods, buy when special offers are on or from the company warehouse. You can get goods that are in perfect working condition but with a major price cut because they are slightly older models.

Accommodation: It is never easy to house wedding guests, especially the outstation ones. But instead of booking rooms in big hotels, try to locate a large farmhouse on the outskirts of the city to house your guests. Arrange for local catering and hire a bus for transport.

This way you save on expensive hotel room nights and excessive room service bills.

Go for Gold: Every girl needs a bit of gold, buy it when it's at its lowest (now!), even if you're not getting married for another three-four years—if you're reading this, then you're planning your wedding, so buy it before it starts climbing up!

Combine Functions: It's easy to say let's have a combined sangeet or mehendi function, both the boy and girl's side can organise it together. But who pays for it? Even if everyone is 'cool' about going half-half, these things tend to create tension, so think twice. Does that mean no combined functions? Well, not really, you can have your sangeet-tilak-engagement functions together. An Indian wedding is a three-day affair—sangeet, mehendi, *pheras* and reception. To minimise costs, you can cut down on the number of functions or simply combine them. Enterprising couples have hit upon the idea of holding the reception and the *baraat* together before the wedding. Similarly, you could hold mehendi with the sangeet. Engagement functions are unavoidable— you will be throwing a big party anyways, so add on to your dance performances and the tilak rituals. You'll have a three-in-one and a complete blast!

Draft in Your Friends: Another saving trick is to harness the talents of your friends. Don't be shy to let those close to you know you're looking for ways to control your wedding budget. They may offer their own skills or help you find a great deal. Your uncle with the classic car may be willing to play chauffeur for the day and your cousin—the computer graphics whiz might be able to create spectacular wedding invites on her computer; all you'll have to do is pay for the paper.

It's very easy to get carried away and there is no limit to how much you can spend. Know when to draw the line.

Hidden Costs that Upset a Wedding Budget

Hosting a wedding is a task that requires a lot of micromanagement. In the frenzy, it is very common to forget several small but very important costs that might upset your wedding budget. Here are some hidden wedding costs that you should be aware of.

POSTAGE

When you're looking at all those fabulous wedding invitations, pause to think about the weight and size of those invites.

What to do

- Take a kitchen scale and weigh the cards and all the elements you'll be shipping in the invitation. Heavy stock paper is exactly that, heavy paper.

MEHENDI

While mehendi for the bride and the bride's mother is a must, getting mehendi done for guests can be costly. Mehendi artists can charge on an hourly basis or a per hand rate. The per hand rate is based on simplicity of the pattern, how long it takes to complete the design on one hand, size of design—palm only, full hand, hand plus wrist, hand plus wrist and extra.

What to do

- Get that information upfront from the artist and decide the cost per guest.
- Decide on the maximum number of guests that can get mehendi applied.

PRIESTS

You may think hiring a priest is the easiest part. But you'll find most priests booked up during the busy wedding season.

What to do

- Find out how much the priest will charge for himself and any assistants he brings.
- Check whether he will bring the necessary items to perform the pujas.
- Book the priest well in advance to avoid extra 'high season' costs.
- Discuss with your priest what events you want covered in your wedding ceremony and in what order. Just because the priest is from your community does not mean he will know how your family conducts its religious rituals.

Wedding Trousseau

The wedding trousseau is not only expensive but an emotional nightmare. Packing up 21, 51, or 101 brand new saris, lehengas, and salwar kameez is daunting for every mother and daughter.

What to do

- Decide how many new outfits you really need. Really really need!
- Can you mix in simpler, western clothing like jeans, skirts and tops?
- Can you mix in part of your current collection?
- Instead of spending money on clothes that can fall apart and not fit in a few years, consider investing the money in a gold coin or a bank bond.

Videography and Photography

This is a well-known black hole. You can be charged for hours of post-processing if you want more photos than in the contract, or if the wedding goes overtime and you are paying by block of hours, or if you want a full set of photos. While the vast majority of photographers are great people, there are plenty that add in costs. Candid photographers who work on the Western pattern are more likely to add on extras; make sure they do not charge you an hourly rate. Indian weddings, unlike Western ones, are long drawn out, so book by the day.

What to do

- Get everything in writing. Negotiate a good rate for extra photos beforehand.
- Sometimes videographers and photographers sneak in extra costs for additional cameras, lighting, assistants, side photo stages and even jumbotron televisions. Cut them out to get rid of extras.

Events, Events, Events

How many events will you have at your wedding? Indians don't do the simple one-day wedding. Cutting out events can cause strife in the families.

What to do

- Think about how to make the events simpler and easier on the budget.
- Does every event need to be in a fancy hotel? Can some of the smaller events be held at your or a family member's home?
- Must you serve alcohol and meat at every one of those events or can you be vegetarian?

DELIVERY AND ADDITIONAL CHARGES

You asked your dress designer to deliver your dress at your doorstep but are you sure he did not add a delivery charge to your bill? Or did you spend a fortune arranging for the best photographer but forgot to discuss his travelling charges?

OVERTIMES

Most of the times, people book their vendors with a set time frame in mind. Everything from the venue to the DJ will be working according to the clock. But sometimes, weddings do exceed their set time. So plan accordingly. If your wedding is going to go on till the wee hours of the morning, then make sure that the venue and the photographer are on board without charging any extras.

TAXES

Each vendor will charge you sales tax or VAT or service tax. The government sets these taxes, and the percentage depends on the city you are in. So check with each vendor individually before giving them an advance. Also, ask the vendors to quote a price that includes all taxes.

VENUE FEES

Yes, we know that the venue fee is usually fixed but there can be surprises here too. After the wedding, the venue management could charge you for debris and littering at the venue. Venue managers can charge you for anything from candle drips to overtime, extra chairs to extra spoons. So, check for all these hidden costs (look closely at all asterisks) before you finalise your wedding venue.

Keep yourself together, breathe and be prepared. If you know there will be hidden costs, the costs won't be so hidden anymore.

Keep enough margins in your wedding budget to deal with such unforeseen costs.

You came up with a number. You did some research. You revised the number. You started planning and now that number's not going to cut it. If you find you've underestimated some expenses, don't panic. Instead, sit down with your fiancé and try to reach a constructive solution. Maybe, you can give up an item or trade one for another (for example, red roses over some exotic flower). If you're coming up short overall, you may have to take on some debt. You might consider obtaining a low-interest loan or using a low-interest credit card. And to keep it from becoming a source of tension between the two of you, sit together and plan out how you will pay out your debt and by when.

Don't pay for your wedding by losing your sanity or your shirt.

Going Overboard...

So, you have the moolah…what better way to show it off than during the grand occasion of your wedding! Oh yes, right from designer trousseau to exotic wedding locales, the world can truly be your oyster. But have you given a thought as to which areas are more important and call for lavish spending in order to have a royal wedding? The following are all-important areas, where no brakes are needed.

WEDDING DRESS

There will be people advising you not to spend a fortune on your wedding dress, which you are probably never going to wear again. But your wedding day won't come again either. And there is no dearth of expert bridal wear designers. So zero onto your favourite one, spend hours going through his collection and finalise an entire new wardrobe.

Ultimate splurge: Request your favourite designer to design a custom wedding trousseau that is studded with crystals or precious coloured stones.

WEDDING PHOTOGRAPHY

Everything will pass but the memories. So, have no second thoughts on hiring the best photographer and videographer in town! Start with an elaborate pre-wedding bridal shoot, snap away your bachelorette, pose for the mehendi-sangeet-cocktail functions, enjoy the wedding day shots and finally follow it up with the reception ceremony. The pictures should tell it all!

Ultimate splurge: Try pulling some strings and get a film director to shoot the entire wedding festivities.

WEDDING DESTINATION

Second only to the bride's dress, research widely to locate the perfect destination for your wedding. Go for the most opulent properties in the country (or around the world), book the entire place for a week at least and let each of your guests have the time of her life. Better still, adorn the properties with a new look each day.

Ultimate splurge: Book an exotic island for ten days for a truly lavish wedding.

WEDDING ENTERTAINMENT

A ten-day grand wedding calls for an entertainment bucket. Wow your guests with an awesome line-up of events. Belly dancers, fire acrobats, magicians, Bollywood and Hollywood stars...let there be no full stop. If you have a sizable number of foreign guests, do not forget to up the India quotient by including authentic Indian entertainment forms.

Ultimate splurge: Let your favourite stars enact your love story in a full three-hour feature film.

WEDDING TRANSPORT

Ferrying wedding guests to and fro during the festivities can be done with ultimate panache. Instead of the usual Mercs, Audis and BMWs, why not up the ante by hiring vintage vehicles? Classy, elegant and royal, your wedding will forever be etched in your guests' minds. Old definitely will strike gold.

Ultimate splurge: As a memento of your wedding, gift customised miniature car models that are studded with precious stones.

Chapter 4

Atithi Devo Bhava

How much time have you spent planning your wedding day? Months, right? Most brides (and their mothers) try and organise their wedding with all the precision and accuracy of a military manoeuvre. It is not called the D-Day for nothing, folks!

But it would be a shame, would it not, if the only thing your guests remember about the wedding is the fact that the chicken tikka was too spicy? In a land, where divine hospitality—*atithi devo bhava*— is a part of our tradition and culture, you want your guests to take away only good memories from your wedding. After all, haven't you spent so much of your time and effort planning it!

Tips to Ensure Guests Have a Great Time
TRADITIONAL INDIAN *AARTI*
In olden days, guests coming home for the first time were greeted with an *aarti*. You could revive this tradition on your wedding day. Have a group of your friends and young girls from the family wait at the entrance of the wedding venue, ready to greet your wedding guests with a traditional *aarti*. It will add a personal touch that your guests will surely love.

Have Fun Dressing Up

Add a touch of traditional glamour to your big day. As guests reach your wedding venue, make them don traditional headgear—*pagdi*s and stoles—chunnis to make them feel extra special and to mark them as a prominent member of the wedding party. You can also hire professionals to tie these up for your guests.

Hygienic and Clean Washrooms

Guests, especially children and elders visit the washroom quite often. So, make sure that the washrooms are well-maintained and hygienic. Arrange for staff to monitor its cleanliness.

Seating Arrangement

Usually the number of guests exceeds the seats available. Choose a venue large enough to spaciously accommodate your guest list and instruct your venue manager to have enough seating so that each guest can be comfortable. Also, suggest he keeps extra chairs handy.

Entertain, but Not Loudly

Rituals and catching up with one another can engage your guests, but only for that long. Why not invite a dance troupe, perhaps a live singer or even an orchestra party to captivate your guests and up the entertainment quotient. Let music set the tone, but ensure the volume is such that it does not obstruct the flow of conversation.

Thank-you Gifts

Give gifts to close friends and relatives who made the evening wonderful for you. This gesture will make them feel special. Also, they will remember your wedding for the love and care you showered on them. Personalised souvenirs are probably the best way to show your guests how much you value them. There are plenty of ideas to suit every taste and budget such as:

- If you are a music buff, then compile a CD of your favourite numbers for a gift.
- An antique finish knick-knack perhaps, which your guests can display in their home as a memento of your wedding.
- Here's one that your lady guests will love: A little change purse that has been gussied up with brocade, lace or silk.

- One of the best stimulants to memory is the olfactory sense. For me, the scent of cardamom is irrevocably associated with my grandmother's tea. Gift your guests a packet of your favourite potpourri or aromatic candle—the delightful scents will remind them of your wedding!

Make Them Comfortable

If you thought that having your reception at a fancy hotel, decorating the reception hall to look like something out of a fairy tale and ensuring that booze flows like water is all you have to do to take care of your guests, well…think again.

- The pet peeve of wedding guests is the long reception line they have to contend with in order to congratulate the wedding couple. In fact, at large weddings, guests spend most of their time at the reception.

Solution: Instead of the traditional 'stage' receptions, perhaps the wedding couple could mingle with the guests. This way, everyone would definitely have a better time!

- Having thirty plus dishes in three different cuisines is good, but only if your guests can actually get to them without starving first. Holding onto a heavy plate while waiting for food is too reminiscent of the lines at school dormitories!

Solution: Let the waiters serve starters and soups before the dinner starts. Have multiple counters for food instead of a single one. And since caterers charge by the plate (on a per head basis), this will not add to your food costs at all. Also, during the meal have breads, rice and papad on the move.

- Musical chairs at a reception? One often has to fight for a place to sit. Why have only 150 chairs at the reception when you're expecting more than 500 guests?

Solution: Ensure adequate seating arrangement for your guests. By adequate, we mean about 60 per cent of the guests you have invited will attend the function, 15 per cent of invitees are unlikely to show up, whereas the rest will be a rotating crowd. With heavy clothes and heavier plates, standing and eating becomes an impossible task.

When you have spent so much for the food, I am sure you want your guests to enjoy it.

- Mother Nature can easily gate-crash your event: Ignore weather conditions only if you're ready to risk your guests running away from the wedding reception or not turning up in the first place. Yes, most of you will avoid having an outdoor wedding during the monsoons but what about when it is too hot, too windy or too cold?

Solution: With global warming hitting us, the weather has become really unpredictable. It is best to check the weather forecasts for the wedding/reception day. If the temperatures are likely to be more than 30° C or less than 10° C, have an indoor reception. If that's not possible, arrange for portable fans and coolers during the summer or heaters during the winter. In extremely cold weather, it is also a good idea to have small bonfires around which the seating can be arranged. In addition to making your guests cosy, they look great too.

So now that you know how to keep your guests happy, go ahead and charm them with these tips.

Preparing the Guest List—A Very Important List Indeed!

This is the most important task as well as the most difficult one. There is no way to sugar-coat the guest list. In a traditional Indian wedding, a large number of extended family members and guests arrive for the wedding, especially if it is the first wedding in the family. Compiling a wedding guest list can be extremely stressful because people's feelings are involved. It calls for extra tact, patience and understanding to avoid conflict. But even among all this fuss, there are ways to make it easy and fun.

Here are some guidelines for building your wedding guest list.

COME UP WITH A NUMBER

Before you start jotting down names on paper, you and your fiancé need to come up with a number: An estimate of how many guests to invite. This, of course, will largely depend on your budget and on the size of your wedding venue. You'll want to get your list established shortly after you've decided on a budget and venue, especially because you'll need to factor in cost per person, a head count versus capacity of your venue and how many invites you need to send.

Stay Put

Of course, you're going to announce your engagement to close friends and family members—that's okay because they're anyways the first ones you'll invite. Beyond your immediate clan, resist calling anyone else until you know the wedding's approximate size and scope. If people know from the start that they're not likely to be invited because it's a family-only or far-flung affair, they won't be miffed when they don't find a fancy envelope in their mailbox.

Both Sides Draw Up Initial Drafts

The best way to start is to take out a notepad and start jotting down names, this is your initial run through and consists of everyone you'd love to have at your wedding. Before creating a master guest list, draw up your individual lists—you and your spouse-to-be as well as the parents on both sides.

- Begin by adding your immediate and extended family those who are like family to you.
- When listing close friends, remember to include their spouses and parents.
- Now consider all those left—who share your life, bring you happiness and will continue to do so beyond this one day. These include close neighbours and colleagues who have been supportive.
- After estimating your total, consider if it would be reasonable to add other possible invitees to your guest list. If it seems feasible, look back to recall all those who have made a positive impact on your life. These may include mentors such as your school teacher and tennis coach. Also, those who may have impacted your life in some way like doctors and counsellors. You might even want to add business relations who continue to stay in touch.

Compile your lists to create a master draft. Next, you need to prioritise by determining the 'must invites', the 'should invites', and the 'could invites'. Does your budget cover all the 'must invites'? If so, move on to the 'should invites' and then to the 'could invites'. This way you ensure that the people most important to both the families make the cut.

CREATE A AND B LISTS

While you're pretty safe assuming that 10-20 per cent of your final list will not attend, it pays to be ready with a second string in case you dip far below your target number or if there's a group of guests you want to invite—like second cousins but as of now don't have the room. If you're shooting for 200 guests, for example, identify 240 guests as your A-list. These are the folks who will get the first round of invites. The rest, in order of importance, become the B-list. Once you get more than forty A-list regrets, you can start working down your B-list, sending out a few invites at a time until you get 200 acceptances. Don't wait too long getting your B-list out—no one wants an invitation the week before an event.

OUTSTATION GUESTS

Next, you need to decide the number of outstation guests in order to make arrangements for them.

You need to consider:

- How many can be accommodated with the family and friends?
- Those who will be put up in guest houses/hotels, how many days will they be staying—how many ceremonies besides the main wedding would you like them to attend?

Once this list is ready, invitees can be requested to schedule the event in their personal calendars. Inform them much in advance so they can get their train/plane reservations confirmed and make arrangements at home before leaving to attend your wedding.

Do not invite anyone out of a sense of guilt. While 'the more the merrier' is good, ensuring that everyone is comfortable is the responsibility of the two families concerned. For you, as host, outstation guests mean expenses of accommodation, transport, meals, sightseeing (if any) and any other foreseeable expense. Here too, it is advisable to keep room for the unexpected.

Cut It Short

Unless you have unlimited funds, you're not going to be able to send a wedding invitation to every single person you like. To cut costs, cut down on the number of guests.

- Make a separate list for close relatives, distant relatives, friends, neighbours and colleagues. Study each list carefully to prioritise.
- If you're having a really small wedding, keep your family invites restricted to close relatives only like immediate aunts, uncles and first cousins. The distant relatives list can be discarded like your second and third cousins. But if your parents are sponsoring the wedding, then ahem, let them do the listing!
- Invite your boss and assistant by visiting them personally at their residence. Avoid the office, as it will automatically set off an office-invite chain reaction! Invite only those colleagues who are your lunch buddies or you might end up spending more by treating them later (after you return to work).
- For co-workers, apply the 'but for' test: If the company dissolves tomorrow, would you still be friends with them? But for your job, do you have anything in common?
- If inviting a particular person means you will have to invite the rest of the gang, which in turn will add up eleven more guests, then just drop that person from your list!
- If you've been staying in the same area for years, it might become necessary to invite some very close neighbours. But if the space is really tight, don't risk it—you can always send them some sweets announcing your wedding (hopefully, they'll understand!).
- Avoid inviting people whom you meet only at events organised by mutual friends. They are not your friends but your friends' friends.
- People, whom you don't plan to call or see, when you visit

their town, shouldn't feel insulted when you don't invite them to your wedding.

- If you wonder, 'What do they want?' when a person calls you, then perhaps they should not make it to your guest list.
- For any potential invitees still on the fence, think how you might relate to this person, five years from now. Will you look at the wedding pictures and wonder, 'Who is that?' Better not to invite!
- Eliminate people you know but haven't been in touch with for years.
- Please don't feel obliged to invite acquaintances who invited you for some wedding, a few years back.

Decide on a cut-down date and make your final list at least five to six weeks before your wedding day. That gives you enough time to get guest responses and learn how many are planning to come. Accordingly, you can give the caterer the final head count.

If you can't invite as many close friends as you'd like, consider hosting a barbecue or a casual cocktail party when you return from your honeymoon. Include all those friends you couldn't call for the wedding and be sure to mention you don't want them to bring gifts.

Don't feel bad about trimming your list. Remember you cannot please everyone. It's a very special day for you and obviously you would like to be surrounded by people you know and love.

Whom Not to Invite?

Weddings are incomplete without guests; after all, everyone needs their friends and relatives around to share these joyous moments. But there might be a few who end up spoiling your mood on your special day. They will crib about the food and the venue, get drunk and misbehave or act as a wet blanket on this blissful occasion. So, here is a list of guests that every couple should keep away from their wedding. And, if their presence is inevitable, then let me also tell you how to deal with them.

THE CONSTANT CRITICISER

They are the ones who always have to criticise and complain about everything. These guests will quibble over everything from your clothes to the food and maybe even your spouse! Keep them at a distance, if you cannot keep them away.

How to deal with them: It is best not to indulge them in conversation as that is an invitation for disaster. You can also leave some waiters on their tail to make sure their mouths stay occupied at all times!

Sob Storyteller

It is either their love for attention or inherent talent that some people can churn out a sob story anytime, anywhere. To gain sympathy, they keep recounting their hard-luck story and whining about life in general. Such guests not only irritate those around but mar your happiness as well.

How to deal with them: If you end up inviting such a guest, introduce her to the constant criticiser. Away from your other guests, these two will have a lot to talk about.

Single, and (Always) Ready to Mingle

People who are just out of a relationship or who have been trying too hard to find their perfect match might become little bitter during weddings. They will sigh at every sight of a happy couple (or maybe ogle at every single person of the opposite sex).

How to deal with them: Pair this friend with your spouse's single friends. Some *Hum Aapke Hain Kaun* moments amongst your guests might make your wedding more interesting.

Interfering Relatives

You will definitely have an aunt who claims to be an authority on the latest styles and make-up trends. And dear bride-to-be, do not think she will shy away from interfering with your make-up artist's work as well. Just as you are getting ready to reach the venue, she will impart her 'valuable' inputs and ensure that she is heard.

How to deal with this: Just smile and thank her for those 'interesting' suggestions. Tell her politely that you will definitely try them out. If she persists, ask your mom or sibling to find some excuse to take her out—even drag, if needed.

DRUNKEN RELATIVES

We all have a relative who just cannot handle his drink. After a few drinks, he loses all control over his tongue—recounting jokes and anecdotes which only he will find funny and bore your guests to death.

How to deal with them: Take your relative's wife in confidence and ask her to take care of her husband. Also, ask your bartender to keep an eye on the guests who are drinking too much. He should offer them some food or watered-down drinks to keep them steady.

YOUR EX

Unless your ex is your best friend, do not send a wedding invite to him. It would be your biggest mistake. He will probably act uncomfortable or bitter, if he still has not got over you.

How to deal with them: Never invite your ex to your wedding. This is a rule that is not meant to be broken.

The comfort of your guests will be your top priority and rules over all lists and arrangements. A wedding, after all, is an official reunion of all the loved ones—it becomes your responsibility to keep them happy.

Chapter 5

Finding a Suitable Wedding Venue

It goes without saying that your wedding day is the most special day of your life. From caterers and decoration, to make-up and bridal dress, everything has to be perfect. But the one thing that is the soul of the entire ceremony is the venue. Finding a suitable venue is no less than finding a suitable boy! The venue, to a large extent, sets the mood for the many ceremonies. A venue should be spacious and offer all the basic amenities.

Since Indian marriages usually take place at certain auspicious times of the year, there is a huge rush for venues during the wedding season. It is therefore imperative to decide and book the venue well in advance to avail a good price.

You must select the venues for the following occasions:
- Engagement or *sagaai*
- Mehendi
- Sangeet
- Cocktail/bachelor/bachelorette party
- Other ceremonies
- Actual wedding ceremony
- Reception

Indian weddings of any faith—Hindu, Muslim, Christian or Sikh, usually come in two parts. First comes the traditional wedding—full of religious ceremonies and complicated rituals, followed by an informal reception to welcome the bride and mingle with the guests. The location of your wedding, guest count and the duration/time of your wedding determine its venue. Here are some venues to consider:

Choices for the Wedding Ceremony

TEMPLES, CHURCHES, MOSQUES AND GURDWARAS

Religious places score high when it comes to choosing a wedding venue. It sends out a strong message about your religious side and also proclaims to the world that your partner accepts your traditions with an open heart. There is just one problem when you choose these locations—not all religious places entertain people from other faiths/castes. Uncomfortable scenarios with guests of other faiths can be quite embarrassing for the couple and the organisers.

COMMUNITY CENTRES OR WEDDING HALLS

If you are having your wedding in a small town then local community centres can be very convenient. These are very well-known and are big enough to hold a sizable gathering. Major cities in South India have specially constructed *Kalyana* mandapams—banquet halls that suit wedding requirements perfectly. For example, there are lots of rooms for the bride, groom and guests to get dressed or rest for a while. They also have huge dining halls and ample parking space, in addition to great acoustics for your music requirements.

RESORTS OR DESTINATION WEDDINGS

Couples these days go all out while planning their weddings. Indian weddings usually have several small ceremonies spread over a week. Booking a resort for the wedding seems a great choice for couples who want their guests to participate in all the small ceremonies of a traditional Indian wedding. Destination weddings are another huge hit with couples these days. This concept combines the idea of a vacation and a wedding to conjure up a dream celebration.

HOTELS AND BANQUET HALLS

Hotels and banquet halls are other great alternatives for receptions. Many couples prefer to hold their weddings in a religious place and then throw a huge reception party in one of the known hotels in town. This works great, especially because most guests prefer skipping the religious ceremonies and come over to greet the couple during the reception.

COUNTRY HOUSES AND FARMHOUSES

There are some country houses which have been turned into five-star wedding venues. They cater only to wedding groups. Located usually on the outskirts of the town, they provide accommodation and other basic facilities for the families, relatives and guests of the bride and groom. Both families are lodged in the same place and it becomes very convenient for everyone to attend all the functions. Since the chalets/cottages/rooms housing the two parties are separate, the specific functions can be performed separately as well.

PARKS AND GARDENS

If the ceremony is planned outdoors, a large open area will be required which can be covered with shamianas, tents, canopies and awnings. Check the weather conditions to see if this idea is feasible. The main ceremonies should be held on a dais so that everyone can witness them.

A wedding is not just about getting all the ceremonies done the right way; it's a forging of bonds between the two families. Any hint of a wrong note can be considered inauspicious. This is another reason why so much importance is given to the venue in Indian weddings. In fact, once the parents decide on the venue, often, the priest vets it. In certain customs, all marriage rituals must be performed facing a certain direction and only the priest can ensure that. Therefore, before taking a final call on the venue and the construction of the mandap, get it cleared by the priest.

Few Things to Keep in Mind

- A wedding conducted according to the Special Marriage Act is usually held in the office of the marriage registrar. If the bride and groom choose another venue, they must check if the chosen venue is licensed to hold this ceremony.

- If the reception is held on the same day but at a separate venue, the general rule is that the reception hall should be just about a half-an-hour drive from the marriage ceremony venue. Your guests will not have to rush or become tired travelling from one venue to another.

Banquet Hall or Beach?

One of the first things you need to decide is whether you want a simple wedding or a grand extravaganza. This will dictate the kind of wedding venue you choose and the location too. You may want to pick from wedding halls that are simple covered areas which can be decorated later or book a palace hotel property to make your wedding a much talked-about event. Couples are increasingly opting for a beach wedding, if it is a gathering of only close friends and relatives. What also matters is your wedding style—a modern minimalist wedding demands a venue starkly different from a royal celebration. Decide on a wedding style early on, finalise the venue accordingly and you might save a lot on decorations.

Follow Your Guest Count and Budget

For a small gathering, a modest-sized hall is apt but a big gathering requires a large hall or house. Remember, the more the budget, the better will be the venue. Cost is important, but not always the deciding factor for a venue. At all potential venues, ask what value they can add to improve the event for your guests. When you do decide on a venue, check the contract carefully for any miscellaneous additional charges.

Do Some Research

Once you have decided on the kind of wedding you prefer to host, research your options well. Make a note of all the things that you want at the venue. Say for example, space, lights and washrooms. You may also need to consider audio-visual requirements, the need for natural light or blacked-out windows and function furniture such as sign easels. Make sure that you shortlist all the wedding locations that are possible. Try and visit as many as you can.

Seek Recommendations

Recommendations from friends and family who have been down the same route can be a great starting point. They may have brochures of places they visited previously and also acquaint you with the key contact points at these venues.

See for Yourself

Once you've shortlisted the suitable venues, start visiting them in person. You may find your weekends very jam-packed for a while!

When you visit venues, pay attention to the little details, like routes your guests will take, what the bathrooms are like, whether there's ample heating/air conditioning and where the power sockets for your band/speeches/DJ/ceremony music are functioning.

Find Out If the Venue is Full Service or Not

There really are two very different types of wedding venues:

- A full service wedding venue most of the time offers everything from table and chair rentals to linens and catering supplies.
- The other provides only the space and it is up to you to fill in the rest. This means you will be responsible for booking all the vendors for the wedding day.

Either way, some venues have fixed vendors whom they expect you to work with. Working with venue-appointed vendors for catering, car rental and decoration does not give you the option to shop around and find a quote that meets your budget. At most venues, you will get all the facilities under one roof. But if not, ask what extra expenses you will need to incur. Make a note of things like water and generator facilities.

Ceremonies and Where They Will be Held?

While evaluating the wedding venue or the garden wedding area, carry with you a list of ceremonies. Make sure there is enough segregated space where each ceremony can be held without disturbing the guests or the bride and groom.

Lighting

Light can make or break the mood and the space.

- If you're marrying during the day, make sure your hall has plenty of windows.

- If it's an evening affair, make sure the room's not too dim or that the lighting can be controlled for the big entrance, dinner and dancing.
- If you're marrying outdoors, say at dusk, will you be able to set up candles if necessary?

Visit the site at the hour you've chosen for your wedding, this helps you assess its lighting. Even if the space looks romantic by candlelight, you may be surprised how different that twenty-year-old carpet looks during the day. You'll also miss a chance to see how sunlight streaming through floor-to-ceiling windows completely transforms the room, if you check it out only in the evening.

The Right Colour

If you're considering a certain theme and colour palette for your party—e.g. a modern lounge style cocktail party, reception done in 'black and red'—those gold cord swag curtains are really going to wreck the effect. The site doesn't have to be done in the exact colours as your planned decorations but the walls, carpets, chairs, and curtains shouldn't clash or conflict with your party's mood or theme. If you want a spring wedding brunch, look for a space that's done in light (perhaps pastel) colours or floral. For classic elegance, consider a room done in neutrals or black and white.

Good Acoustics

If the hall seems to echo, it could give some weird reverb to the music, not to mention making it difficult for guests to hear one another talking. A tile or wood floor, for example, will amplify sounds, while a thick carpet will tend to muffle them. Check out the room's sound quality during an event. And tailor your music to the acoustic conditions.

Think About Your Guests

While booking a wedding venue, always think from a guest's point of view. You might like the venue but it might not exactly be comfortable for some of your guests. For example, try and choose a venue that is on the ground floor to make it easier for elderly relatives, who find it difficult to climb stairs. Though often less emphasised and discussed, the parking facility at a wedding venue does matter. It's pointless inviting huge numbers and then keep them hanging outside, looking for parking space. Appoint enough parking attendants or valets to take care of the guests' vehicles.

CHANGING ROOMS AND REST ROOMS

Indian weddings are long affairs that go on for hours. Children tend to fall asleep as the mahurat—auspicious time for weddings is often at odd hours in the night. Ensure the wedding venue has some rooms or enclosed tents available for guests to change, rest or refresh themselves.

CATERING SERVICE

Some wedding locations also provide catering services; here you can book the location and the food together. Some wedding halls have tie-ups with large catering services and will allow only their affiliate caterers. In such cases, make sure you evaluate them separately on the menu, food quality and price. Most would happily invite you for a tasting session. If possible, request an invite on a day when there's a wedding function going on—you'll not only get a sneak preview of what your wedding could look like but also the taste of the food that will be served.

CORKAGE

A great number of venues rely on making a profit from the sale of drinks, and therefore do not encourage you to bring in your own alcohol. Every venue will have a different policy but do bear in mind, it's entirely normal to have to choose from their spirit list or pay a corkage fee if you wish to bring your own. Often, the corkage fee plus the cost of your spirits is more than some of their basic house spirit prices, so unless you are bringing in a very special spirit that you have bought at a very good price, it doesn't make financial sense.

WEDDING DECORATION SERVICES

In most cases, wedding decoration services are included in the wedding venue package. Ensure that you are comfortable with the kind of wedding decoration options that the venue offers. If there are any changes that you want, ensure that you pass on the instructions to the decorator well in advance.

Learn to Bargain

Mostly, wedding venues set up a price and tag themselves as non-negotiable. Do not feel obliged to pay them what they ask for, just because of their 'fixed price' tag. Bargain as per the wedding budget in your mind. The time or the number of hours allotted by the wedding venue is an important factor. Generally, wedding venues are allotted for about six-seven hours, after which they charge extra.

Ask Questions

Before booking your venue, there are many questions you need to run through the banquet manager. No matter how silly or trivial they may seem, don't hold back. You are paying a lot for the venue, so you need to be completely happy with the service and have complete confidence in the venue manager.

Ask questions as to where will the bride and groom sit? Is there a toilet attached to the bride's room? Where will the guests be accommodated? Ask whether the venue authorities will provide a DJ or you will have to get one on your own? Are there any particular restrictions such as the use of fireworks or candles? Just be sure of everything you want from them. It is always better to ask whether or not the place has any restrictions with regard to using any of its facilities, lest there is a problem at the last moment.

Late Licence?

Always ask until what time does a venue have its licence—both for serving alcohol and playing music. Midnight is usually the norm for music to finish and the bar to shut down but there is an option of an extended licence (usually for an extra fee) until one o'clock or two o'clock, which the venue has to secure from the local authority. Even if there is a residents' bar, there is usually a 'music-off' time.

Don't Commit Straightaway

The importance of booking the venue early and getting everything on paper cannot be stressed enough. Equally important is to seek a full breakdown of all the costs in an itemised list that shows what is and isn't included in the price. This may include the room hire, caterers, decoration, waiters and staff to manage your wedding and cutlery.

Check for hidden costs and review the logistics before you book. Make sure that you read the fine print. Check whether VAT and service tax has been included in the overall price. Ask what happens to your money in case of cancellation from either side.

Enquire About the Deposit First

One popular misconception is that all wedding venues follow an industry standard when it comes to booking your date and making that initial payment. Wedding venues actually charge anywhere between few thousands to forty per cent of the total rent. If you want to reserve a specific date urgently, call the vendor beforehand and ask how much is the deposit.

Booking Dilemmas

Asking the right questions and planning far in advance means fewer last-minute mistakes. Note how promptly your main point of contact at the venue—normally the banqueting manager, responds to your queries as this may determine whether you should go for that venue or not. This will be the person managing your wedding. Any delays are just not acceptable!

You may want to go for a hotel where they will give you a complete package for your event which will include hotel rooms for guests to rest and change, as well as the all-important honeymoon suite for the bride and groom. You may also want to consider this package if the hassle of catering decisions is not your cup of tea. Known hotels generally have top wedding caterers on their panel and you are obliged to work with them. These caterers are normally vetted for quality and health checks and will remove the uncertainty associated with new suppliers.

Check Before You Book

- **Time**: On the wedding day at what time will the venue be made available to you? Your decorators, florists, mandap supplier and caterers (if there are outside caterers) will need early access, often as early as six o'clock to set up properly and in time.
- **Restrictions**: Are there restrictions on decor, flower petals, music or fire restrictions for the mandap?

- **Size**: Is it big enough to host your guests and all the activities you hope to include in your wedding? Think beyond eating and dancing—do you plan to have any entertainment and is there enough space for it? Is there a good spot for non-dancers to catch up over cocktails?
- **Table Setting**: Does the venue provide anything for table decor? For example, tea lights, candles, ornaments, etc. What table settings are available—white tablecloths or are there other choices? How will the tables be arranged? Do they have sample table plans?
- **Weather**: If you want to have an outdoor wedding, what are your options for keeping guests comfortable in all types of weather? Does the venue have a backup plan in case of rain? What if it's scorching hot on your wedding day in July? Does the venue provide shaded or air-conditioned indoor areas for respite? What if it's cold? Is there heating and plenty of cosy indoor space for guests?
- **Decorations**: Will the venue take responsibility for decorating the tables and providing the materials?
- **Lighting**: Who will be responsible for the lighting at the function hall? Can the lights be adjusted at certain times during the wedding?
- **Speeches**: You might require audio-visual capabilities that day; will they arrange it? Will there be someone on hand if there is a technical fault with the equipment?
- **Drinks**: How do they charge for corkage? Can the drinks be pre-purchased and served using their staff? Can the drinks be purchased through the venue?
- **DJs and band**: Will they allow them to set up prior to the event start time? Will they provide them with food and drinks, as required? Are there restrictions on the noise levels during the event? Till how late can the party continue? If you dream of dancing until the wee hours, make sure the venue doesn't have an early curfew.

- **Seating Plan**: Will the venue provide the full seating plan including buffet set-up and starters on the go?
- **Menu (if they provide catering)**: When does the venue require the final menu details? Can they cater for special dietary requirements?
- **Staff**: How many staff will be working at the venue on the day? Who will they be reporting to? Will this person be available to you?
- **Car parking**: Can the guests use the parking facilities at the venue and will it be provided free?
- **Accessibility**: Some necessary items/requirements may have to be brought in and it should be convenient to bring them to the venue.
- **Cloakroom**: Will there be a cloakroom area provided for the guests?
- **Rooms**: How many bedrooms are included in the package for the immediate?
- **Others**: If the wedding is in the morning and the reception in the evening, make sure there are changing rooms and rest rooms that can be used by the guests.

It's also worth questioning the venue managers about their recommended suppliers. Does the venue, for example, insist that you use their suppliers? Are the businesses they advocate, recommended on merit and experience of working at the venue? Or are suppliers paying to be on the list? Will you have to pay extra commission? If they do insist you use certain suppliers (as they normally do with caterers), then also get independent quotes from these suppliers prior to booking.

Finally, do ask who will be your main point of contact throughout the planning process and on the actual day itself. At this stage, you may be dealing with the sales team and only once booked, will you work with the events team before finally dealing with the banqueting team on your wedding day. For peace of mind, you may prefer to deal with one person throughout but if that isn't an option, consider working with a wedding planner who can oversee everything for you.

Dos and Don'ts

DON'T RULE OUT VENUES AUTOMATICALLY

If you have the time, give yourself free reign to visit any and all wedding locations that pique your interest whether they're must-sees or just maybes.

DO TAKE THE BARE BONES INTO ACCOUNT

It's easy to transform a venue from nondescript to stunning with drapery, lighting and centrepieces. However, these decor elements come with a hefty price tag, so you may consider selecting a place that you can see yourselves getting married in, with just minor retouches.

DON'T LOSE SIGHT OF YOUR PRIORITIES

During the wedding planning process, it's easy to get swept away and overspend thinking that this is once-in-a-lifetime event. Every bride has her moments, where judgment jumps out the window.

DO TAKE ADVANTAGE OF WORD-OF-MOUTH

Those three little words mean so much to vendors—most brides take into account what kind of experience their friends and family members may have had at a particular wedding venue. Tell your assigned sales representatives about couples you know who got married at their establishment and recommended it to you. Perhaps, they may throw in some small extras in return or lower the price a smidge. It doesn't hurt to try!

DON'T FORGET THE PHOTOGRAPHER

Let them know once you have the venue organised so they can visit and get a feel and check out the best places for photos.

The right wedding venue is that crucial piece of the puzzle that can bring all your ideas together. It's all too easy to fall in love at first sight, but make sure your head rules your heart. Select the venue only after thorough research.

Chapter 6

Theme Your Wedding Uniquely

All Indian weddings are characterised by vibrant colours, gorgeous clothes, energetic dancing, foot-tapping music and mouth-watering dishes. A wedding turns unique when it reflects the individual personalities and tastes of the couple.

Today, you can bring about a 'marriage' of the traditional with the new and exotic. A little planning can lend an unusual touch even to your regional rituals. Every Indian wedding comprises the following elements; see how you can make them distinct and special:

- Invitation cards
- Venue and decor
- Food
- Attire
- Wedding entry/exit

You can turn your wedding exclusive if you prepare well. You need not have a large budget. You can keep things simple and low cost and yet have a one of its kind wedding.

A theme is simply a style choice that you apply to all aspects of your wedding day—from invitations, to decor and even your table settings. The theme itself could be anything from a specific colour—perhaps you love green, a distinguishing motif such as a peacock feather, to a definitive look you may fancy, such as a Rajasthani wedding.

On its own, a theme provides you with a cohesive look for your day. It will typically give you a day that is easy to label. Picking a theme can make things simpler when you plan your reception and wedding.

Ideas can spring from anywhere. You may have a favourite movie, book or place that inspires you. Try to come up with a concept that can be translated into an intelligent and relevant design such that it adds depth and meaning to your special day. Take the time to think about who you really are, what's important to you and what you want your wedding day to say about you. How you want it to affect you and your guests...the emotions you want the day to evoke. Now put your stamp on your event—ten years later, as you flip through your wedding album, your personalised motifs will stand out and still look amazing. The keyword in theme weddings is homogeneity.

Choosing a Theme

This depends entirely on the bride and groom. It could be based on:

- A hobby or personal interest
- A film that you enjoyed
- A specific historical period—a Mughal wedding perhaps. You may choose to wed at a historical site that holds special significance for you.
- A retro theme such as the 1950s or the 1980s
- A season such as spring, summer, monsoon or winter
- Someplace else—for instance on a ship, a jet, or a desert setting
- A fantasy such as the Arabian Nights
- Something as indigenous as a village theme
- Romance
- Your favourite city—Venice, Paris, Mumbai, Delhi...anything
- Do you have a unique cultural background? Import all the special rituals and traditions into the ceremony and reception.

Let everything from your attire to the menu reflect your heritage.

- A floral theme. Sometimes, just one kind of flower can make up the whole theme—the rose theme, marigold theme, orchid or arum lily theme.
- One colour theme—you can use different shades but the basic colour remains the same.

Keep the following in mind when creating your own theme:
- Decorations, including the backdrop
- The attire (including make-up) of the bride and groom as well as the families concerned
- Dress code (including make-up) for all guests
- Food and beverages—even if you serve a different kind of cuisine, the table settings and service as well as mode of serving will have to match the theme
- Make sure you see the whole thing through to the last detail and have enough time to make it happen
- A mantra that never really goes wrong: Keep it simple.

THINGS TO CONSIDER

- The theme should suit the personalities of the bride, the groom and the families. Never forget that an Indian wedding is a social event and if those attending are not comfortable, there will be room for criticism.
- All thematic details should be carefully worked upon by the couple or a professional. The end result should be completely authentic.
- The budget is of the greatest importance when planning a theme wedding. A royal, romantic or fantasy theme spells great expense as you have to create the right ambience.
- Check if the elders in the family are okay with your chosen theme and find it feasible. Ask the priest too, if your family insists.
- Make sure that nothing inauspicious is incorporated.
- The same theme can be extended to all pre-wedding rituals and post-wedding ceremonies. Of course, if you decide on a

different theme for the reception, choose one that blends with your wedding theme.

- The table decor as well as the favours should reflect the theme.
- Even if you have hired a wedding planner, participate in all the major decisions. This way the theme will embody what you find special.
- Wedding indoors or outdoors? Your theme will have to be adapted accordingly.
- Outdoor weddings will naturally be more expensive—they call for more elaborate decor and lighting.
- Colours are very important in Indian weddings. Whether the ceremony is a Christian one or a nikah, in India, besides the specific colours at the ceremony, it's standard to have shades of orange, red, maroon, pink, with lots of zari and gold.
  Colours are important in a retro theme as well. So, consider psychedelic colours for the 1960s, hot pink (and very little or preferably no black as it is considered inauspicious) for the 1950s, and neon colours for the 1980s.
- In case you have chosen a floral theme, note that jasmine, roses and marigolds rule by tradition. Now, orchids, gerberas and carnations have become popular.
- Certain leaves are traditionally used in the ceremony, these will have to be included in the decor.
  - Banana leaves with the stem is usually placed on the four supports of the mandap. It stands for prosperity.
  - Betel leaves bring good fortune.
  - Mango leaves signify prosperity, happiness and purity.
  - A *tambool* which is a combination of a betel leaf, an areca nut and lime is exchanged during sagaai to seal the alliance
- Your music must match the theme to set up the right ambience. You could play traditional instruments like the *shehnai* or *nadaswaram* to welcome the guests or to lend ambience to a ritual. But other than that, whether you choose to have a live band, a DJ or soft background music, the mood must follow the theme.

Theme Ideas

Here are some popular theme ideas and how you can incorporate them into your wedding.

Beach/Nautical

Shades of blue and green work well with this theme. Send a message in a bottle to invite your guests. Or dress up a simple invitation with some sheer ribbon, shells and starfish. This gives them a sneak peek into things to come. Glam up your wedding accessories with silver starfish charms. Have your guests wear flip-flops and place large shells on each table. You can have your mandap by the sea.

For the reception, instead of draping lot of tulle, use decorative fishing nets, which you will find at craft or home decor stores. Sand, seashells, starfish and sea glass can be used to create eye-catching centrepieces. Serve tropical drinks with umbrellas and themed cocktails.

Winter/Christmas

Create a winter wonderland. The Christmas before your wedding, haunt the stores and you should be able to find everything your winter themed heart desires. If your wedding is near Christmas, churches will already be decorated for the season. For Christmas, think in reds, greens, and gold. Place a majestic Christmas tree at your reception site. Decorate it with candy canes and ornaments that can be later gifted to guests. Use poinsettias for centrepieces. Have a hot chocolate or eggnog bar for your guests.

If Christmas is not your thing, stick to the winter theme. Blue, silver, snowflakes and ice capture this setting very well. Your reception area can turn into an ice palace with white draping and blue lighting. Set up ice tree centrepieces. Consider a traditional Christmas dinner for your reception.

Country/Western

Ask everyone to dress up—the men can don cowboy hats and boots. You can also find western style tuxedos at places that rent costumes. If you really want to give this one all, make a memorable entry— gallop in like a cowboy on a horse.

Use bales of hay for the backdrop. Bandanna and gingham fabric or ribbon looks good. Consider putting your centrepieces in small galvanised buckets. Buy miniature cowboy hats or buckets, fill them with candy and present to your guests. Sunflowers can adorn your bouquet and other arrangements. Serve barbecue at your reception with plenty of ice tea. Play country music.

VILLAGE WEDDINGS

Go for a rustic setting. Light up with lanterns. Earthen pots and bullock carts can create the right ambience. Invite folk dancers and serve ethnic fare on banana leaves. See if you can arrange for your *baraat* party to arrive on elephants.

GOAN WEDDING

A Goan wedding theme is especially popular in cross-cultural weddings. In India, beach weddings are a novelty. A Goan setting is not just unique; it is also quite romantic. The glorious sunsets and the endless sea are sure to impress guests and herald a happy future for the couple-to-be.

ARABIC/ROMAN/EGYPTIAN WEDDING THEMES

While these themes are not very popular in India, they certainly charm Indians living abroad. They call for a more elaborate decor, so it helps to have a professional wedding planner decide on the thematic elements. Paintings, artefacts and drapes at the venue must conform to the respective styles of the region. For example, in a Roman theme, paintings of the Colosseum, mock chariots, landscape gardens with fountains can recreate the magic.

Go by these popular themes or conjure up something completely different—the possibilities are only limited by your imagination.

It's your story, tell it creatively.

Chapter 7

Flowers, Lights and Colours!

Wedding planning isn't easy at all! While some aspects can be managed, most require an insane amount of effort and preparation. Choosing the right wedding decoration can be as intricate and mind-boggling as buying the perfect wedding dress. A lot of research must go in to put all aspects in place. Be it lights, flowers, furnishings, drapes, everything should be in symmetry.

Make your wedding day more special and exquisite with these decor trends.

Flowers
Fresh flowers are an inseparable part of an Indian wedding. Whether you prefer chic, sophisticated wedding decor or a traditional fiesta, flowers can enhance the beauty of the occasion. But go for the right colours. If it's in winter, vibrant earthy tones are just perfect to perk up your senses. Subtle shades of blue, pink and yellow add a cool exuberance to a summer wedding. Make sure the flowers adorning the mandap, reception stage, wedding area and dining space are in harmony.

Lighting Styles

Lights add life to the wedding decor. But you must strike a blissful harmony amid lighting style and hues to create that magical aura. Some of the latest trends in wedding decor lights are—up-lighting, pin spotting, lanterns, LED mood bars, monogram projections, etc. Use them for a chic or sophisticated look. Chandeliers can give things a traditional look.

Colour Trends

If you have a budget constraint but want your decor to be unique, play with colours to create a mystical charm. For summers and monsoons, create a look with drapes and furnishings in blue, pink and citrus. For winters, experiment with a bright, joyful palette of orange and red. A blend of subtle colours can look ravishing.

Wedding Area Decoration

Team fresh flowers with candles and lanterns (all together) for an ethnic look. Let candles or lanterns light up the dining tables. Also, wrap up the pillars with light strings and flowers for greater effect.

Guest Space

Your guests need to feel most special. Decorate guest tables with exquisite pin-up flower bouquets in roses, carnations or tulips. Drape guest chairs in colourful combinations. Move beyond red and white to try out new combinations such as purple and mustard, black and gold and cream and pink.

Car Decoration

A car overloaded with flowers is definitely not in vogue. For your wedding car, the mantra is 'keep it simple'. A few strips of fresh flowers or a pin-up bouquet in the front are good enough.

Exquisite Idols and Showpieces

Idols and showpieces can make the place look magnificent. Place them near the mandap, entry gate and at the centre of the dining area. Decorate the area around them with flowers and up-lights.

The Exclusive Look

The look of your wedding leaves a lasting impression on the guests' mind. There are so many extensions to decor that are not just limited to look and feel. You also need a number of things for the ceremony which a florist/decorator provides. Here is a checklist of decor items you must discuss with your florist/decorator:

- **Flowers for the hair**: A lot of the brides like to adorn their hair with fresh flowers. Be it a *gajra* made of tuberoses, roses or even orchids—these can add immensely to your hairdo.
- **Bouquet for the bride**: Bridal bouquets can be as simple or elaborate as you want. Recently, I saw a bouquet of roses with rhinestone accents which looked absolutely gorgeous!
- **Bouquets for the bridesmaids**: The bridesmaids have simpler bouquets but see that it matches the bridal bouquet.
- *Milni* **garlands**: A lot of families have the tradition of *milni* right after the *baraat* arrives where the men in the bride's family greet and garland the men from the groom's side.
- **Flower petals for puja thalis and *aashirwaad***: Flower petals are used in various offerings during the ceremony and are used to decorate the *aarti* thaali—the bride's mother does *aarti* of the groom. Also, family and guests shower flower petals on the bride and groom during *aashirwaad*—blessing the couple. Do remind your decorator therefore to bring extra flower petals.
- **Trays for *jaimala*, *milni* garlands and puja supplies**: Ask if your decorator can provide trendy trays for this purpose.
- **Ganesha/statues of god**: Idols can be used in your decor, especially to decorate the entrance of your ceremony or reception area.
- **Diyas or lamps**: You might want to incorporate diyas or oil lamps in your decor.
- *Jaimala*: These are the garlands exchanged by the bride and groom.
- **Aisle decor**: This includes pillars, fabric swags, floral arrangements and flower petals.
- **Ribbon to block the aisle**: This is crucial to prevent your guests from walking along the aisle.
- **Mandap**: This includes the mandap structure/pillars/draperies,

its floral decor, mandap chairs and cushions, as well as the fire pit or the *havan kund* (very important!).

- *Doli*/**Palanquin**: This is totally optional but definitely adds a nice touch to the ceremony.
- **Decor for the ceremony and reception chairs**: This could be pomanders, sashes, bows or chair covers.
- **Boutonnières and Corsages**: These are again optional. But often, the groom and groomsmen would wear boutonnieres for the reception.
- **Gift box/Birdcage**: You might ask the decorator to provide and/or decorate these.
- **Centrepieces**: You will need these for guest tables, sweetheart table/head table, cocktail tables, place card table and guestbook/pictures table.
- **Tea lights/Votives**: You will need these to accent all your centrepieces.
- **Sweetheart table set-up**: These days more and more couples are going for sweetheart tables with very creative set-ups. Discuss the different options with your decorator.
- **Flowers for the cake**: Fresh flowers look gorgeous on the cake.
- **Special linen or overlays**: You can order specialty linen or overlays for the guest tables, buffet tables, etc.

To avoid too much confusion, here are some pointers to help you select the right florist.

References Always Help

The internet, social media, websites, magazines, TV shows have no doubt become the voice of experts and go-to avenues for everybody. But when it comes to weddings, there is nothing better than asking around your known circle of people. Even your other vendors can help you get a better deal.

Visit Multiple Florists

Hasty decisions can be really risky. So pay personal visits to their stores and assess their style. Check out the flowers on display. If they aren't looking fresh, it's better to strike them out of your probable list. Go through pictures of their arrangements at previous weddings.

Get Price Quotes and Book in Advance

Only after securing a general estimate from the decorator should you go ahead and explain the concept and theme of your wedding. You don't want to waste your time and energy dealing with decorators who charge exorbitantly.

Book well in advance because florists and decorators are reluctant to take up new projects just a month before the peak wedding season. Moreover, state your requirements, terms and conditions clearly and consider every aspect of decoration. Even neglecting a small detail like the choice of flowers for the centrepiece can skyrocket your decoration budget.

Design Philosophy

Finalise the florist only if you share a good rapport and a somewhat similar design philosophy. Even if arguments erupt, the aim should be to create a look that satisfies both the parties.

The Extras

A good florist won't just stop at decorating the wedding venue. Make sure you have a clear idea about the flower arrangement for other areas like the washrooms (ladies definitely), staircase of the venue and single rose (or small bouquet) at the rooms of outstation guests. It would include the groom's car and any other thing that needs some decoration.

Check the Schedule

The Indian 'wedding season' means multiple weddings on the same day, which in turn, means a shortage of resources. Hence, before you finalise a florist, please check his schedule. It is pointless if he is doing five weddings on a single day. Do not ever compromise on quality.

Budget It Right!

You might be tempted to spend some big bucks on the pretty orchids and lilies. But no matter what, your floral budget can never take up more than 30 per cent of your total decoration budget. Inform your florist accordingly.

Mandap is Most Important

It is the four-pillared canopy or marquee under which all the religious ceremonies pertaining to a wedding are conducted. These days, mandaps are designed as beautifully as the reception stage itself—resplendent with flowers, drapes and other artistic material. So much so that the bride and groom look like two deities tying the knot in an ethereal setting.

- Highlight the mandap as the showpiece of your wedding decor.
- The latest trend is to experiment with different shapes to give the mandap more appeal.
- Add chandeliers and other accessories to enhance its look. Make sure it goes with the theme though.
- For closed-roof venues, you can opt for open mandap styles.
- Simple mandaps are four-pillared while more complex tomb style structures are eight-pillared. Make sure the mandap is sturdy and in harmony with the overall venue design.
- Go for a simple domed structure and glam it up rather than opting for triple domes and then falling short on funds to decorate it.
- A wedding mandap should be spacious enough to accommodate the holy fire, the bridal couple, the priest, various things that will be required during the rituals, the photographer and the videographer and four to five relatives at any given moment.
- Flowers like orchids and carnations can make your mandap more colourful and vibrant. But the choice of flowers will directly influence the budget, so select them wisely and in right proportion.
- Drapes are the real charmers. You can recreate a fairy tale setting or build a typical traditional mandap with your drapes. Organza is the most preferred choice of material but you can

also try using crystal and stone studded fabrics to create a
glittering effect.

- The current trend is to install the statues of Indian gods and
goddesses inside the mandap to lend an auspicious touch.
Needless to say, Ganesha along with his escort Lakshmi is the
most preferred deity.

Light Up Your Big Day

Consult your wedding planner or the decoration-in-charge for the
lighting options that work best with your chosen theme and colours.
Let the lights announce the transition from one ceremony to another
for a greater effect. In between, just keep a tab on expenses. Make sure
the wedding sparkle does not blow your budget.

There is no dearth of design and layout ideas. It all depends on
the effect you want to create, the mood you wish to reflect and the
statement you want to make. Check out the latest illumination trends.

Up-lighting

Remember those big lights, those bucket-like lamps pouring out
light from above? This conventional mode of lighting just took a very
unconventional form—now they illuminate the room bottom up,
filling the entire space with a soft romantic glow. The effect is totally
mesmerising as light travels upwards, embracing the walls and trying
to graze through the ceiling.

Pin Spotting

Highlighting selected decoration and design items with smart use
of colour lighting is a very popular trend. Against an overall wash
of a uniform colour, the pin spotted pieces appeal to the senses. Pin
spotting is highly recommended where floral designs dominate the
decoration theme.

LED Mood-bars

These are segmented lighting units and are around six-seven feet tall.
Placed strategically along various edges of the wedding venue, for
example, the entrance or the aisle, they can create a soft welcoming
effect. The segments can be set in different colours or one solid colour

for the whole evening. The colour play is programmed or remote controlled, further enhancing your options for a brilliant lighting effect.

MONOGRAM PROJECTIONS

Use wash lighting against stencils to project the custom designed bridal monogram. It lends a personal touch to all the important parts of wedding decor and makes the couple feel that it is truly their day, their moment.

LIGHT BULBS

What about the good old power saving light bulb that is a staple in our homes? Hang them from the ceiling and let them dangle like pendants above the reception tables—you'll score major points from all those contemporary art types.

FAIRY LIGHTS

Four words: Solar, powered, fairy, lights can be the greatest combination. All you need to do is stick the solar panel in the ground for five to six hours, let the sun do its thing, and you've got some seriously magical shimmering for the rest of the night. Drape these babies through trees or cascade them down a wall.

LANTERNS

In all shapes, forms and colours—be it paper, glass, metal, round or square—lanterns look stunning and very romantic in any setting. Use it as a single prop on a table or string a few of them from the ceiling or adorn them with flowers. Depending on the type of lanterns and manner of use, they can accentuate different themes from whimsical to rustic, vintage to ethnic.

It's not just for the evenings. Use lanterns in your decor even at day time—it will still look beautiful and romantic. But for a day wedding, do not light the lantern. Instead fill it with flowers or coloured paper. Turn on the lantern to light up your evening event. Flame lanterns can evoke different moods in your wedding day.

CANDLES

Candles add to the romantic ambience and can be used in so many ways. The wedding candle decorations lets you customise the look—it's easy then to complement a specific style, colour or influence. It's all on you—how creatively you display them, the holders you use or the accents you pair with.

- Decorate along the aisle with candles secured in hurricane glass or lanterns
- Add taper or votive candelabras on the guest dinner tables
- Create or dress up the reception centrepieces
- Accent the cake or guestbook table
- Use as unique wedding favours

Colour Coordinating to Match the Theme

I should point out that overdoing it with a matchy-match look is entirely possible. (You don't want your guests thinking, um, yeah, lavender…we get it.) Begin with the five essential wedding elements—attire, invitations, flowers, cake and favours, and see where you can or should add more colour. Then consider details such as napkins, candles, signature drinks, your *jaimala* and your buffet tables—do you want them in the same fabric and colour as the decor?

- **Attire**: Your attire doesn't have to be solid red or purple, especially since colour accents are increasingly available. Mixing and matching dresses in varying shades—pink and orange, or pale green and yellow—can sometimes make a stronger statement. So you and your groom can incorporate just a dash of the colour, maybe in some embroidery or a dupatta.
- **Invitations**: Your invitations set the stage for the event, so remember the mood you want to evoke. This is your time to show it off. Coordinating the invitation colours with those of the wedding can be as easy as choosing a colour font, ribbon or monogram or as elaborate as layering colourful cards.
- **Flowers and decor**: No matter what colour you've chosen, you'll surely be able to find flowers in that shade. However, it does not mean the blooms will be available or affordable. If your dream flowers aren't an option, use neutral white flowers with centrepiece containers or other decor elements in your colour.

- **Wedding cake**: The cake is one of the easiest places to add colour—just mix it right. White icing makes a marvellous background for colourful sugar flowers, sugar paste stripes, polka dots or other effects. Fondant can also be created in any number of shades. For instance, a yellow and brown country-chic wedding might have a wedding cake iced in a light brown basket weave and topped with fresh sunflowers.
- **Favours**: Ultimately, it's more important to give something meaningful rather than something that matches but it can be a nice touch to pack favours in your colour scheme using themed gift tags and ribbons.

Chapter 8

How to Cater?

A wedding calls for a grand feast—you need a wonderful menu and scrumptious cuisines. In Indian weddings, food is given the utmost importance and maximum care is taken to serve delicious food to the guests. Our wedding menus are based on religion, region and culture. In most Hindu marriages, cuisine is limited to vegetarian, especially in South India. However, in certain North Indian communities and in Christian and Muslim marriages, non-vegetarian forms the main course of the wedding food.

Earlier, family members of the bride used to take care of the menu and personally supervise the food preparation but today's busy lifestyle drives most to opt for catering services. So if you do not have the time to manage the wedding kitchen, you can still arrange a grand feast by hiring a professional caterer for your party.

For the feast you will have to opt for one of the following:
- Professional caterers
- Home cooks or professionals who specialise in vegetarian/non-vegetarian cuisine
- Hotels/restaurants
- Members of the family

You will need to cater for the following occasions:

- *Sagaai*
- Several days over which pre-wedding rituals are held
- Wedding day
- Days on which the post-wedding ceremonies take place

It's Not Just About the Wedding Day

The first meal that the two families have together is when the alliance is finalised, which is the *sagaai, roka* or the engagement. It is important to plan it with care. Ideally, a vegetarian meal is served but in some communities a meal without a non-vegetarian dish is unthinkable.

In any get-together, irrespective of the time, tea and snacks along with sweets or assorted biscuits are served. This is an absolute must. Usually, guests start arriving at the bride as well as the groom's place from about ten days to a week before the wedding. All guests who drop in are served snacks and invited to stay for a meal. Relatives who decide to stay with the families of the bride and groom would naturally have all meals with the family.

Guests who have been put up in guest houses or hotels close by will also have all their meals with their hosts.

Home Catering

In many traditional homes, an outdoor oven and cooking marquee is put up where professional cooks with their helpers set up the kitchen. Non-vegetarian dishes are cooked in a different part of the marquee—care is taken to keep the cooking utensils and dishes serving non-vegetarian separate. The home kitchen is at times used for this purpose.

In case members of the family are taking over the whole business of cooking with help from cooks and helpers, the cooking will probably be done outdoors, as described above. If the home kitchen is big enough, cooking can be done inside too. In either case, both the indoor and outdoor kitchens will be used.

The areas that usually fall in the domain of catering are:

- Menu planning for all meals and snacks
- Setting up the kitchen with all necessary items

- Table decor, including centrepieces on the tables and buffet
- Cutlery and crockery
- Table linen
- Uniformed waiters
- Buffet arrangement with burners to keep the food hot
- Bar
- Soft drinks and other beverages
- Wedding cake, if so decided

Deciding the Menu

The first thing to do is to decide your menu. Agreeing on the wedding menu is one of the most important steps in a new relationship. It is the first time that the two families, with very different tastes, come together and reach a compromise. If this happens peacefully, the couple doesn't have much else to worry about!

Since this is a festive time, full of fun and good cheer, menu reflecting different cuisines should be planned. One universal favourite is the chaat—a savoury item and most weddings have a live chaat counter going. Snacks, drinks and beverages are in demand throughout the day, so specific arrangements have to be made and different cooks need to be assigned to this.

The Indian wedding feast usually begins with appetisers—possibly a mix of vegetarian and non-vegetarian items to cater to all guests. You could have traditional starters from your specific region. Appetisers assume special importance for they create the first impression and you would definitely like to put your best foot forward. Also, don't forget that there will be guests who feast only on the appetisers. Serve a scrumptious meal of delicacies so they can have their fill.

In some regional weddings, alcohol is also served. At times, there are even separate counters or stalls for beverages. These serve soft drinks, cocktails, mocktails, wine, whisky, etc. The main course follows next. It usually contains at least four to five vegetable dishes, different types of dals, pulao—rice and breads. An assortment of salads and condiments complement the meal. The main course traditionally reflects the culture and regional cuisine of the wedding couple or is derived from the theme of the wedding. It is the heaviest and grandest meal of all and should showcase the best delicacies of any cuisine.

After the meal, the guests are treated with desserts. The sweet section comprises mouth-watering ethnic fare. Seasonal sweets and ice creams are given preference due to their universal popularity and appeal. The Indian wedding feast culminates with the paan or *vida*. This is prepared by stuffing a betel leaf with betel nuts, spices and sugar, according to taste.

Ideally, a meal would include:

- **Welcome drinks**
  - Fruit juices
  - Ice cream based drink/milkshake
  - Soda based drink
  - Non-alcoholic drinks, as per your preference
- **Starters**
  - Equal number of veg and non-veg items, served over a span of two-three hours
  - Open up the soup and salad counters with the starters
  - It is followed by all the live stations, roti counters, and dessert counters (some traditions insist guests eat a bite of the dessert first). Keep them open for three hours.
- **Main Course**
  - The main course would have at least five vegetable dishes (more if it is a purely vegetarian meal), three or four non-vegetarian dishes, different types of dals (pulses), various rice preparations, an assortment of breads and a variety of salads and curd preparations.
- **Desserts**
  - A large selection of desserts including traditional Indian sweets and some cakes are laid.
  - Seasonal fruits and ice creams (including the indigenous kulfi) are part of the dessert too.

In the end, tea/coffee, paan and other mouth fresheners.

SAJJAN GHOT

In some cultures, a sit-down dinner has to be organised for the immediate family of the groom. You have to serve them when they sit down to eat with the bride and groom. Allocate about an hour for it. One can design a special menu also for it as it is generally not possible to serve all the items on the wedding spread.

Coffee or tea is usually not served but offered on request.

The couples may start planning their wedding spreads around three to six months in advance. The menu should be decided keeping in mind your budget. Remember the idea is to choose a good caterer who can provide food of your choice, within your budget.

- Make sure the menu has dishes that both the bride and groom like.
- Try not to repeat ingredients.
- Do give importance to colours. A balanced buffet has a red tomato-based sauce, a green spinach curry and a white cashew or curd-based dish.
- Pasta counters are a favourite at weddings but take care that the pasta is prepared fresh.
- Another list of ingredients that must be served fresh include rotis or any Indian breads, dishes like Thai curry or other coconut-based items and anything with cornflour.
- Our tastes have evolved and shifted more towards oriental food such as Thai, Malaysian noodles and laksa soup.
- Live dosa and appam counters are great but these only work with smaller crowds. Otherwise, queues become too long.
- The trick with larger crowds is to open up multiple serving stations and avoid a pile up.
- If the ceremony stretches till long hours, arrange for food and drinks to be served to the guests who stay back to attend.
- Keep in mind the requirements of older people and children as well, because their food habits are specific and need more care and attention.

Your Catering Budget

To decide your catering budget, ask yourself how important a role food and drinks play in your wedding vision. And keep in mind, there are many types of receptions to choose from. Catering costs are determined by a few factors: Number of guests you host, number of courses and food choices you offer, cost of ingredients, rentals, the way the food is served (buffet style, seated service or tray passed), and finally, the caterer's level of expertise. The more flexible you are about these variables, the more wiggle room your caterer has to create the best menu for your budget.

It is important you get an early indication of catering costs and what they include. Enquire about all the available options. If you are on a limited budget, share it with your caterer—ideally they should be able to provide a package that suits your needs. Closely consider what all is included in the price; this tends to vary a lot from one caterer to another.

The big things to look out for:

- Does your quote include VAT/service tax—you really don't want to get stung if this is overlooked.
- Caterers may or may not include tableware and linen hire within their quotes, so make sure you run this past them. You surely do not want to budget for such extras, right before the wedding.

Your wedding caterer and his professionalism decide the budget of your wedding catering. So choose your wedding caterer wisely.

Menu Planning and Catering Tips

The caterer influences much of your guests' experience at your reception, from the food and drink to the service, even sometimes decor. But don't let this daunting detail intimidate you. You may spend lakhs on the wedding and all people remember is the palak paneer. So here's how to make the food a hit.

- **Know your time and place**: Before you choose the menu, you need to know which meal you're serving. This depends mostly on the time of your wedding—lunch (12:30-3:30 pm) or dinner (6:00-10:30 pm).

- **Get your numbers right**: Unless your wedding budget is mammoth, the number of guests will play a vital role in deciding what to serve. You may love lobster but lobster for 400 guests might be out of question. You also have to think about how long it will take to serve the food—one of the biggest problems when serving party food is the lag time between its preparation and presentation. In case you decide to go for a small affair, you can serve a 'menu with a difference'.
- **Vote for variety**: While choosing your menu, be it a lunch, sophisticated aperitif or a lavish six-course meal, you need to make sure you feature variety in flavour, texture, appearance, temperature and colour to keep your senses stimulated. For example, if you're having a dessert buffet, you would not want the entire spread to consist only of ice creams. More importantly, remember to have a spread such that everyone finds something they like.
- **Culinary sophistication**: A growing number of to-be-weds are forgoing traditional 'banquet hall fare' for more adventurous cuisine. Why serve dal makhani and butter chicken when there's an oriental soiree! Even if you want an Indian menu, there are plenty of interesting yet economical ways to serve variations.
- **Sample the cuisine**: Taste the food before you finalise on a menu (or a caterer, for that matter). But don't just go by your taste buds. Pay attention to its presentation too. Do the dishes look attractive? Has the food been served with imagination? Do all the dishes complement each other? Ask yourself these important questions.
- **Stay in season**: Great cooks plan their menus around seasonal food—whatever is freshest in that month or season. On chilly winter evenings, indulge your guests with rich traditional cuisine. Ask your organiser to light a bonfire and hire a specialist bartender to keep the spirits up, all through the night. For summer weddings, avoid serving too much of rich Indian curries. Go for salads, pasta, fresh juices, chaat-papri, etc.

- **Drink and be married**: An increasing number of Indians consider liquor an inseparable part of the wedding menu. Factors that apply to food also apply to the bar—time of the day and type of reception, your budget, and more importantly, the tastes of your guests. Let somebody from the family handle the bar to ensure good service and control on usage.
- **How you serve**: The most popular way is to lay a buffet. However, you could have something in between a sit-down meal and a buffet—some fare is served to the guests at the tables while the rest is laid out. Having a 'live' counter where snacks are prepared in front of the guests adds to the appeal.
- **Seating**: You may have a very elaborate and fanciful menu. But does the seating arrangement ensure the guests can eat in comfort?

As roughly 30-50 per cent of your total wedding budget is allocated to your food, choosing the right caterer is a must.

Choosing the Wedding Caterer

A good caterer should listen to your ideas, relate to your overall vision for the day and then draw from their wealth of experience to build upon your ideas and deliver in line with expectations.

DECIDE ON YOUR BUDGET

The first and foremost point is your budget. Look for the best service provider within your budget. With some caterers, there is room for negotiation as their quotes are usually 'cost per head'. You could also substitute some items in the menu that may be expensive.

NAIL DOWN YOUR VENUE

This decision impacts your caterer at so many levels. For one, some locales, especially hotels, may require you to use their in-house caterers, so shopping around isn't necessary or allowed.

Second, if you're renting a space without a kitchen or one too small to really accommodate preparing dinner for 1,500 people, you'll need a caterer who is experienced in making meals at remote locations. He should have generators and all the other necessary equipment to serve a meal anywhere.

Third, having a venue in place also settles the theme of your wedding, which in turn, shall influence the kind of food you'll want to serve.

While many couples prefer the freedom of choosing their own caterer, working from a 'preferred list' of vendors isn't necessarily a disadvantage. Caterers listed on your site are likely to deliver good work as they would have your venue's seal of approval. They're also familiar with your site's kitchen, layout, coordinator, etc. Even if your venue allows you to hire outside caterers, ask the site coordinator for recommendations.

PLAN THE MENUS

Decide on the meals you need to cater. Plan the meals for each day and ceremony to get an overall picture. Do you want the caterer to provide snacks or will these be prepared by other cooks or even by family members in the home kitchen? Maybe, a mix of options can help you stay within your budget. It is also a good idea to plan a buffer, just in case you exceed it.

BOOK EARLY

Check out various options with regard to caterers and their rates, at least six months prior to the wedding. The sooner you book the caterer the better.

- Weddings happen by seasons and someone else may snap up the caterer you like.
- The rates rise closer to the wedding date. It would be easier to negotiate if you book much in advance.
- The best caterers are in the greatest demand, so book as far in advance as possible to ensure you get your top choice.

CONSULT FRIENDS

Ask your relatives, neighbours and friends to refer a professional wedding cook who is popular in the area for his preparations. Do not try an unknown cook under any circumstances. Though you can get an exhaustive list of catering service providers online, it is always better to trust the word of mouth. No one knows better than the customer whether a caterer does a good job. Check with friends who share your taste. Shortlist five or six caterers who come highly recommended.

Make the Call

Query each shortlisted caterer on phone first to get the basic input. Check if they are available on your wedding day and work within your budget. Once you learn who all are available and affordable, schedule interviews with your top three-five picks. During these interviews, answer questions about your event and ask a few of your own, like:

- What range of menu options and courses can you offer in my budget?
- Do you offer any rentals? If not, can you coordinate rentals including pick-up and return with third party? Can I bring in my own rentals, if the cost is less?
- How much time do you need to set up and break down?
- Do you provide liquor? What is the cost per drink/bottle? Will you buy back unopened bottles?
- Can I bring in my own liquor and if so, is there a corkage fee?
- Who will oversee the event and catering staff?
- How many servers will be there at my event?
- How will the caterer arrange the food on the buffet table or on plates? Is it possible to see photos of previous work displays?
- Do you provide bartenders? If so, how many do I need?
- Do you charge extra to pour coffee for guests?
- How do you handle guests who require vegetarian, Jain or special meals?
- Do you require a list of minimum or maximum number of guests?
- Will you provide food for the photographer, videographer and other vendors?
- What kind of deposit do you require to hold a wedding date?
- What is the payment schedule?
- What is your refund or cancellation policy?
- Are gratuities (generally sweet boxes for guests) already figured into the total price? If so, what percentage is being charged?

- When does the menu need to be finalised? When will you provide the final per person cost?
- When do you require the final head count?
- Do you offer menu tastings?
- Where will the food be prepared? Are there on-site facilities, or do you, the caterer and the site manager need to make additional arrangements? If the caterer brings in his own equipment, is there an additional fee?
- Will the caterer be willing to include a recipe you provide like a special family dish or an appetiser that has some sentimental significance?
- Will the caterer also be working on other weddings that coincide with your wedding (the same weekend/day or time)? You need to be sure they can devote sufficient attention to your event.

Ask What They Do Best

You need to know what food options they can provide. If they offer just the basics and you are considering something more adventurous, then look beyond the regular wedding caterers. A wide and varied menu is usually preferred. A caterer may boast he can give you any cuisine you envision but every caterer has his specialty. Find out what he thinks is terrific on his menu and decide how well that blends with your own sensibility. The caterer should be able to provide traditional dishes as well as some local delicacies. Take care to select the right caterer for your required menu. For instance, a caterer specialising in non-vegetarian items is not the best bet for a traditional Brahmin marriage having a vegetarian menu.

Know What They Supply

Generally, caterers also provide the china, table linens, utensils and glassware on the tables, serving dishes, presentation platters and other accoutrements for buffet and passed appetisers. Caterers even bring the wait staff and provide the bar service for your affair. Sometimes, the reception venue or decorator may provide these items. Find out if they handle table decoration as well. If you are not convinced, take no chance. The decorator at the venue can handle the table decor.

Quality of Food

Look for stunning presentation paired with sensational taste.
Go through the caterer's work portfolio to see pictures of his special
offering. Ensure that your caterer is well equipped with all necessary
professional and commercial facilities and a team of talented
individuals to serve your guests on the wedding day. Check on
the quality and sustainability of the produce they source. Creating
seasonal menus will enhance the quality and taste of your meal.

Don't just take the caterers' word—seek proof of where they
source their ingredients from. Check their references from previous
customers. Bear in mind that some people can be incredibly fussy,
so take what other couples say with a pinch of salt. A personal
recommendation from someone you really trust is the best way to go.

Tasting Session

Check if the caterer offers a tasting experience. A tasting tells you about
the quality, style and presentation of their food and gives you the
opportunity to explore how your own ideas can be worked into their
existing menus.

- Caterers with storefronts will usually give clients a sampling of
  reception fare.
- Others host tastings a few times a year.
- Some caterers only provide tastings once a contract is in place.
- Others require couples to pay for tastings.
- Some don't offer them at all.

If a caterer you're considering doesn't offer you a tasting, you
need to double-check their references. How about paying for a sample
menu for two to see how it goes? With so much of your wedding
budget at stake, this won't be a bad investment and you and your
fiancé can make a date of it.

Setting the Scene

A caterer plays a crucial role in making your big day a bigger success.
Besides providing quality food, your caterer is likely to be the last
supplier to dress your tables before the celebrations begin. Ensure that

apart from the menu, the caterer is also good at table decor—a good meal must also be presented well.

Check that the decorations:

- Are homogenous
- Match your theme
- Are aesthetic and elegant
- Allow for space as waiters, guests and children will be moving about

You also need to decide whether you want a sit-down meal or a buffet. Arrangements have to be made accordingly. In a sit-down meal, you need to plan the seating for:

- The bride's family, relatives and guests
- The groom's family, relatives and guests
- Office friends and colleagues
- Vegetarian and non-vegetarian guests

The caterer should be knowledgeable about cocktails and other liquor that is being served and the glasses they are to be served in.

Most Indians eat with their fingers. A washbasin or some kind of arrangement for washing and wiping hands and rinsing the mouth is a must.

Traditional South Indian meals are served on banana leaves. In many cases, the guests sit on the floor on white sheets.

Also, in some cases, custom may dictate that there are separate areas for men and women to eat. Sometimes, long trestle tables are set up as the first ceremony begins and these are taken down after the last ceremony is over.

Nominate a Catering Manager

Even if you have hired a caterer, do nominate a family member as the catering manager to oversee the whole wedding food segment. He must supervise the food preparation, see that it is ready on time and perhaps do a tasting as well.

Service

Finally, service is extremely important, equal to the quality and style of your food. It's important that you receive excellent service, right from your initial enquiry, through to your tasting session right up until the end of the wedding day itself. Your caterer should serve you with the enthusiasm and expertise your wedding deserves!

Check if the caterer will take care of the food service as well. Else you appoint your relatives and neighbours to help out or hire waiters to handle the service at your wedding ceremony. The caterer's team is bound to know the food and service well, so it is safest to go for the caterers and their own staff. Make sure you know the ratio of staff to guests and that the staff comes suitably dressed. Bear in mind that apart from the catering staff, you may need additional waiters and waitresses to supply drinks and snacks to the guests.

Classic Buffet Goof-ups
- Pasta becomes soggy and begins to spoil if kept out for too long
- Rotis, naans—Indian breads, must be made fresh (ideally use a portable tandoor)
- Coconut milk-based curries don't work if left for long
- Fried starters or koftas become limp and need to be changed every thirty-forty minutes
- Decide on hot or cooler food based on the weather (soup for winters and sandwiches in summer)
- Make sure the ingredients you decide are available

Keep in Mind
- First check if your caterer is available on your wedding date. Find out what the booking and payment process is. Be sure to understand at what point your date becomes secure and when payments are needed. The last thing you need is a sudden shock and unexpected bill just before the wedding.
- Insist your caterer visits your wedding venue to check the kitchen arrangements. He has to plan the utensils and cooking requirements. You or your nominated person has to organise the caterer's requirements properly and on time.
- Avoid preparing too much or too little quantity of food items. Assess your invitee list and expected number of guests to avoid unnecessary expenses.

- Prepare and serve food on time. Delay in service will reduce consumption and food will go waste.
- Have an exclusive counter for beverages or nominate a team to serve it.
- Decide from where to source the vegetables, fruits and non-vegetarian items.
- The caterer should be open to your ideas and suggestions, with regard to recipes and spices to use.
- For a personal touch, some of the bride's family members could stand behind selective food counters.
- If you are specific about something like a royal cocktail service or some special local cuisine, you must instruct your caterer clearly, right at the beginning.

Add an Extra Edge

Earlier, a Café Coffee Day or Domino's logo had nothing to do with a wedding. But things have changed now! New trends emerge each season! From branded stalls and live stations to unique presentation styles—food served at Indian weddings has dramatically changed. Let's check the latest trends in cooking at big fat Indian weddings this season.

Presenting in Style

Wedding tables now don a lush look with stylish centrepieces and fine linen. Next comes exquisite cutlery. Use creative utensils like porcelain spoons, mini cast iron skillets, shot glasses, miniature cups and unique forks for that extra edge!

Brand It!

From local brands like Haldiram's and BTW (Bitoo Tikki Wala) to multinational chains like Domino's and Costa Coffee—all are making the big fat extravaganza even bigger! These add to the opulence and make it look stylish. These, of course, don't come cheap. Reportedly, for a typical Indian wedding, you may need to shell out five-eight lakh rupees to treat your guests with premium American ice-cream Häagen-Dazs.

Chapter 9

Click Perfect Memories

Wedding pictures are a cherished keepsake, passed down through generations. They are the commemoration of the thousands of hours and lakhs of rupees spent to plan the most important day of your life. So choosing your wedding photographer is not a decision to be taken lightly.

You should not compromise either on the quality or on the number of professional photographs. A distant relative may offer to play 'wedding photographer for the day', but would you trust an inexperienced person with your life's most treasured memories? Photography buffs in your family or friend circle may suggest they want to photograph everything as well but tell them politely that you prefer them to be your guest and just enjoy themselves. Flashes from other cameras may set off lights that the photographer has set around the room.

Professional photography isn't expensive—it's priceless. Your wedding day will be filled with unforgettable 'once-in-a-lifetime' moments that you'll want to relive and share. No matter what your budget or style preferences, your once-in-a-lifetime wedding deserves unique, specialised services that will capture and preserve your treasured remembrances in a top-of-the-line, heirloom wedding album. As the years go by, you will come to appreciate it even more. Good photographic ability ensures that the essence of you, your relationships and your events are preserved—you will have hundreds of professional images (in black and white, colour, sepia and mixed effects) for your album.

Photography Styles

No two weddings are alike, likewise for photographers. Photographers come in many different personalities and styles. Some stick to one specific style, others shoot in a variety of different styles. Then we have the real innovators who create their own style. When it comes to wedding photography, it's always good to understand the differences, so you know what to expect from the different photographers out there. The most popular styles of wedding photography in today's market are as follows:

TRADITIONAL

Classical wedding photography comprises a series of contrived posed or 'set up' photographs of the wedding party and the two families. Traditional wedding photographers tend to follow a 'shot list'. Lighting and backgrounds are tightly controlled by the photographer, resulting in well-exposed images.

Disadvantage: The couple spends too much time in getting their photograph taken. Images can look visually pleasing but stiff due to their static and contrived nature and are predictable. You probably don't want to rely too heavily on formal portraiture or you will miss out on the energy, passion and raw emotion surrounding your wedding. Most couples want to include some candid, photojournalistic photography in their wedding albums, alongside the formal shots.

PHOTOJOURNALISTIC OR REPORTAGE PHOTOGRAPHY

Wedding photojournalism appeals to couples seeking a series of unique photographs designed to 'tell a story' or narrate their wedding day. Wedding photojournalism has grown very popular—it is the art of capturing moments unobtrusively. You will barely know that the photographer is there—he covers the wedding as it unfolds. Wedding photojournalism is not about poses. It documents the emotions and energy surrounding the occasion.

Disadvantage: Wedding photojournalists do not manipulate or create events. The resulting images therefore can be unpredictable; some consider this a drawback. Personally, I find this aspect beautiful—it is a true record of your day.

If you choose a photographer who shoots exclusively in this style, couples may regret not having any traditional photographs in their album. Also, with reportage wedding photography, you are relying on the photographers' interpretation of your day.

ILLUSTRATIVE OR CONTEMPORARY WEDDING PHOTOGRAPHY

Photographers, who shoot weddings in this style, highlight the design element by placing their subjects in settings of interesting composition and backgrounds. Contemporary photography often involves unusual or 'off the wall' ideas and strange camera angles. This photographer is usually a very creative person who not just directs his subjects but also encourages them to interact in order to get a more spontaneous feel. This brings out the photographer's artistic creativity and compositional skills rather than simply capturing a series of moments.

Although, this style of photography may be less popular, when done correctly the results can be fantastic and make your wedding album unique. You will often see this style featured in glossy wedding magazines.

Disadvantage: The downside is that it doesn't really provide a true record of your wedding day. You might be disappointed if your album ends up like an art exhibition

CANDID PHOTOGRAPHY

It is that click which requires no preparation or posing on the part of the person because the emotion itself is magnificent enough to be captured. Candid photography will provide you something that you can share with friends. Even if you see it many years down the line, you will still be able to connect with the emotions of the occasion.

At the end of the day, there's a world of difference that a truly skilled candid wedding photographer can bring. You get a neatly woven story of your wedding in pictures. As they say, a picture is worth a thousand words—a photo of the bride shedding tears during her *vidaai* (departure from parental home) or the groom smiling secretly at his bride even as the priest rattles off something complicated in Sanskrit, is something that will be immortal and priceless!

Candid wedding photography services also involve dedicating a photographer to the couple, a photographer for parents and other close family members and one for a theme-based portrait session. The portrait session is designed according to the requirements—the couple's love story, their likes, etc. For example, if a couple has been together since school/college times, a pathshala kind of environment can actually be created for the portrait session. Focus on a portrait session doesn't mean that the happy mood surrounding the wedding is ignored. The album is a mix of mood captures and portraits, and together they make up a great wedding album.

What to Look for in Your Wedding Photographer?

It's always sensible to have one team of photographers for both sides. Besides reducing the photography budget, it also filters the number of photographers at the wedding which means the couple is less camera-conscious and more relaxed.

EXPERIENCE AND TRAINING

There is no magic number for years of experience, no level of training which ensures a professional or business will serve you well. Sometimes, a talented and conscientious newcomer to the profession can give you service equal to that of an established professional who has less talent or enthusiasm or fewer principles. Find out how many weddings the photographer has shot. He may have been a professional photographer for fifteen years but does only one wedding per year. Along with the number of years he has been filming weddings, ask how many actual weddings he has photographed. Weigh the information you learn about a professional's experience with the other characteristics that follow.

COMPETENCE

Check their work portfolio. Viewing a few albums will tell you if their working style matches your need. You'll get to see the detailing and finishing techniques they use. Ask for formal references.

REPUTATION

In the wedding industry, word gets around if a business is trustworthy or unethical, if the staff is helpful or pushy, if the prices are reasonable or expensive. Weddings involve a lot of money, hence, if the couple did not get what they wanted or expected, they tend to broadcast the bad news. Some customers though are unsatisfied because of their own unrealistic expectations. Compare favourable recommendations against your own needs and expectations.

OFFERING

Whether it's à la carte or a fixed package, fully understand what all you will be getting. Is there room for changes, if yes, will that cost you? How much time will he spend? What if you need more time? Make sure you know what's coming. Ensure there are no 'hidden costs' and both parties are clear on the deliverables—digital copies only/albums/size/pages of albums.

COMMUNICATION

A responsible professional will make an effort to inform you of his practice, limitations, timetables and any problems which may occur. He will try to answer your questions and address concerns, if any. Pay close attention to what he says and abide by his guidelines.

STYLE AND PERSONALITY

In your mind, you want something a little alternative, artistic and candid. Some photographers shoot in this fashion, some don't. There are also photographers who are so militant about the integrity of their work and their candid style that they will outright refuse to take a posed photo of you and your Usha Aunty (true story.) Choose a happy medium. Although everyone has their own way of expressing themselves, look for a professional with whom you can work effectively. You must agree with your photographer's methods and trust him to handle your wedding shoot and any crises, which may occur.

Truth in Advertising

If you are dealing with a studio that employs a number of wedding photographers, make sure you are shown samples of the actual photographer who will be assigned to your wedding. Meet him face-to-face before your event.

Equipment

Just like every photographer should bring along an assistant to help him during your wedding, every photographer needs backup equipment in case his original equipment fails. Flashes, lenses and cameras should all come in multiples. Extra batteries and memory cards are also a must.

Enthusiasm

A consistently apathetic or negative professional may be a poor choice. Once you have a contract in place, breaking the agreement may be impossible or expensive, so try to gauge the interest of the professional early on. His enthusiasm to work with you must be evident.

Comfort Factor

Regardless of how much you love the work on their site or the pricing and packages they offer, it's crucial to feel comfortable with this person being in your intimate space all day. Take the time to get to know this person, interview more than one photographer and really weigh up the decision with a lot of questions.

Timely Delivery

You want to implicitly trust the photographer to deliver the images to you in a timely fashion and more importantly, capture images that you will love. I know people who have waited years for their photos and photographers who have lost entire weddings and tried to go rogue and shirk the responsibility. So do your research—speak to their previous clients and look up bridal blogs.

Hiring a wedding photographer is one of the first things you should do because the top photographers book their schedules even a year in advance. If you want outstanding pictures, start searching for your photographer when you have decided on the date. If you will be celebrating an 'in-season' wedding, book your photographer at least six months in advance. The following steps can help you select the best photographer to record your big day.

- Decide what level of service you want from your wedding photographer. Perhaps, you only need photographs of your ceremony/reception, so just one-three hours of photography may be enough for you. Other couples may prefer a complete package that may include a pre-wedding engagement session, sangeet, mehendi, other smaller events, bridal portraits and newly-wed photos.

- Decide how many images you would like. Higher-end photographers often capture thousands of images for you to keep forever.

- Figure out how much time and expertise you have to process your images yourself. Many brides choose photographers that only give them a disc of their images (no album, prints or other items) and later find that they lack the time, software or knowledge to create their own albums, properly edit the photos (crop, colour correct, etc.). Often, years later, these couples just have a stack of dusty, cheaply processed proof photos or photos on a disc that cannot be lovingly displayed to remind them and their family members and friends of the wedding day.

- Decide how you will use your pictures. Do you plan to purchase just an album for yourself or also pictures for your walls, prints to give to friends and family or even put the images on stationery, invitations, calendars, mugs, T-shirts, and magnets?

- Good wedding photographers have a reputation of success, and therefore are relatively well-known. They should be the easiest to find. Seek recommendations from friends and family who have held weddings prior to your event. Ask if they liked the photographer. Go through their wedding albums. Additionally, ask your wedding planner, venue manager, caterer, dress designer, florist and banquet director to refer known professionals. Check out 'real wedding' features in bridal magazines and blogs. Talented photographers have often shot these, which is why they're being featured. Make a list of photographers who seem to fit your criteria for price and available format.

- Visiting websites of photographers can help you shortlist them. Call for references and check their standing with local event management teams. See if your styles match. Consider how well they perform in different settings/environments. For example, for a beach wedding, find a photographer who is stronger in filming outdoors.

- Interview shortlisted candidates on the phone. Ask if they are available on your chosen date, how much experience they have, whether they specialise in weddings, how soon after the wedding can you expect your prints or disc. Strike out names that do not conform to your preferences or are unavailable on your date.

- Make appointments to meet each finalist face-to-face. Go to these meetings with your spouse-to-be if possible.

- Look at samples of their work, get a brochure with details about wedding packages, discuss your wedding with them and observe how much of it they understand. The photographer is likely to show you two or three wedding albums. Make sure that at least one album you see features an entire wedding—from start to finish. After examining all his work closely, ask if you can see another set of photographs from a recent wedding. This way you get to see both his best work from the pre-selected albums as well as his average daily work.

- First, examine the basics of the pictures such as colour, clarity, exposure, graininess and composition. Then determine the photographer's style—does he shoot photos that are adventurous and unique or are they standard and ordinary? This will also help you zero onto the style you prefer. Pay attention to the photographer's ability to capture the emotion of the day.

- Notice how polite they are. Ask yourself, 'Is he someone who will understand my state of mind and work around it—I may be stressed, exhausted, dehydrated, overheated, and ready to faint in that heavy lehenga! Or is he the type who takes pictures without much passion.'

- Discuss wedding photography equipment. Although you may not be a professional photographer yourself, you should know what type of camera and equipment your photographer would be using during your event.
- Finally, find out if the photographer has shot at your wedding venue before. If he has, he may know of places to get good shots or ways to capture the best moments.
- Discuss all the photographers you visited with your fiancé. Compare available packages from the photographers you both like. Decide which photographer and package best fits your needs and expectations. As with any major decision, sleep on it.
- Call your chosen photographer and ask them to pencil you in on their calendar until you can come back to sign the contract. Make an appointment to sign the contract.

Signing the Contract

- First, negotiate price. Contrary to what you may have been told, everything is negotiable including price, packages and wedding proofs. This means knowing exactly what type of service and package of photographs you will be getting. What is being offered can vary from one photographer to the other! Right from the option to get only soft-copies, online galleries, slide shows, wedding album, artwork, DVDs, wedding films, photo booths, video booth, the list goes on...
- Then make sure that the photographer you want is the photographer you will get at your wedding. Some larger companies may do a bait and switch.

The contract shall be a record of the services you both agreed upon.

- Confirm, confirm, confirm! This is the golden rule of wedding planning. You must confirm appointments, plans, reservations, etc. several times—once during contract signing, a second time three-six months before the event, and again one-two weeks before the wedding, when you work out last-minute details, changes and requests.

- Introduce the photographer to important members of the family and your close friends to ensure they aren't missed out in the coverage!

If you are having a destination wedding, a local photographer has his own benefits:

- Your search for a wedding photographer located in your wedding destination is pretty much going to start and end online. But you could also seek recommendations from the hotel/resort you book, your event manager, decorator or any friends/family you may have locally.
- Once you've found someone with an online portfolio that catches your eye, email to learn what they offer. While not a perfect test, you can get a feel from their replies.
- The downside, of course, is the lack of real contact. But make sure you meet them at least once before the wedding. You will probably be travelling to the destination once prior to the wedding to double-check your bookings and arrangements.
- You can also ask them to provide references from previous clients. Also, check with your resort or wedding planner to learn if they have worked with the photographer before.
- There is some amazing talent to be found in these destinations. These local photographers also know all the best locations to make the most of the destination for your bridal portraits. This kind of insider information on unique and picturesque settings can make the difference between great wedding photos and amazing wedding photos.
- Another plus for local photographers is the cost. Your budget won't be eaten up by flight tickets, work visas (if it's a foreign destination) and accommodation costs. These savings can perhaps help you buy those extra special favours you were eyeing for your guests!

At the end of the day, you have to choose a photographer whose work inspires you and who makes you feel comfortable.

Add the next two things in the bucket of things you desire from the photographer.

Have a 'wish list': Don't be shy to discuss with your photographer exactly what you want. Present him your 'wish list'. For example, you may request a close-up shot of the various decorations, photos of you with certain guests, etc. Ask for multiple shots of all important moments—the exchange of *varmala*s, the *phere*, sindoor *bharai*, etc.

Studio shots: You may also want to have some studio photos taken with your fiancé, anywhere from a week to one day before your wedding. This allows you a controlled, unrushed environment to ensure some good quality photos with both of you looking impeccable. Some brides are reluctant to appear before the groom in their wedding attire until the wedding day. That's entirely understandable. Postpone the studio session then to a day or two after the wedding.

Some Latest Additions
SHORT MOVIE STYLE WEDDING VIDEO (CINEMATOGRAPHY)

The film opens on the facade of a lavish Rajasthani palace flanked by lush gardens. The camera takes you inside where the bride, resplendent in a gem-studded lehenga, descends a spiral staircase. The groom, wearing a bright red *pagdi*, awaits by the open door. The camera pans across the lush grounds behind, goes on to focus on the festivities of an outdoor wedding reception even as the sound of a *shehnai* grows louder. Later, in a quiet corner, the father of the bride sheds a soft tear and the daughter's mehendi-embellished hand gently wipes it away. The couple in this film are real, so are the tears, the pandit and his slokas.

It's the modern, professional avatar of the traditional wedding video. You are definitely a star at your own wedding—with all eyes on you, your designer clothes and gorgeous make-up. What if you can capture all the emotions of that day and relive them over and over again? Photographs are good but what if there was a better alternative?

A personalised wedding film, wherein you and your husband are the lead pair, your families and friends feature as the supporting cast—you have the typical song and dance routines, drama, comedy, action and emotion. Yes, all this and more. It'll come with a two-minute trailer, followed by the main film. Now, what's better?

Gone are the days when the videographer roamed around the wedding venue with his equipment to shoot a five-hour-long video that starred badly edited 'candid' moments of the wedding (not even sparing the decked up aunty while she opens her mouth to gorge on the gulab jamuns).

SLOW MOTION PHOTO BOOTH

This new trend in wedding photography and films is expected to become one of the 'must have' deliverables for a photographer/videographer because of its fun quotient.

A slow motion video is nothing but shooting multiple frames at higher frame rates and then playing them back at a lower frame rate. These videos however, look more interesting than the actual event! Currently, a slow motion photo booth for a wedding event can be very expensive but that too is likely to change.

You can't recreate a wedding, or any of the moments within it. It's the ultimate documentary assignment and your photographer, whoever they turn out to be, only has one shot. So choose wisely.

Wedding Photo Checklist

MEHENDI

- Photos of the decor
- Bride applying mehendi
- Bride with her friends and relatives with hennaed hands
- Candid shots of the bride and guests

SANGEET

- Photos of the decor
- Bride and groom dancing together
- Different shots of the various performances
- Candid photos of the couple

HALDI

- Close-up shot of the haldi and other ingredients
- Haldi being applied on the bride

WEDDING

- Shots of the groom's sherwani and accessories
- Groom getting ready
- Groom with his friends
- Father of the groom helping him get ready
- Full-length shot of the groom when he is ready
- Groom with his parents and siblings
- Shots of the bridal lehenga, jewellery and other accessories
- Bride getting ready
- Bride with sisters/friends while getting ready
- Candid shot of bride with her mother
- Full-length shot of the bride after she's fully dressed
- Bride with her parents and siblings

THE CEREMONY

- Exterior and interior shots of the venue
- Candid photos of the *baraat*
- Bride's family welcoming the groom
- Close-up shot of the groom waiting for the bride
- Bride walking to the dais
- Candid shot of the bride and groom
- The couple exchanging garlands
- Bride and groom greeting guests
- Candid shots of the guests
- Shots of the different rituals
- Food counter
- Bride and groom feeding each other
- Bride bidding goodbye to her family
- Candid shots of the bride's family after the ceremony

AT THE GROOM'S PLACE

- Shot of the decorated car
- Welcoming the bride at the groom's house
- Shots of the couple as they take part in the wedding games

RECEPTION

- Shots of the couple getting ready
- Photos of the venue
- Detailed shots of the decor, table settings, centrepieces
- Shots of guests arriving and greeting the couple
- Candid photos of the couple
- Shots of the couple dancing
- Shots of family members dancing
- Musicians/DJ performing
- Full-length shot of the couple

Capture the Romance—Pre-wedding Photography

Have you recently gotten engaged? Congratulations! You deserve unique engagement and romantic pre-wedding photos. Photos that tell your own story—photos that make you laugh, cry, scream, smile, howl or even kiss your fiancé. Pre-wedding couple photography or fun-filled romantic couple photography is now an inseparable part of wedding photography. Pre-wedding shoots were unheard of ten years back. But today, they are a mandatory ritual for so many couples.

Why Go for a Pre-wedding Photo Shoot?

A pre-wedding shoot captures the chemistry of a couple before the actual wedding—those special feelings and emotions, which will soon be replaced by deeper intimacy and greater acquaintance. Couples scout for locations and themes for their shoot and want to make it one of the most special events of their wedding. Some couples recreate scenes of their courtship—take their photographer along to their favourite haunt, places where they dated or proposed. Some get their first love letter photographed and preserved forever. Others leave it to the photographer to candidly capture their love.

Pre-wedding photography is a welcome switch from the traditional wedding day photography to contemporary fashion photography. The concept is to improvise the wedding album tradition to fashion-forward pictures that are relatively flawless.

A pre-wedding portfolio is an aggregation of photo journalistic and posed images shot by the professional candid wedding photographer.

It reflects both 'beauty and love' in a fashion portfolio that a couple can flaunt and cherish forever.

Couples also get to know their photographer a bit during the pre-wedding photo sessions. Sometimes, the wedding day itself is a bit rushed, making it tough for the bride and groom to focus on their pictures.

Pre-wedding photography can capture flawless and independent expressions, embracing your love in pictures for life.

Pre-wedding shoots often require the couple to pose, and each shot has to be pre-conceived, planned and staged. Most of the couples are a little anxious at an engagement/wedding photo shoot, as for many, it's their first introduction to a professional photo shoot. After going through a pre-wedding photo shoot, the couple would be more relaxed. When it comes to their big day, they then know what to expect and the photographer knows what works best for them. I, thus strongly recommend that all couples opt for a pre-wedding photo shoot.

The most important part of any couple shoot is to bring out the authentic emotions between the two. Every couple is different, having unique stories and personalities. A photographer's job is to put these personalities, in their true sense, in pictures, depicting their unique love story.

Flaunt Your Pre-wedding Shoot

Pre-wedding photos look great in the guestbook too—show them around to family and friends when they check in. You can also make a short slide show video of selected photos, which can be played at the wedding or reception venue on plasma screens or as an entrance video before you make your entrance. You can also have your favourite photographs from the shoot mounted in a frame and placed beside the entrance for guests to see as they enter.

You can also get a pre-wedding documentary style video shot—it's perfect to play at your wedding reception. You can use parts of the pre-shoot within the trailer and give the option of recording messages to one another.

Pre-wedding photography is one genre that's picking up very fast in India post the social media revolution. People want to preserve these early memories and can also use them as a teaser for the big day.

Some couples even do thematic or conceptual pre-wedding destination wedding photo shoots. It could be as exotic as a beautiful beach at a far-off location or a simple and serene temple or church setting.

How to Prepare for Your Pre-wedding Shoot?

- **Do not show pictures taken by other photographers to your photographer**: That will kill his creativity. If you like that other photographer, go ahead and hire him. Remember, photos cannot be recreated. You are special and your photographs will also be special and unique.

- **Zero in on a date and time for the shoot**: Your photographer might want you to reach the venue before sunrise. Don't request him to delay the shoot—the morning light is soft and will lend a glow to the pictures. The high and harsh afternoon lights are bound to play up the deep shadows around your eyes.

- **Decide the venue for the shoot**: Location is important as it provides the background, which influences the total effect of the image. Shuttling from one venue to another is not a good option as you end up wasting time in travelling and lose the soft morning light which is a must for the shoot. If you intend to have your pictures taken in different locations, book separate sessions.

- **Discuss the dress you would like to wear**: Your photographer might suggest some colours depending on the setting. If you are contemplating a change of clothes in between the shoot, know beforehand when and where you are going to do so. Finding a place to change might be a challenge at some locations.

- **Props play a vital role in a romantic couple shoot**: The handbags you carry, the dupatta, shoes and other accessories on you—all become an element in the picture. So select them with care. The engagement rings, flowers, balloons, an umbrella, a luxury car or any other wisely chosen creative prop can create magic.

- **Be well-rested before the shoot**: However, get up early in the morning to have enough time for your make-up. The pictures can only be as good as you look. The photographer will enhance them with good composition and his artistic flair. But you indeed should look your best.
- **Last but not the least, enjoy your day**: If you are in a good mood, it will reflect in the pictures. Be happy, dance and play with your beau. If you can do just that, your photographer can give you some great pictures to cherish for the rest of your life.

So there you go, all ready for the shoot. Have fun!

Chapter 10

Wedding Invites and Stationery

An exquisite wedding invitation card can be the perfect beginning for an event as important as your wedding. Pronounce your big day with style and flair.

First impressions last forever and wedding invitations set the tone and theme for the entire affair. Typical accompaniments to the marriage invitation cards include boxes of traditional Indian sweets, dry fruits, money-stuffed envelopes and some gift items in a handmade paper bag or something that goes with the marriage theme. Lots of interesting gifts and accessories go along with the invites these days. These include graphic printed stoles, divine idols, fragrance, candles, etc.

The wedding invitation must be stamped with a logo or a motif that corresponds to the wedding theme and also acts as your personal style statement. The logo will be repeated all the way from the pre-wedding invitations (save-the-date cards) to wedding cards, and even wedding 'thank you' cards. Plan ahead for beautifully crafted and coordinated wedding stationery.

The card serves as a regular reminder of your wedding. The matter inside the wedding invitations should be well-organised; the words must make the guests feel special. The importance and beauty of the cards lie in the polite and elegant way they invite guests to your marriage.

Put all that together and it's easy to see the central role invites play in your big day. But remember, this is supposed to be fun! Take a deep breath and consider the following invitation details to guide yourself through the process intact.

Hint the Theme

Thematic wedding invites are designed taking into consideration many aspects of the wedding that include the decor, theme of the individual functions, venue/city. In case of a destination wedding in Bangkok, Dubai or Mauritius, classic themes like Buddha Bar, Oriental, Arabic or French could be used. Your invite can become the trailer for your chosen theme. For this, the designer must visually illustrate the theme in his work of art. The invites should hint at the theme, but subtly.

Many brides struggle to create the perfect theme for their weddings. In my experience, brides begin with a theme in mind, but it goes out the window once they see invitation samples they love. Keep an open mind about invitations, especially if you have no locked-in theme or colour scheme. My best advice when it comes to planning a wedding is to stick to a colour theme. Narrow design themes can eliminate choices before you've even considered them.

Today, there is no limit to creativity! For example, a natural wood tropical wine case, with intricate etching of the invite and a custom labelled wine bottle inside can be the perfect invite for a beach wedding. Tropical flowers and sea animals could inspire the graphics.

Popular themes conceptualised successfully in the past include, jewels of the Nizam, French garden, Baroque, Greece, masquerade, paisley, etc. Another novel concept is based on the theme of Indian art—the invite box styled in the form of a coffee table book in real canvas.

Innovative Design

Couples today wish to reach out to their friends and family in fun and creative ways, even when announcing the date of their wedding!

The tradition of handing out conventional marriage cards with a simple motif and boring colours has long faded. But what one bride loves, another may refuse. For example, a more outgoing bride may feel that a metallic pocket fold with a satin ribbon and rhinestone buckle perfectly sets the stage for an elaborate, flashy wedding. On the other hand, traditional brides may prefer classic invitations, featuring a white cotton card stock with black, gold or silver lettering that appears simple and elegant.

We all love to see bright colours and some funky designing in cards. Imagine receiving a business card holder in the mail. Open it to find a business card wedding invitation for each function. This small and stylish invite can be the talk of the town—it promises a unique experience for the guest, who anticipates it will be a very 'original and modern' wedding.

With brides and grooms getting increasingly involved in the design and execution process for the wedding invites, a lot more youthful and eclectic cards are landing in our mailboxes. From monochromes to neon, colours take the lead. While the classic earthy and pastel tones shall continue to be the staple, more couples are experimenting with bright colours for an added punch.

Laser cuts are also gaining popularity with their intricate and delicate detailing. Also, watch out for geometrical, clean lines and attention to detail. The latest trend for wedding cards is vintage regalia invites inspired by the British Raj, the grand life of the royal families, Indian architecture and Nizam's jewels. Typically this would mean:

- Antiquated finishes that makes the invites look royal and elegant
- Colour palette will be a beautiful mix of ivory, camel, distressed golds, chocolate and natural wood with real gem colours
- Filigree work and monumental jalis

Much is New in Print Technology

The beauty is in fusing timeless Indian craftsmanship with cutting-edge print technology to create finely crafted invites. Be it printing on newer materials, trying new styles of printing or using a primitive technique in the most unconventional manner—a lot is new in wedding invites.

Buying expensive invites will not make your wedding classy or unique…you need to have an eye for detail and style. At times, even the simplest of invites can come out extremely elegant. There are people who like very unstated elegance and cannot stand garish stuff at all—their invites are generally muted in all aspects, except for style and sophistication.

Research Before You Shop

Ease your invitation stress by researching a little before you contact vendors. Know roughly what you want but keep an open mind. Shopping for invitations online can save brides a lot of time, money and stress. Wedding e-marketplaces are also gaining momentum in India. They offer a vast selection of vendors who provide custom design invitations to fit each bride's unique requirements.

Hunt for Reasonable Deals

Invitations can get pricey. What's the fair price for the quality and detailing you require? Only by comparing vendor prices on wedding e-marketplaces and the local market can you get reasonable deals. Some vendors offer free guest address printing on invitation envelopes, while others offer free shipping. It's important to consider each aspect of a price to get the biggest bang for your buck. Invitation cards start from as low as twenty rupees per invite and then there is no limit. Today, people spend a lot of money to make that unique first impression.

Wedding Invite Etiquette

Families often send out more than one invitation card to the guests; one for the actual wedding day and two more, one for the sangeet—a wedding function in which people sing with instrumental accompaniment and another for the reception. No matter which part of the wedding ceremony it refers to, the text on all wedding cards should sound formal and courteous.

Although your card decision would be guided mostly by your budget and personal choice, there are some standard norms to abide by.

Keep these essential aspects in mind while designing wedding cards and sending them out.

- Always use vibrant colours, unique styles and high quality paper to make the cards. The invitation should reflect the extravagance and elegance of the event. Remember, these wedding cards are sent to make the guests feel warm and welcome.

- It is an Indian custom to have separate cards from the bride and groom's side. And a lot of guests actually receive two different cards for the same occasion. Why not have a single card to cut redundant costs and make your guests feel extra special on being invited by both sides. It would also symbolise the unity of two families.

- When addressing the recipients on the envelope, don't miss out any of the three—the title, first name and the last name. Also, check that the names of your guests have been spelt correctly.

- Indian wedding invites must suitably represent the religious and cultural traditions of the family. Consult family elders to ensure all necessary aspects have been included before the cards go in for printing.

- Indian marriages comprise several events, each having a significance of its own. Generally, the wedding starts with *sagaai*—ring ceremony, followed by mehendi, haldi ceremony, *jaimala* and then the marriage reception. In case you wish to invite your guests to all these events, you need to mention the same on the card, with their respective timings. Check the timings once again before the card goes for final printing.

- Irrespective of the chosen pattern or layout, it is wise to refrain from wordy content. When you write too much on the card, it becomes difficult for guests to fish out the important and relevant bits. So avoid flowery and ornamental language as far as possible. Keep it short, sweet and to the point.

- Make sure all RSVP contacts are mentioned correctly on the card with their respective contact numbers! You might wish to include directions to the reception with a map overleaf or an extra insert.

- Plan the printing schedule in advance, so that invites can be sent out on time. Refrain from sending last-minute invites to anyone. It makes them feel like a 'last-minute inclusion' on your guest list.
- If you're planning to have *pheras* at eight o'clock, do not put down 7:30 pm on your invitation. Perhaps, you kept that margin to ensure no one misses your grand entrance. But this way, guests who came on time would be kept waiting and that's not done.
- Your invitation sets the tone for your wedding and that starts with the envelope. Now, we're not saying you need to hire a calligrapher but it adds such a personal touch to address them by hand. Ask a friend or relative with nice handwriting to help out. Or try this calligraphy cheat: Using a fancy font in a very light grey, run each envelope through your printer, and then trace over the printed address using a calligraphy pen. Your guests will never know your secret!
- Ideally, wedding cards should be sourced from a trusted vendor so that you get what you want and the consignment is delivered within the promised date.
- It is considered inappropriate to mention 'no boxed gifts', or 'no gifts' or 'no flowers' on an invitation. Gifts should not be expected from your guests and therefore should be left out of the invitation.
- Make sure you proofread the invitation content, especially the way the names are spelled and for any grammatical error. It is always wise to make someone else also proofread it.
- The general turnaround time for a good customised invitation suite ranges anything between four-eight weeks, so plan accordingly.

Final Thoughts

I recommend you purchase a sample before placing a full order. You can physically examine the quality of the invitation this way. Remember that actually viewing a product can make all the difference. Check for a minimum order size. Some printers require a certain number of invitations to be ordered and will only print more in pre-set amounts.

Give yourself plenty of planning time—accounting for production, proofing and mailing the invitations to your guests.

There's never been a couple quite like you, which is why you won't settle for anything short of completely custom—completely you—when it comes to wedding invitations. From formal to fun, classy to sassy, you can easily design wedding invitations that match your personality. Browse online or visit local vendors until you see something that resonates with who you are as a couple. Once you find it, take some time to play around with colours, design elements, typeface, text and placement. You want it to be perfect and when you see it with a fresh eye you'll know exactly when it's there. In my experience, it doesn't take the bride and groom long to figure out exactly what they want.

Getting the right theme, one that makes your wedding invitation stand out could set a trend for others.

Add-ons—Wedding Stationery
SAVE-THE-DATE CARDS
The first checklist once you've decided to marry consists of a ring and a wedding date.

Once you have finalised these, you can begin figuring out your save-the-dates.

A save-the-date is often the first form of communication between the wedding guests and the happy couple. It reveals that the couple has decided to get married and announce their special day.

Save-the-date cards are a relatively new trend in Indian weddings. They show that you respect your guests' time and would like to ensure they attend the wedding. In good etiquette, send these as soon as possible, months before the wedding to 'reserve' your big day on their calendars.

As destination weddings and three-day weekends have become more standard, so have save-the-dates. And if you're marrying during high-travel times, like a holiday weekend or summer in a beach town, a save-the-date is an expected courtesy. Of course, you don't have to send one if you don't want to but it will give guests the heads-up about your wedding plans. Between travel arrangements and busy schedules, sending a save-the-date will increase chances of guests attending your celebration. And that's the goal, right?

A save-the-date for a destination wedding need not be anything fancy. You can send out a traditional save-the-date card or something different like a fridge magnet. Firing off a simple email may also do the trick.

This is not only for your guests but you too. Your guests will be able to indicate whether they can attend your wedding or not. Having an idea of the numbers early on will help enormously in your planning, making things such as venue selection, supplier booking and finding appropriate guest accommodation a lot easier and simpler.

For save-the-dates, the wording doesn't have to be anything exceptionally formal. Something like 'Save the weekend: Megha and Rahul are getting married on Saturday, 24 April, in Goa. Invitations and hotel information will be sent in early March.' This way, your guests know what to expect, and they'll be able to get in touch with you if they have any questions. Include the year after the date, if you'd like. Just make sure that everyone who gets this card is someone who will definitely be on your final guest list: Once you tell them to save your wedding date, they're as good as invited and there's no turning back.

Avoid having 100 people asking you, 'Where's the wedding?' by including the city and state on your save-the-date (no need to put the actual venue at this stage). Many of your guests will still have to travel and possibly book overnight accommodations, so give them a heads-up as a courtesy.

Some couples mention their wedding website on the save-the-date. This is a more acceptable way to direct guests on the format of your wedding and what accommodations they can stay at for the wedding and so on...

As with any printed/written item for your wedding day, there are some save-the-date etiquette mistakes you'll want to avoid:

- **Sending them out immediately upon your engagement**: You're all excited about the wedding plans, you booked the place then made a guest list that includes everyone you've ever known. But as time goes on, all of those deposits for the venue, the videographer, photographer, florist, caterer and more add up. You could find yourself in a money crunch that requires you to cut down your guest list…but you can't now for you sent everyone a save-the-date. This is the #1 save-the-date mistake. Asking guests to reserve a block on their calendars and then not inviting them to the wedding is just not done. So take your time, make sure you know the strength of your budget and send out the cards only once you're sure about the numbers.

- **Going off-colour**: Your friends might think a wacky save-the-date card featuring a dog with cartoon eyes, swigging a bottle of tequila is fun but your relatives will wonder about you. Keep the save-the-dates on the classic or classy side, and personalise them with a photo of the two of you, great colours, a border and so on. There's a lot you can do to be original and still show taste.
- **Not putting enough information**: Along with the date, always make sure you include the wedding location such as your hometown or the destination wedding locale, so that guests can make travel plans. Just having the date is not enough. Guests need to know how many days they'll need to take off from work.
- **Invitation to follow**: Be sure to state on the save-the-date cards that the 'Invitation will follow' or 'Formal Invitation to Follow'. This will minimise confusion and save extra phone calls. Leaving the guest confused would defeat the purpose of sending the save-the-date card.
- **Right timing**: As a general rule, for a faraway destination, it's best to start spreading the news, at least four-six months prior to the ceremony. This gives the wedding guests plenty of time to book their travel, save a bit of cash and ask for days off from work. Any earlier, and they may toss the notice aside. Any later, and it might as well be an invitation.
- **Avoid enclosing confetti**: Or anything else that will fall to the floor and be a pain in the butt to vacuum/clean up. A better

enclosure is a sheet of vellum with a poem or something that can be kept or tossed with ease.

In the case of a wedding abroad, it really is 'the earlier the better'.

Wedsite—The Wedding Website
WHY MUST YOU HAVE ONE?

The caterer is running late. The band says they're down a bass player. The chairs aren't the right colour. And the *varmala*—where's the *varmala*? There are plenty of things to worry about on your wedding day. Whether or not your guests have all necessary information shouldn't be one of them. This is the Information Age, for god's sake! A wedding website could be the answer.

If you're having a destination wedding, then all of your guests will be travelling in from various locations. You're too busy being the bride/groom to play travel agent, so a wedding website could be the place to post pertinent travel details such as hotel information, local dining options and other fun things to do during wedding downtime.

Even if it is a local wedding, you'll probably be having some outstation guests. If you don't want to clog your invitation with too many details, share the extra information on a wedding website. Include the website URL on an insert that gets mailed with your invitation/save-the-date.

CONTENT AND PURPOSE

Your wedding website can be as simple or as detailed as you want it to be. In addition to travel and location details and directions, some sites are set up to let guests RSVP online. Some sites allow you to store guest email addresses and send them updates as more details become available.

But wedding websites don't have to be all work and no play. They can also include fun anecdotes about how you and your fiancé met, a Q&A about the bride and groom, and of course, lots of pictures. You can even have a page where guests can upload their stories and memories after the big day. Some couples love their website so much that they repurpose it as a Mister and Mistress Page to keep their loved ones updated on their lives. And no worries, if you're a privacy hound, opt for a site that offers password protection, so that only your nearest and dearest have access.

You could build your own website, take the help of companies or simply create one with any of the numerous free online wedding websites. Wedding websites range from free to around ₹3,000-5,000 for a year. But as the old adage goes, you get what you pay for.

The free wedding websites offer basic design with few, if any, customised features. You'll probably have to deal with a couple of ads on the page too. Most pre-fab wedding sites offer packages at different price points, so you can upgrade to the one with the bells and whistles you want. The advantage of picking a service like this is that you don't need design or HTML skills. The downside is that you'll probably end up having to choose from one of their design templates, so you may not get all the customisation you like.

You could also pick another couple's site that you like and find out what she used. If you want your website and your wedding invite to have the same colours and design motif, you'll probably need to hire a pro, which will cost you a little more.

Still not sure? You may want to read ahead and see why a wedding website may be an ideal tool for you.

- **Focus on what's most important** rather than spend your time fielding questions from your guests, let your wedding website communicate all your wedding plans for you. You focus on planning.
- **Change of plans? No problem**. Last-minute location change? In-case-of-rain information? Hotel updates? While major changes to the big event can make for one hectic couple, making the change on your site takes five minutes of your time. Plus, you can add updates as the date gets closer.
- **It's easy to stay in contact with your guests**. One of the best features in a wedding website is the interactive guestbook. Guests can leave their best wishes, make comments or even offer suggestions. Ask guests to sign the book or enter their email addresses to be notified of site updates or changes. Then happily send one email instead of making hundreds of calls.

Some of the newer wedding websites allow your guests to subscribe to updates you make. If a wedding website provider offers RSS feeds, then you can even share your updates on social networking sites like Facebook.

- **Guests need not call for directions**. Google Maps, for example, allows you to embed maps and directions directly on to your web page. Google Docs has different forms that you can use to organise and plan the day. It has an RSVP form that you can also embed onto your website. It's an easy way for your guests to RSVP and it automatically enters the information provided by your guest into a spreadsheet.

- **It's eco-friendly**. No matter how you use it, your site will probably save you cash on paper and stamps, not to mention the trees you've saved by using less paper and carbon emissions you've spared by not loading the postman down with a whole lot of envelopes. Whether you prefer to go completely paperless and use your site for everything or just for a portion of your wedding-related festivities, every little bit helps.

- **Save on printing costs**. If you're having invites printed, you know how quickly the price will rise by just adding another piece of paper to the mix. By directing everyone to your site in any engagement party, shower or wedding correspondence, you'll save time, money and effort on printing costs.

- **Sharing your Big Day**. Not everyone can make it to your wedding. All those special people who missed out on your big day can share your memories and keep in touch with you through your wedding website.

A wedding website can help preserve your memories—you can upload photos of your special day. Unfortunately, many wedding website providers offer websites that expire after one year. Your memories don't expire, why should your website?

Tips to Build Your Wedding Website

WELCOME AND THANK YOU MESSAGE

Start by welcoming your guests/website visitors and thanking them for taking out time to visit it. Introduce your site, say something sweet but keep it short. This will be your home page, which has in addition, your very 'in love' picture.

THE COUPLE

Of course, everyone wants to hear about the people getting married. I like to believe the majority of your guests find this to be the most interesting part of a wedding website. Fill this section with pages on how you met, the proposal and lots of pictures.

EVENT INFORMATION

This section differentiates your wedding website from a regular Facebook album. List down all the planned ceremonies and event locations with addresses, dates and timings. Basic directions, including nearby landmarks, are essential on a wedding website.

RSVP INFORMATION

Whether you have mailed out invitations or sent invitations online, an RSVP section should be included. This is mostly just a reminder in case the guest has mistakenly deleted the online invite.

GUEST LIST—WHO IS INVITED?

Most people are curious about your guest list; go ahead and indulge them by creating a page that lists your invitees. Have the time? You could make it more personal by adding stories and information or little tit-bits about each guest.

MUSIC

Yes, music can be a good accompaniment to your love story. But not everyone can focus with background music, so include an option to pause the music.

GALLERY

Pictures add life to your site. Feel free to include: High school/college pictures, courtship and engagement pictures and more. Just don't go overboard—no one needs to wade through all 749 photos from your last vacation together.

SHARED WEDDING TIMELINE

Add a page where your guests can upload their best photos and create a shared timeline of your wedding.

Always test run your website before you make it live. You may work on this for weeks, so you may not spot errors that a fresh set of eyes can. Ask someone else to test run it as a visitor and make sure you are good to go.

Set up your wedding website early on in the planning process, at least six months before the wedding. You can then add your personal website address into save-the-date cards to your wedding guests with as much information as early as possible.

As a couple, you will want to plan and share your wedding with people who matter the most to you. A wedding website facilitates this and so much more.

Programme Cards/Book

Most wedding etiquette books will not insist on a wedding programme but for certain types of weddings, programmes are more necessary than others. If the couple is having a traditional ceremony, a large wedding, destination wedding or a particularly long one—spread over a few days, wedding programmes are a must. It gives guests clear directions on the various events and also something to read as they wait. Since Indian weddings are spread over a couple of days to a week, different ceremonies take place on different days and at different timing. So having a wedding programme makes it convenient for the guest to plan their day and attend the rituals.

Elements of a Wedding Programme

- **The cover**: Typically includes the date and/or the names of the couple. It may also include the location and a picture or design element such as a flower and scroll.
- **The order of events**: If you haven't already included your names, wedding date and location, consider listing that information on the inside, just before the order of events. Then list the happenings of each day in the order they will occur. You can also list what will happen during each event, including greetings, prayers from your religious books, exchange of vows, etc.
- If it's a destination wedding where guests stay in for a couple of days, a map of the resort with directions to reach the banquet or event area will make you a wonderful host.

- If you are having a sangeet with dance performances, you can have a full list of songs with names of artists.
- Inserts may include directions from the wedding ceremony to the reception, lyrics to a song or even explanation of ceremony rituals as guests generally are of diverse faiths.
- It can include a request for audience participation in certain parts of the ceremony.
- You may also include the seven vows given in your religious books. But I would prefer each groom and bride write his and her own set of vows and publish it on the programme book for added charm.
- Few words on the significance of the location or theme (for example: The reception will be held at Golden Palms resorts, the site of the bride and groom's first date).
- Other than these basic points, you can do whatever you want. Include the story of your proposal or short description of how you two met or a humorous anecdote about your first date; a thank-you message to your families and your guests; a note from the couple describing each other—anything that's important to you.

Remember that the programme is a wedding keepsake, so really make it your own. But before deciding on making programme cards, think again.

- **Programmes can be expensive**. You'll need wedding programmes for each guest (or at least one per couple), which can add to the cost.
- **You'll need to have someone pass over the programmes to guests**. Or place them in a Welcome basket (for destination weddings/outstation guests). Or perhaps, near the entrance, so guests don't miss it.
- **Wedding programmes are only used for a brief amount of time at the wedding**. You may feel like you're not getting your money's worth if your ceremony is very short.

They say the devil is in the details but I happen to think that personality is what makes any wedding shine. One of my favourite places to add creativity is in the wedding programmes—they don't have to cost a fortune to be a winner with guests. From whimsical to romantic to modern, here are a few of my favourite things.

Some Unique Ways of Presenting Programme Cards

- Consider having your vows calligraphed or printed on envelopes and stashing programmes inside. Hang the envelopes by their flaps from satin ribbons that you knot around the chairs near the mandap or loop over the ends of pews.
- Having a summer wedding, and one of your events is planned outdoors? The guests will be baking out there, so you may want to cool them off a bit. Have programme information printed on fans. If you'd like your wedding programme to double as a wedding favour, then this beauty is a thoughtful gesture for warm summer days.
- A foodie? Hand over small goodie bags as a welcome kit to your guests. Inside each bag, add a programme and recipe book featuring, among others, the caterer's recipes.
- For a couple that frequently travels, a booklet resembling a bundle of luggage tags is an inspired choice. The card-stock pages can be tied together with sturdy string and a floral print cover gives the package a charming yet casual look.
- For a cool weather wedding, why not give programmes their own woolly wraps? Felt pouches bring a cosy touch and bursts of fall colour to the ceremony and make pretty mementos for guests.
- I've seen bubbles used at so many weddings and it would be wonderful having your guests blow some bubbles like kids and enjoy a day event in the open. Pack the programme card with a bubble gun with a label suggesting they blow some wishes to the beautiful couple.
- Share your love story with a newspaper-inspired wedding programme! Plus, the back can have a personalised crossword puzzle, which will keep guests entertained during wedding downtime.

The general rule for length is that brevity is best. But one can find all sorts of programmes—from single sheet of paper outlining the ceremony events to pamphlets that include short descriptions of each event, special notes to guests, maps and pictures of the couple through the years. All of these are great ideas! However, keep this advice in mind: Guests should be able to read the programme rather should want to read it. So, make it look as interesting as possible.

There are many different options for wedding ceremony programme formats: A single card, a multiple-page booklet or a tri-fold, among others. Make sure your wedding programme coordinates with the rest of your wedding stationery and that you proofread your programmes before printing.

Wedding programmes are not required but can offer a personalised touch to your ceremony.

Menu Cards

With all the hustle-bustle and long queues before the buffet tables, guests usually tend to pick up items they can readily access. Menu cards can help guests decide what all they really want to eat.

Whether tucked into a white linen napkin or placed on the table, a menu card adds a classic touch to any wedding reception. They are a nice addition to the table decor.

Guestbook

In older times, a wedding guestbook helped a newly married couple recall who all came to their wedding, organise thank-you notes and start a formal address book. Have your guests sign a memento that you can display in your home, keeping the memories out in the open rather than up on the bookshelf.

Thank-you Cards

Believe it or not, back in the 1950s, pre-printed thank-you cards were the norm. How and why did this change? Over the years, weddings have grown in size and cost. Guests are flying in from all over the world, spending thousands to attend a wedding. Somewhere along the line, it was decided that guests deserve a more personal 'thank you' for their time and effort.

Chapter 11

Wedding Favours—
Token of Appreciation

Your wedding day wouldn't be as much fun or memorable without all your loving friends and family, who travelled from near and far to celebrate with you. Gifts given as tokens of appreciation can be the perfect way to say thank you to your guests for sharing your special day. These gifts, also known as wedding favours, need not be extravagant or expensive—it really is the thought that counts. Giving wedding favours is an age-old tradition that has evolved tremendously over the years. A wedding favour is traditionally given just before the guest departs but it can be a part of your welcome basket too. These small yet intricate tokens of appreciation will help your guest remember and treasure your special day.

When choosing a favour, be original and pick one that is meaningful to you and your family. Or see that it complements your theme—blending well with your colour scheme and wedding design. Personalised favours are extremely popular because it is a fun way to add your own stamp to the wedding day.

Start your search for the perfect wedding favour:

- Flip through your favourite magazines, browse websites. Several online vendors offer a wide variety at competitive prices.
- Stop at specialty shops like chocolatiers, gift stores and stationery boutiques.
- Gather ideas on innovative packaging and sample flavours and find trinkets that catch your eye.
- To spot current trends and get ideas, go through the favours you received at recent weddings but try to be unique with yours.
- Pick a favour associated with your wedding location to create the right ambience. In some cases, it can also be practical—personalised sandals at a beach wedding come in handy for a walk on the beach.

Now filter these ideas, keeping in mind the theme, practicality of the gift, availability and most important, budget. Lastly, remember that the best way to thank your guests is by choosing favours that they will enjoy and truly appreciate.

Give your favours a stamp of approval by branding them in some way. The constants: Your names and wedding date. Your medium can range from rubber stamps to elegant calligraphy. A monogram can be designed with the initials of the couple, which can then be used to personalise gifts like bedroom slippers, tote bags and cosmetic bags.

Some gift ideas that will get you started on your own ideas:

- A photo of the guest celebrating with the couple is a perfect gift for any budget and for every theme. Frames could be ordered well in advance, keeping in mind the theme like a meenakari frame for a Rajasthani wedding or one with seashells for a beach wedding. If on a budget, thick paper printed frames can be made (prints reflecting the theme). Want to give a keepsake, go for silver frames.
- A box of home-made chocolates, Indian sweets, dry fruits, cookies, scented candles, music CDs or silver coins are natural choices. Personalised monogram printing on the box can add an edge.

- Giving away eco-friendly items at your wedding is one of the best ideas. Handwoven baskets, table clock made from recycled wood and organic linen are some options. Available in many vibrant colours, they make a perfect return gift.
- Send guests off with miniature cookbooks filled with your favourite recipes.
- *Vaastu* and feng shui items will show your concern for the happiness and prosperity of your guests. So, gift them a pair of romantic Mandarin ducks, Chinese guardian lions or a laughing Buddha. Even lucky crystals and wind chimes.
- This is one gift that will definitely be liked by all and sundry—statues of Lord Ganesha, Radha-Krishna, Shiv-Parvati or any other idol you want. Idols come in various sizes, metals and designs, so make sure you pick something unique for your guests.
- Fortune cookies in handsome red-ribboned boxes stamped with the couple's monogram. Share handwritten romantic wishes with your guests in home-made chocolate cookies. Inside the box, pack two fortune cookies—one vanilla and the other chocolate. The fortunes can be written in English or any language you want.
- Paintings look wonderful in every house. You could gift Madhubani, Rajasthani, Tanjore or even modern art.
- Hand-made products are beautiful and look special. Hand-made clutches to wooden hangings—options are many, but these gifts might be little expensive.
- If you have decided to incorporate the sand and sea into your wedding, give everyone a personalised seashell. You can have your names and date engraved on one side, while the other simply says, 'Our love shell last forever'. You can also buy seashell bottle openers or a tea light shell gift set for every guest.

Select a Seasonal Send-off

For winter, offer warm blankets or hot cocoa kits, complete with powder mix, marshmallows and a spoon or a lip balm. Hand out sunglasses, hats or mini personalised sunscreen bottles at a summer affair. As for spring, the idea of sending guests home with potted plants and growing instructions is wonderful. Choose a longer lasting reminder like a beach towel or bag for a seaside affair and hand warmers or neck warmers in your signature colours for a mountain wedding.

For Nature Lovers

Some wedding trends may change with the times but saving the earth will never go out of style.

SOME SUGGESTIONS FOR ECO-FRIENDLY WEDDING FAVOURS

- Find something that is local to the area like tea leaves, coffee and nuts. Personalise it with monograms.
- Send your guests home with a bottle or half of locally produced organic wine and they will have good reason to toast you in the months after your wedding. If you can buy unlabelled wine, dress up your bottles with personalised wine labels to brand your special day.
- Why not send your guests home with seeds of happiness? Get back to nature and give out seed packets to all your guests. The seed cards can even be custom printed with your names, a personal message and the date of your event.
- Or gift a tree for merely 350 rupees using web portals like http://plantatreeindia.org/, which will be planted in their name in the Himalayan regions of Uttarakhand.
- Another great idea is to give herb or orchid centrepieces in nice ceramic pots decorated with ribbon in the wedding theme colours.
- Nature lovers will like a pot of lucky clover. Or you might consider giving your guests a mini palm or a lucky bamboo plant. They'll bring your guests luck that'll last long after your wedding!
- Natural soaps, lotions and handcrafted lip balms can make amazing gifts. The lack of chemicals and the handcrafting process used to make these items minimises the likelihood of

any skin irritation or dryness. In addition to smelling nice, the essential oils in these products are believed to have their own healing powers. Lavender bath salts can help your guests relax while a bar of peppermint soap will help wake them up the next morning. So if your wedding goes late, they'll have just what they need to recover from the festive evening!

You may find that eco-friendly favours cost a bit more than the alternatives but you only have one wedding. Favour your guests and the planet at the same time. In doing so, we preserve the earth for the generations of children that are certain to result from so many happy unions.

Donate to a Good Cause

Your guests' presence at your wedding can do more than support the two of you—it can also support a worthy charity. Making tax-deductible donations to the charity of your choice by giving away a certain amount per guest is a wonderful thought indeed. Add a note to the programme or inside the escort card that reads: A donation has been made in your name (the name of the charity). If you wish to explain why you chose a certain charity, you may want to create personalised donation cards (but of course this will use more paper, so make sure it's recyclable), or you can have individually tailored informational videos describing the gifts (to play on your wedding website or at your reception). Some possible wedding favours may include purchasing in-kind gifts (such as a pack of crayons per guest or a first-aid kit per couple) for needy schools and clinics.

Pass the Flame

Soy wax candles burn for twice as long as petroleum-based paraffin candles and they produce less soot. Soy wax candles are also cheaper than beeswax (another natural wax alternative). You can consider gifting some to your guests.

Music Lovers

If your wedding is rooted in music, hand out iPod minis loaded with your favourite tunes. Or present your guests with a CD of your unforgettable songs. Adorn CDs with a custom CD label showing a song list. Package your CD favours in a glassine envelope or metal CD case and top with a personalised designer label that says, 'Thank you, thank you very much', in Elvis style!

Quirky

If you're feeling lucky and want to spread your luck, why not buy all your guests a lottery ticket and put them at their table.

Personalised playing cards, poker set, shot glasses, wine glasses and coaster sets work well too.

Themed Wedding Favours

Themed weddings are all the rage now and with such a wide selection of favours available online, you can find a favour to complement any theme you can dream of. Even though the favours tie into an overall theme, they should still reflect the personality of the bride and groom. Themed favours can be elegant, simple, practical or whimsical.

Look at your budget, figure out what you can afford and then what you want to potentially present to your guests. Many couples present an inexpensive, yet personal, favour to each guest, while other couples present a more elaborate favour to each couple or family. Creativity is the key here. If you are under a tight budget, then consider making your own favours.

Make Your Own Wedding Favours

Do-it-yourself wedding favours give you the opportunity to showcase a hobby or special interest.

Before you begin, think about what you would like to communicate through your wedding favours. The following questions might give you some ideas:

- What is the quality or characteristic that defines you two—the bride and groom?
- What is your favourite hobby?
- How did you meet?
- Is there an activity you and your fiancé enjoy doing together?
- Does your wedding have a theme?
- Will your wedding take place around Diwali or Holi?

Once you have decided on a message, design a favour that will convey your ideas.

Make favours that fit the theme, such as presenting heart-shaped candy tins for a Valentine's theme, movie CDs for a Bollywood theme or beautiful diyas for a wedding near Diwali. Whatever you choose the fact that it was handcrafted by you with your guests in mind will guarantee success.

It is wise to make the favour as simple as possible, so it's easy to assemble. This is especially important for large weddings. The trick is to wrap favour ideas into creative and distinct packages.

Here are some ideas for inexpensive wedding favours:

- For summer weddings, a card stock hand fan can be made by hand where a recipe to a favourite cocktail or summer drink may be printed on one side with a monogram and wedding date on the other. Add a personalised gift tag that says 'Thank you' for a classy, finishing touch.

- Sweet treats like candies, cookies, chocolates, mints and nuts can be packed creatively for a perfect do-it-yourself wedding favour. Candies wrapped in mini acrylic favour boxes, scalloped-top favour boxes or organza bags with personalised wedding labels or thank-you tags on them, finished with a satin ribbon, would surely be a crowd pleaser. Mini glass jars filled with your choice of cookies and nuts, labelled with personalised tags or stickers can make for a sweet experience.

- Just make a powdered mix of a favourite treat or drink and place them in elegant or quirky favour pouches. Liquid mixes are possible too; just trade the pouches in for a mini cocktail shaker.

- For the scent enthusiasts, there are plenty of how-to-dos online for soap bars, potpourri and candles. These can make for fabulous favours with the right packaging. Tin cans for candles, organza bags for potpourri and pillow favour boxes for soap bars. Be sure to finish off with a personalised label.

- Guests will recall your wedding while they browse through their reading list if you provide them with bookmark favours.

Even a great favour can fall short if not wrapped properly. From simple brown boxes and clear cellophane bags to tiny tin pails and slim silver canisters, your favour packaging can make as much of an impact as what's inside them.

One note: Make sure your favours aren't so matchy-matchy that they get lost and blend into the decor. Choose packaging that coordinates—not perfectly matches—with the decor and flowers. And play with texture too. Rather than setting your favours in flat corrugated boxes, go for fabric-covered boxes in various shades.

Whether you decide to give one favour per guest or per couple, be sure to have extra wedding favours on hand. Many couples also send favours to friends and family who were not able to attend your wedding. If you expect a lot of children at the event, have a separate type of favour for them.

Wedding favours can be a wonderful way to share your love and add that special finishing touch to your wedding day. After all, it's all in the details. Guests will appreciate any token of thanks that you decide to give. So present something from the heart to serve as a lasting memory of your special day.

Welcome Basket

A few months before the wedding, it is a good idea to prepare the welcome basket.

You may have guests not only from out-of-town but even abroad. Providing a basket of hand-picked goods in the guest room is not only courteous but a nice way to thank them for travelling the long distance to celebrate with you.

How Should You Start?

- Think of what your guests may need during their stay. Maps and city guidebooks are a great idea!
- Think of the area specialties. Is your town known for its tea? Or silk, perhaps. Buy local products that you think your guests will enjoy. They will also appreciate bottles of water, coffee, tea, snacks or even a bottle of wine (don't forget the cork screw!).

- You may also find great items in your local souvenir shops. If you are in New Delhi, include a miniature Qutub Minar or Lal Qila. In Jaipur you may find a miniature Hawa Mahal.
- Other alternatives are scented travel candles, personalised sewing kits and beautifully packaged soaps.

You don't have to purchase the biggest items, even a small thing will do. Think of something that will put a smile on your guest's face.

CHOOSE A CONTAINER

You can always go with a traditional basket but you can also be creative! Get pails for a beach wedding. Or even beach totes. Paper gift bags are always practical and less costly. A unique idea is to dress them up with personalised labels and beautiful ribbons.

You may also want to write a welcome note and attach it to the basket. Include directions to the venue and back, and a list of shopping places in the area. If you are having a wedding weekend or if your ceremonies are spread over a couple of days, do include a programme for your guests.

A day or two before your guests arrive, take the gift baskets to the hotels where your guests will stay. Make sure you write your guests' names on them and instruct that they be delivered to each guest upon arrival. I'm sure your thoughtfulness will be greatly appreciated!

Chapter 12

The Perfect Wedding Attire

The wedding day for any girl is the most important and glamorous day of her life and no one can look as gorgeous as the bride.

The great Indian wedding is a myriad of colours that makes it vibrant and festive and unforgettable for the bride and the groom and all who participate in it. The gorgeous attire of the bride takes centre stage, lending beauty to the entire event. Be it the red zardozi border, a *Banarasi* sari or the gorgeous lehengas of the north, the bride looks resplendent in all. From the cream and red bordered *Panetar* in a Gujarati wedding to the dark green *Paithni* saris in Maharashtra or even the traditional rich bordered Mysore and *Kanjeevaram* from the south, they all glam up the Indian wedding.

From clothes to jewellery and make-up, the bride needs to take care of every bit to ensure that on her wedding day, she looks nothing less than perfect!

In order to get the best out of her designer, the bride needs to first get in touch with her own ideas, then find a designer who will understand her sensibilities to create that amazing work of art for her to wear. Today's bride has everything at her fingertips—she's ambitious and knows what she wants. Exposed to both the rich tradition of India's cultural landscape as well as the diversity available overseas, she knows what appeals to her.

It's important to do your research: Your bridal dress will have to gel with the theme and location of the wedding to make the right style statement. For a Goa/Bangkok wedding, the colour of the sea, the sky and the availability of local flowers have to be considered when designing the outfit.

Most designers today are aware of the price sensitive market and offer different price ranges that cater to everyone's budgets. A couture garment can take anywhere from two-four months in production, so plan early.

First bridal mantra: Brides generally forget a very important element—elegance. Having always heard that 'more is better' you end up overdoing things. Your mantra should be 'simple and elegant'.

Brides often get confused between clothes being too heavy or too light. I personally have only this to say: The art here is to look like a million bucks and create a statement without going overboard. As long as one is elegant, there is absolutely nothing to worry about.

Clothes, jewellery, make-up, hair and accessories are the key components that complete the look. The key is to balance it. So spend some time with your stylist, make-up artist or simply in front of the mirror and be honest.

Traditional is not boring: We practically live out our lives in contemporary clothes, so this is the occasion to embrace your tradition. Shake off the false notion that traditional clothes are boring and dated. Well-made traditional clothes, with just the right amount of sensuality, in fact, look breathtaking and timeless.

One of the most ubiquitous outfits for a modern Indian bride is the lehenga. Pairing a top or tunic with a long skirt maintains the elegance of a traditional sari but adds a layer of comfort, without the worry of six yards of fabric wrapped around your body! Whether it's a short choli top or a long-jacket tunic, whether you drape a dupatta over your head or pin it to one shoulder, it's a custom piece, with numerous style options to fit every bride's personality and preference.

A deep red lehenga for the ceremony or a multi-coloured design for the reception—you can play around with colour combinations to make a unique statement. While a brightly coloured piece is perfect for a festive and traditional function, a pristine white outfit will perfectly emulate the contemporary elegance of a white wedding gown. Versatility is definitely the strength of the Indian wedding wardrobe.

With the trend of destination and theme weddings catching up, the look is more relaxed. For the wedding day, the 'look' is still very traditional. You can experiment with colours and styles for the pre-wedding functions though. At the cocktail, engagement and reception, the bride can opt for more western looks whereas functions like sangeet, mehendi and wedding call for a more traditional look.

Formal can be fun too: Functions like mehendi and sangeet are all about fun. So add drama to your clothes by adding lots of bright shades like yellow, fuchsia, orange, lime green, turquoise, etc. For the cocktail and reception—neons, acai blue, vivacious pink or coral with embroidery in Swarovski beads impart that contemporary look. Embroidered *anarkali* kurta and churidars are great options—these empire line outfits add length and look graceful. Interesting brocade or velvet borders are extremely 'in'—embellish your *anarkali* kurta as well as the dupatta. Flaunt new styles to make your sangeet more fun. Wear embroidered bolero jackets, adorn your hair with *gajra*s or wear a sexy backless kurta. As the D-day nears, things are going to get more formal, so this is the time to have fun.

On the wedding day, colours preferred are more traditional like samba red, poppy red, Indian hot pink and oranges. The bridal colour palette is no longer restricted to single flat colours; it's more a mix of flaming hues.

Tips

Comfort should never be compromised: If you are not feeling very experimental, stick to jewelled colours and traditional silhouettes. It is all about personal style and how comfortable you are with your look.

Never buy your wedding attire too *early*: Keep a gap of not more than four-six months from your wedding date. Although saris won't have any fit issues, but lehenga and cholis can be a matter of worry if you grow notably thin or otherwise. While buying or getting your outfit tailored, make sure there is room for adjustments, in case of last-minute weight gain/loss.

Get in touch with the designer about four months before your event. Two weeks should be enough to freeze the designs and then about three months to execute the same. Keep two weeks in the end for fittings and minor alterations.

Buy what you like: At the end of the day, it's your opinion that matters. You should be comfortable with your choice. No bride would want to feel self-conscious on her wedding day.

No last-minute trials: Don't leave anything for the last minute, especially your dress trials.

Comfortable innerwear: Wearing comfortable lingerie is as important as your wedding attire. Make sure that it complements and supports your attire.

The Perfect Indian Wedding Attire: Traditional to Stylish

A soon-to-be bride devotes almost all her time to choose her perfect bridal outfit.

SARIS

Saris are the most traditional wedding attire for an Indian bride. This six-yard wonder looks great on almost all body types and comes in an extensive range of colours, fabrics and designs. From traditional to casual, Indo-western to region specific, you will find saris of all types. Even the way you drape it differs from region to region. A Bengali sari is very different from a Kerala sari, so keep that in mind when the shopkeeper shows you those saris.

If the huge range of saris confuses you, go on and design your own sari.

SALWAR KAMEEZ

Some customs expect brides to wear the traditional salwar kameez or Punjabi suits. You could go for a rich, pure silk salwar with zardozi work on it, or a more comfortable georgette fabric. Some of these dresses are embellished with precious stones for a dazzling bridal look.

LEHENGA CHOLI

Lehenga choli is the sexiest Indian wedding dress ever. A short blouse combined with a flowing lehenga and a beautiful dupatta makes this bridal dress a hot favourite among brides. You can find lehengas in almost any kind of fabric—silk, chiffon, georgette, velvet, and so on.

These sensual wedding dresses are more expensive than saris, yet are most preferred. There's usually a lot of work on the lehengas, which can make them really heavy and uncomfortable. Ensure that you pick the right fabric with just the amount of work you can carry.

VARIATIONS

Designers these days love to mix and match.

- You can go for ghagra style saris, where the pallu is made to look like a dupatta while the rest of the sari is like a ghagra.
- Teaming a long kameez with a lehenga is another look to try.
- Indo-western bridal wears are a rage—tube tops, corsets and noodle straps are making a great style statement.

Be it traditional or modern, your ultimate wedding attire will be based on your body type and complexion. So, factor these in before making your final choice. After all, it's you who has to look good in them!

Your Lehenga Guide

You want your wedding lehenga to be exclusive and perfect but that does not mean you have to pay an astronomical amount for it. Many brides end up buying heavily embellished lehengas, which cannot be used anywhere else. They look at the designer's name, not the design, silhouette or the versatility of the outfit.

SET A BUDGET

It is very easy to go overboard when you don't have a specific budget in mind. Designers charge anything from ₹20,000 to a couple of lakhs for a wedding lehenga.

DON'T RUN AFTER TOP DESIGNER LABELS

It's normal to seek designers who are well-known or feature in bridal magazines. Remember, their garments are going to be overpriced.

Why not seek out lesser known designers and boutiques. You may find great lehengas at a fraction of the price. Also, don't forget that these designers are likely to be more open to suggestions and customisation.

Go for Quality, Not Just Exclusivity

Exclusivity is one factor that pushes brides to pay exorbitant amounts. But what guarantee do you have that a famous designer will not have a similar piece stocked in another store. So, do not hanker for exclusivity, instead look at the quality of the lehenga. Is the fabric comfortable? Does it fit you like a dream? Does the lehenga overwhelm you or does it accentuate your overall look? Ask yourself these pertinent questions as you try them out.

Think Beyond Designer Lehengas

Designer lehengas often end up costing more because of their expensive embellishments. Swarovski crystals, real gold and silver thread and semi-precious stones are a few things designers use to hike the price of their garment. Do not fall for such gimmicks; opt for a lehenga which looks good on you and falls in your budget. Delicate thread embroidery and artificial stones, if used well, can make your lehenga stand out, too.

Steer Clear from Weighty Issues

Many a time, designers cram every possible type of embroidery and work into a lehenga. You may have heard of brides wearing a 30-35 kg lehenga, which cost them several lakhs. Don't go for a garish, heavy piece just because it is expensive. Keep your comfort factor in mind. On your wedding day, you would want to look serene and happy, not irritable and tired.

And if your choli and lehenga are heavy, then go for a simple dupatta. Don't overdo things just because a designer tells you so. Think about your own style and comfort, first.

Become a Designer

If you have an innate sense of fashion and style, why not design your own lehenga. Look for a fashion student who can bring your design to paper. Hire a good tailor and skilled craftsmen. Buy your own fabric and embellishments and create a beautiful piece. It would be your own personal style statement. Seek opinions from close friends and family. But in the end, always follow your own instinct. We know this will be a slightly tedious process. But, here you wouldn't have to worry about exclusivity and budget because both will be in your hands always.

Never buy wedding attire online: When you're looking at a gorgeous wedding dress online, the 'purchase now' button can be mighty tempting. But it's an outfit you've never tried on (or even held in hand); you should take a breather before you buy it.

To Get the Most from Your Bridal Shopping Experience

Shopping for your bridal attire is one of the most fun and enjoyable experiences. Unfortunately, it can turn into a nightmare, if friends or family try to impose their own style or opinions on the bride. So choose your shopping companion wisely. Take along one or two people at the most.

First, shop at a reputed bridal shop that has an experienced bridal consultant. After gathering some information from you and observing you, an expert bridal consultant can usually choose several outfits that you will not only love but that will flatter your particular body type and style, and be appropriate for the formal occasion. An expert consultant can also help you put together your 'complete look' for the wedding.

Chapter 13

Wedding Binder—Your Best Friend

Whether you have helping hands or have to plan it all alone, a wedding binder is the one thing that is needed at every stage of the wedding process. This binder will collect your thoughts and keep all the ideas in one place, so you are not constantly hunting down that last website you were at, or trying to find a picture of that dress you found in the window last weekend. That makes it the top tool for organised wedding planning.

Besides your future spouse, your wedding binder will be the closest thing to a best friend that you'll have during your courtship period. It is essentially a 'home' for all wedding-related information, with each topic occupying a specific area. That makes for quick referencing and retrieval.

Three-ring folder: Get a folder to which you can keep adding materials. The size of your wedding and how many 'extras' you incorporate into your wedding day will determine the size of your binder. Pick a binder size that reflects the size and type of wedding. Bigger and more formal weddings entail more planning, so consider a three-inch binder. For regular weddings, a two-inch binder will probably suffice. (Note: You might want to buy a binder with clear plastic on the front/back so you can insert a picture of the two of you, picture of your wedding location, honeymoon destination, etc.)

Besides the binder itself, you will need:

- **Dividers with pockets and tabs**: Divide your documents into three main sections, starting from pre-wedding events to the actual wedding and including the honeymoon. Be sure to add dividers within the three main sections. For example, within the wedding section, place dividers for categories like budget, attire, venue, decor, photography, bridal party, guests and entertainment.

- **Clear protector sheets**: Place a few sheets in after each divider or where needed. You can insert things like magazine tear-outs, swatches, brochures and sample invitations—basically any odd-size or fragile documents that you can't punch and file in your binder. Sheet protectors are especially good to hold contracts—so you don't punch through any of the text.

- **Printouts**: Add printouts. Using the pastel copier paper, printout checklists and worksheets found online or copied from wedding planning magazines. Some checklists and worksheets that you are going to need in your binder: Guest lists, budget analysis worksheets, contracts, ceremony sites, rental company worksheets, stationery, wedding planning checklist and so on.

- **Business cardholder**: Buy sheets of business cardholder pages that fit standard three-ring binders to keep track of the different vendors. Write small notes about the vendor on the back of the card to help differentiate.

- **Resealable bag**: Attach a resealable bag to collect your receipts and swatches. Zipper pouches will enable you to access them easier than if you slipped them into a protector sheet.

- **Reinforcement stickers**: Finally, you're going to be flipping through the pages pretty frequently, so add reinforcement stickers to the punched holes or they may start tearing.

- **Paper hole puncher**: To punch and put all of your contracts in the binder

- **Add the filler paper**: You are going to be taking a lot of notes as you plan your wedding. In addition, you will be conducting a lot of interviews with vendors. Place the filler paper in the front of the binder for easy access while you're on the run or on the phone.
- **Imagination and your own decorations**: Pictures, glitter, stickers, etc. (Make your wedding planner as attractive and fun as you want—you'll be looking at it from the start of your planning until your wedding day. You might even want to keep it as a memento of your wedding planning.)

Other supplies that help you stay on track with your wedding plans:
- Camera
- Coloured pens/pencils/paper clips
- Computer and printer
- College ruled paper
- Tape/glue

Take your ideas and prioritise. Sit down together and figure out what is most important to you and what you will not give up for your wedding day.

Next is research. Take weekends together to go looking at different things such as flowers, venues, invitations, wedding clothing and styles, and favours. Be sure to take pictures or printouts of that webpage you found to be a treasure trove of ideas. If you are in stores, grab business cards to attach to your photos for contacting vendors later.

Organise your research by separating your ideas out in different sections or by labelling them with different colours (with coloured pens). This will help you keep things organised so the binder does not look like a chaotic mess of wedding ideas.

The tab dividers in the binder can be set up in any number of ways. The number of sections depends on what you want for your wedding. Below is a list of categories from which you can choose. It includes subdivisions of the categories to help you take care of all details. Of course, add any other categories that you want.

Some categories you can have in your pocket folders:
- Catering
- Photography
- Bridal attire
- Transportation
- Ceremony
- Honeymoon

One **two-sided pocket folder** usually has enough room for the paperwork of one vendor. One side of the pocket folder is for ideas and research while the other side is for estimates and contracts. Keeping these different types of information separate will allow you to locate them and retrieve at a moment's notice.

Assemble the pocket folders in order of importance to you. If you are constantly making calls to your caterer, place that folder towards the front of the binder. Already know what favours you want to give out? Place that folder towards the back.

Now the sections you divide the binder into rest completely on you. However, you can do some of the following:
- **Important**: This is where colour swatches, timelines, checklists and vendor contact list live.
  - Your planning timeline and checklist (from nine-sixteen months before, all the way up to the week of the wedding)
  - Wedding timeline
  - Day of the wedding checklist
  - Wedding day timeline
  - Emergency kit
  - Vendor contact information
  - Wedding party contact information
  - Family contact information
- **Inspiration**: Every time you find an image that inspires, be it online or in a magazine, clip/print it and place it in style board form. It's really nice to have one place where you can start to form your vision.
- **Budget**
  - Budget worksheets

- Ceremony budget worksheet
- Reception costs, food and drinks, flowers, photos, transportation, music, etc.
- Even if you house spreadsheets (budget, payment schedules, etc.) on the computer as you constantly update them, it's always nice to be able to look at a printout of it all.
- **Fitness**
  - Fitness log
  - Fitness plan
  - Weight and measurements at the beginning and end of planning
- **Bridal attire**: To start with, this is a good place to store photos of lehengas/dresses and accessories you like. Later, it can be replaced with the receipt for bridal attire and accessories, including quotes and coupons from multiple designers/rentals.
  - Schedule of trials
  - Bride's attire
  - Jewellery
  - Bag
  - Shoes
  - Lingerie
  - Tuxedos/formalwear and accessories
- **Guests**: This is where you keep information on the room block, favours, etc.
  - Bride guest list
  - Groom guest list
  - Final guest list with phone numbers and addresses
  - Guest list tracker
  - Guest hotel information (if outstation guests)
  - Welcome bags
  - Transportation
  - Favours
- **Invitations**
  - Calligrapher
  - Postage

- Wording
- Programmes
- **Programme**: This is where you can have the list of events you want to include in your wedding with their probable dates and timings. Each of these events forms a separate tab with details of venue, caterer, theme, budget, etc.
  - Bachelor party
  - Bachelorette party
  - Engagement party
  - Sangeet
  - Mehendi
  - Cocktail
  - Reception
  - Sufi night, and so on
- **Example of one of the tabs**: Reception
  - Location
  - Decorations
  - Lighting
  - Table plans
  - Floor plan
  - Flowers
  - Menu and beverage list
  - Music
  - Photo shot list
  - Rental items
  - Transportation
  - Programmes
  - Photo booth
  - Set-up information and instructions
  - All relevant contracts
  - Entry and exit plan
- **Photographers**: A list of all recommended photographers with some research on their work. Quotes from all the photographers that you would want. This is where you keep

the signed contract along with all of the photographer's pricing and information, once it is finalised.

- Contract
- Must-have photo list
- List of everyone needed for photos—break this down into names
- Any props

- **Flowers**: Pretty self-explanatory, this is where the many floral quotes are housed, along with a few images of flower arrangements you like. Once you commit to a certain vendor, remove the other quotes and make this a place for receipts and other related information.
  - Contract
  - Pricing and budget
  - List of arrangements for all wedding functions
  - List of any other specifics needed

- **Vendor list**: Contains the details of the selected vendors. Once you commit to a certain vendor, add the vendor to this list along with his quote and the advance given. This is a quick reference sheet.

- **Beauty**: This is where you can collect brochures from different salons and make-up artists for pre-bridal and bridal packages. Later, replace them by appointments and details of the one finalised.

- Hair appointment for different occasions
- Make-up appointment for different occasions
- Nailcare appointment and beauty appointment
- Bridal consultant

- **Wedding stationery**: Sample invites, programmes and contact details of all the vendors. This should later be replaced with the finalised sample along with correspondence and receipts.

- **Caterer**: A list of all recommended caterers along with their quotes. Also, alongside have details of the food tasting experience so that decision-making gets easier. Some of you might want to split this one up for different occasions. This is where you can keep the contracts and details and the menu for the big day. Here you should also have details of all rentals and staff the caterer has agreed to provide.

- **Entertainment**: Brochures from DJs, bands, etc. Later, it can be replaced with the signed DJ contract and an ongoing list of songs on your must-play list.
- **Honeymoon**: Hotel accommodations, flight schedules, activities, etc.

Of course, wedding binders aren't one size fits all, so use this as more of a starting point than anything else. Choose which categories you need and assemble the sections in order of importance to you.

What other information can be stored in your wedding binder?

- A list of gifts you've already received
- Payment schedules
- Email/phone list of all your vendors at one place
- A list of favourite wedding websites/resources

Really, you can include anything you need!

Benefits to Using a Wedding Binder

- **Money-saving benefit**: You're prepared when a vendor wants to talk about price. If someone quotes you a price in writing and you can't produce the paper it's written on, they might try to overcharge you for their services.
- **Time-saving benefit**: Since all your information has a 'home', you won't be wasting your time printing duplicate information off the internet or repeatedly asking for the addresses of your guests.
- **Sanity-saving benefit**: All your wedding information is in one place. No need to take apart your living room looking for what you need.

Keep your wedding binder updated and always carry it with you for vendor meetings. You'll have all the information you need to compare prices and make educated decisions. You will be organised, prepared and in control of your special day.

Chapter 14

Words of Wisdom

Prepare yourself for unforeseen mishaps so that your day goes just perfect!

Missing Vendors

Appoint a wedding party member to try and track them down. Hopefully, you will have all their contact information at your wedding and reception site. If the vendor stays missing, look for alternatives listed in your binder. Your venue manager or wedding planner will possibly be able to come up with names of reliable last-minute substitutes.

If you can't find a substitute, here are some other suggestions:

MISSING FLORIST

Have a wedding party member run down to the nearest florist and buy as many flowers as you can afford. If possible, convince the florist there to come and help decorate your venue. If flowers are not readily available, consider tall pillar candles for their romantic ambience. Candles can also make simple centrepieces. Or build centrepieces out of fresh fruit and votive candles. Your guests will never know that the florist didn't come!

Missing Photographer

Call up your guests and ask them to bring cameras. If you hadn't already planned to have cameras on the table, get a wedding party member to run to the camera store and purchase some disposable cameras. After the wedding, set up an online page where guests can exchange photos (such as on Flickr or Kodak). You may end up with far more creative shots than you would have with that good-for-nothing photographer anyway!

Missing Priest/Pandit

This could really be something you can't do without. Ask your relatives, if they know any priest, or send someone to the nearby temple to get one. If nothing works, download an online copy of the wedding rituals and required mantras then ask a friend to lead the wedding. While you won't be legally married at the end of the day, you will still have had a memorable and spiritual wedding. Later, you can go to the temple and make things legal, or get married by a religious leader in a more intimate way.

Missing Printer and No Wedding Programmes

Make use of the blackboard and write down the wedding programme at all visible places. You can also type out the programme in the format of a welcome letter and get it photocopied. No one will notice that you didn't have programmes.

In the end, the important thing is to breathe. While you may believe that your wedding day is ruined, remember the important thing is to celebrate your love together, in front of your loved ones. As long as that happens, what could go wrong?

Untold Facts

Every girl dreams of what her married life will be like. However, sometimes a bride needs to also consider that life can be full of surprises. The unexpected can happen, but if you plan ahead, your married life might still be close to perfect.

Take Time to Enjoy Your Engagement Before Diving into Wedding Planning

Being engaged to the love of your life should be the most joyful experience ever, so embrace it. Before heading to the magazine stands and flipping through hundreds of pages of wedding dresses, jewellery and venues, take a few weeks out just for you two. You'll learn to appreciate your love for each other more. Trust me; there will be plenty of time for planning!

Everybody Wants to be Involved

Prepare yourself for the fact that everyone from your closest family members to pushy friends and cousins will have an opinion on how your wedding is supposed to look like. Some of them will be more considerate, they will keep your wishes and preferences in mind and try to come up with constructive ideas, which you may or may not want to take into account. And others…well, there will always be a few who believe their taste (regardless of how tacky it might be) is so good that you absolutely must take it into account! Don't freak out and always have a few polite ways to say, 'No'. Sure, a brutal approach is way more effective but it will also create unnecessary tension and give you a bad name you absolutely don't want.

It's Exhausting!

Planning a wedding, even a really tiny one is actually pretty exhausting! If you want to save by planning your own wedding, you'll really have to be organised and get as much help as you can. Don't leave it all for the last moment. But if you have to organise everything on short notice, keep a few easy, hassle-free solutions ready to pull out, in case your plan A proves to be too difficult to follow through.

Something Will Go Wrong!

From huge catastrophes to tiny details, brides tend to blow everything out of proportion—unless you're living a perfect life and have enough money to own an emergency crew to put down every tiny fire that breaks out, you're bound to see something go off course. That's where a good SOS kit and a 'calm down and count to ten' strategy comes into place. And since I've been through all that, there's one useful wedding tip I can offer, 'Don't let anything get to you so much that it ruins your day! A drunken guest, a tiny stain and even a misplaced *varmala* won't really matter three days from now, and if you let those things ruin your day and make you feel bad on your own wedding...well, you'll remember that for the rest of your life.'

Wedding is Just a Test

While a marriage is the closest thing to a compatibility and adaptability test, a wedding is the opportunity to see who your close friends and 'good' relatives are. And once the whole thing is over, you'll know exactly who is who—you'll be able to single out the ones who came to celebrate your happiness on your big day from the ones who came just to eat, drink and gossip.

'No Gift Policy' is Completely Acceptable

The 'cash over presents' rule is actually more popular than you think. Half of the recent marriages that I have been invited to or discussed with friends, have been the 'don't-bring-us-presents' type of weddings. Why not! Truth be told—most of our married friends wish they had been bold enough to do it too because exchanging all the doubled/tripled/unwanted gifts later on is really stressful and time-consuming.

Stay Organised

When you do start planning your wedding, keep everything in a certain area, where you know you'll be able to find it. This will lower your stress level significantly. I bought a large three-ring binder and page protectors and organised everything in there. That way, when I wanted to look for a brochure I received or a business card I had, I knew right where to find it. This might not work for everyone, but I also bought a big tote box and kept all my magazines, pictures, 'thank you' cards and anything else momentous in there, so I knew just right where to look.

First Wedding Night isn't All Fun and Games

In fact, most newly-weds agree the wedding night was the least eventful one ever! I couldn't agree more—I was like, 'I'm going to brush my teeth and I'll be back in a second,' and he was sound asleep and snoring before I even had a chance to finish that sentence! I followed his lead of course and dove into bed three minutes later looking forward to a full night's rest, which I craved for well over a week! The second night after the wedding as well as the honeymoon will, on the other hand, give you a chance to put that fantastic set of bridal lingerie into a good use, so remember this first of my wedding facts and don't get sad or mad, in case the wedding wears both of you down.

Nothing Really Changes that Much

All that wedding talk, movies and the oh-my-gosh-you're-getting-married gasps made me believe something really big is about to happen! I literally woke up every morning expecting to notice something different! What? Can't say for sure but there was that inexplicable feeling of knowing something is about to happen and expecting it to happen. And guess what? Nothing! Nothing happened! Might not be the most useful wedding tip ever but it will sure help you hold it together and avoid wasting precious mental capacity. You'll stay the same, your husband will stay the same and you'll love each other and enjoy spending time together just as much and that, my ladies, is good left as is.

Don't Forget the Reason You are Getting Married

The small wedding you envisioned with close family and friends could turn out to be this huge wedding you never expected. Opinions get hurled at you from all angles. Sometimes, both families get involved and before you know it, you're trying to make everyone else happy and not thinking about what you and your significant other want.

Before you start stressing about all the details of the wedding though, remember the reason for the day. At the end of that big day—which you've spent all this time planning for—you're married to the person you want to spend the rest of your life with. It's not going to matter what the colour of the mandap was or whether there was a Russian dancer or if chicken was served rather than steak. What matters is that you and your other made it through that day and you can begin life together the way you want.

So what's the point of these wedding facts? Well, let's say I've decided to write them down because I want you all to know that as magical as it is, the wedding day isn't a movie. And guess what? All those little mishaps and downsides are what make it so unique and fun.

So get ready to face some bumps down the road, prepare yourself well and remember to have fun because that's all that matters!

Avoid What Can be Avoided!

Mistakes will happen, more so in a wedding, where there's so much you have to do and so much is at stake. But if you just pay attention and are organised, I promise you won't make nearly half as many wedding mistakes! So let me give you a heads-up by listing a few that we tend to overlook.

Not Having a Clear Understanding of Your Own Expectations

Many problems are caused by conflicting expectations. Until you've planned a wedding, you have no idea of the number of choices and decisions you will need to make and the great emotional turmoil that can be attached to many of them. Attempting to separate fantasy from reality will nip many issues and is the key to defining your own expectations.

Before you start making specific wedding plans, decide what is truly important to you. Do your reading early on. Buy a wedding book and some bridal magazines and get a grip on your needs and situation.

Lack of Budget Priorities

It's super easy to get caught up in the fun of wedding planning and forget about your budget. Put your budget on top to save yourself money and inessentials that might not matter in the end!

Don't let the almighty money ruin what should be one of the most enjoyable experiences for you and your family.

Not Communicating Effectively

Communicating openly with both sets of parents, your fiancé and anyone else who is helping you financially with your wedding is of utmost importance. Once you have gathered your information and considered what is important to you, it is time to sit down with everyone who needs to be involved.

Throughout the wedding planning process, express your desires and expectations clearly. Remember, it's not what is said and done, as much as how it is said and done. Feelings can be hurt and there can be lifelong ramifications.

Clearly communicate areas in which you feel comfortable making your own decisions and areas where you need input from others. Gentle reminders may sometimes be necessary when someone is intruding on your territory or desires.

During a confrontation, respond in a calm, yet firm voice: 'That's a good idea, however, xyz and I discussed it and we've decided to do this.' Or, 'I appreciate your help (opinion) however, I really think we're going to do it this way.'

Peer Pressure

Wedding planning isn't something that just the bride plans, there is typically a ton of other people involved, and I got to say, the biggest wedding mistake most brides make is allowing themselves to be pressured into something they don't want. For example, do you really need to have the biggest suite at the hotel? Do you really need the three lakh rupees wedding dress? Scale down and listen to your own words!

Repress the urge to impress other people. Imagine that you're in a safe little bubble, where you're unaffected by peer choices. You'll be more likely to stick to your budget.

Not Having a Plan

With tons of people involved in wedding planning, having a blueprint of who is going to plan what and who is going to take care of what is huge! This will not only save you time but also money.

Not Being Flexible

To remain sane while planning a wedding, you must decide what is important to you. Think positive and then be willing to go with the flow. Compromise is the key. Be willing to give and take.

Express your desires, but don't get hung up on details. Invite ideas from others and try to be spontaneous. If you're a control freak, do yourself a favour and choose only one or two things to obsess over.

Not Looking

A lot of people, when they are getting married, just leap before they look. You walk into the first reception venue on your list, fall in love and reach for the pen to write a deposit cheque. Sometimes, that works fine. Other times, it doesn't. A week later, you may hear about a place that costs less and offers more services. Impulsive moves usually don't help your budget. So spend some time investigating. If you're the spreadsheet type, plug in the details—cost, services, extras and terms—for every vendor you consider. Even if you end up going back to that love-at-first-sight place, you know that you did your due diligence.

Don't Over Research

Once you've selected a site, stop thinking about other better locations. Once you've chosen the florist, photographer, etc. halt your research. Trust yourself to make the right choices, think positive about them and move forward. You have a lot of other things to do.

Too Many Guests

Once you get your mother and mother-in-law involved—which is a norm—they will have you inviting everyone you've ever met and never cared to see again. Brides tend to go crazy inviting too many people which is a bad idea for several reasons. First of all, you will end up spending too much on invitations and postage—especially when you invite people who you know have no intention of coming. Secondly, you will be paying for that plate of food and other expenses for each guest. Third, you don't want to waste an hour of your reception (especially if you have limited time) greeting people whose names you don't even remember!

So, when you're planning a wedding, have a cap on your guest list. If you are planning on 150, cap it at 150.

Not Sampling the Food

When selecting your wedding reception venue or caterers, the most important thing is to try the food before you commit to using their services. Presenting hungry wedding guests with a cold plate of undercooked food is not the recipe for a happy wedding reception. Your guests may have special needs—it will not be courteous to skip vegetarian options and consider only the non-vegetarian majority.

Remember, you are the host, so everything that happens on your wedding day is a reflection of your taste. Make sure that your wedding meal is as lavish as you envisioned it.

Overfeeding Your Guests

You're so afraid that your wedding will be the one where guests go home hungry or unhappy that you over-order food. Or you try to dazzle everyone with a seven-course dinner extravaganza rather than a more modest but perfectly adequate one. Rest assured no one at your wedding will starve: A reputed catering company will never underestimate how much food you'll need. What this means is that you might not need to have sixteen appetiser choices, sticking with just a few will probably be fine. And keep in mind, the more choices you offer, the higher the cost.

Always be sure to tell your caterer what your budget is and what types of food you want to include in the meal and then let them work their magic within your given parameters. Remember, you're paying for the wealth of their expertise, so trust them to do the job right!

Skimping on Food

Just because it's a buffet style wedding doesn't mean your guests should be rationed portions of food. Nothing left for second helpings? If you think your future mother-in-law can be a little unpleasant now, just wait until you see her on an empty stomach. Being short on food is a big etiquette no-no. Buffet style dinners are fine but you need to make sure there is enough food, plates and napkins to go around.

Work with your caterer ahead of time to make sure you have a menu that's within your budget but still allows you to serve well. There's no point adding an extra appetiser, if it means you'll have a limited portion. Food is one place where it's best not to cut corners. Instead, try saving in other ways like by throwing your wedding on a Sunday (cheaper than Saturday) or simply trimming down your guest list.

Going Overboard with Booze

Your guests will most certainly appreciate a well-stocked and open bar but that doesn't mean you need to provide premium-shelf liquor and a large variety of wines. Survey your guests' drink preferences and buy accordingly. One brand of white and red wine, a couple of varieties of beers, basic liquors (whisky, vodka) and some cocktail mixes will gladly do. Also, try to work with vendors who will reimburse you for any unopened bottles. Finally, avoid fast depletion of your bar stock by passing around a signature cocktail. This also avoids long lines at the bar.

Not Delegating Responsibilities

Delegating responsibilities, wedding preparation tasks and roles is vital—you cannot do everything! Family members will be helping out with the important duties of the wedding day, so why not create a shortlist of responsibilities for each friend? Ask them to run a few errands or make calls for you. Just make sure you ask someone you know will get the job done on time.

Part of the wedding experience also depends on a number of people, who require detailed directives from you such as the caterer, photographer, florist, transportation and/or drivers and DJ. Discuss your ideas in detail with them so that they operate on the same wavelength and avoid embarrassing mistakes during the actual reception.

Lack of Creativity

A lot of weddings speak nothing of the couple's personality. Now, I'm not saying everyone has to have a theme wedding but shouldn't this most important day of your life reflect something of you?

Let's say, your sister chose to have dozens of long-stemmed red roses in tall crystal vases on every table at her reception. Must you follow suit, especially since you know fully well that this option is rather pricey?

Be imaginative. What if, instead of the red roses, you chose local blooms? Or what if you asked a florist to create one centrepiece that you and your friends can use as a template to make the rest yourselves? You'll save lots on the labour that the florist would have to put in.

Not Knowing How to Get Your Groom Involved (I have written a whole chapter on it to help you...)

We know it's not the Stone Age and there are plenty of guys out there who want to see their wedding as an event that reflects their style too.

Have a serious talk with your groom and get a concrete idea of his interest in various details. Decide on tasks he wants to be involved in. You definitely don't want to drag him into decisions that don't interest him. Your fiancé might just surprise you with his contribution and innovative ideas.

Not Having an Assigned Overseer or Consultant for Your Wedding Day

Have at least one person to oversee all services and details—the tent is set up correctly, the flowers are the ones you ordered, the caterer has arrived and is working, etc. You and your immediate family should not have to worry about details on your special day. A dependable friend or preferably a wedding day consultant can free you and your family to enjoy your wedding day.

A wedding consultant can help you as much or as little as you think necessary—help plan the whole wedding from beginning to end or just help you for your wedding day and/or reception. A good consultant can actually save you money by suggesting less expensive alternatives that still enhance your wedding. However, the biggest advantage of a consultant can be your savings in time and stress.

Not Hiring Wedding Professionals

There is no substitute for experience and expertise; this holds true at least this one time. References are important when hiring a wedding professional but that gut feeling of 'woman's intuition' can serve you well. If you have lots of doubts or unanswered questions, you probably need to do some more shopping!

If you want a smooth and relatively worry-free planning process, wedding and reception—rely on the experts. No one knows their business better than they do. They've seen it all, making them the best source of creative ideas and experts at handling any challenge.

Think twice before you ask friends or accept offers from relatives to handle major responsibilities for your wedding. Stories abound of relationships being stretched to their limit, when well-intentioned friends and relatives end up causing wedding catastrophes that range from major to minor. From the mismatched table and mandap decoration to important pictures being missed by the bride's amateur photographer friend, whose camera flash was not working correctly. It has been said, 'It's better to make a friend out of a wedding vendor than try to make a wedding vendor out of a friend.'

There are wedding professionals to fit every budget. Check references so you feel confident that you are choosing a professional you can count on. With weddings, you don't get a second chance to get it right!

Not Communicating with Your Vendors

Don't assume that because they are professionals with years of experience, they automatically know what you want. Each bride's vision is different. Vendors want to avoid disappointing you, so share the details of your dream with them from the beginning.

Micromanaging Your Vendors

You're choosing talented professionals who understand your vision, so let them do their jobs! We know it's tempting to control every detail but you won't have the time and you certainly don't have the experience your vendors do. After your initial meeting, trust the pros to get it right.

Not Getting Signed Contracts

If you only have a verbal agreement, they can call you a week before the wedding and cancel for whatever reason, such as a double-booking or a closure. A signed contract will also have a lot of useful information such as set up times, serving details and any extra fees that might incur.

Not Paying Attention to Fine Print

It's crazy how so many brides and their families don't pay attention to the fine print! Don't skip reading anything and if you have questions—no matter how seemingly insignificant—ask immediately, especially when it comes to clarifying payment terms. You want to know exactly when payments or balances are due; if there are any minimum charges, corkage fees for liquor or any other possibly pricey unknowns. If your wedding is a little time away, be sure to block in guaranteed prices on catering and liquor.

Never ever sign any contract on the spot; always take it home and read over everything, noting down your questions and concerns. If a vendor pressures you to sign, take that as your cue to move on to the next vendor. Nothing is so urgent that it can't wait overnight.

Choosing a Friend as Your Photographer

You've got a friend with lots of professional grade equipment and a really great eye—you should just see her albums on Facebook! She'd be a great photographer and she'll do it for practically nothing. Though it might seem like a great idea, it usually doesn't turn out well. When the wedding is over, all you are left with are your wedding photos. You don't want them to be blurry or out of focus. And who's to say, on the night of your wedding, your friend won't decide to act more like a wedding guest and less like the photographer! It usually just pays to hire a professional.

Spending Too Much Time Taking Pictures

There are photographs of special moments that you must have, pictures of spontaneous moments that are fun to have and staged photos that become a nuisance beyond a point. Don't be afraid to say no to your photographer when you've had enough.

Too Many Extras

Finally, it's really easy to get sucked into the details of a wedding. If you scale down on some of the extras, I promise, you'll save a ton of money in the long run!

Not Having a Backup Plan

Outdoor weddings can be beautiful but not if it rains. As a wedding planner, plan every outdoor event as though it's going to be raining sideways with gusting winds. Consider a tent or a backup ceremony location. You don't want to be wet in your gorgeous wedding attire and your guests to probably sit in their cars and watch from afar.

Not Asking for a Discount

Everything is negotiable in the wedding industry. Tip: Instead of saying, 'I want X, Y and Z. How much does that cost?' Say, 'This is my budget. What can you do for me?' True story: I got some bridal accessories free with my wedding attire just by asking! It's always worth a try.

TRYING TO DROP TWO SIZES BEFORE YOUR FINAL FITTING

You've found the wedding dress of your dreams; though it's not exactly a perfect fit on the real-life you. Your plan: Order the dress two sizes smaller and then do whatever it takes to make it fit. Or so you think. Making a commitment to eat right and exercise is great when you're planning your wedding. On the other hand, crash dieting and chaining yourself to the gym is a course likely to end in disaster and a dress that doesn't fit.

Instead of losing more sleep than weight, find the attire you love and order it in your current size. If you want to work on your body during your engagement, that's great—go ahead, but be sure to make your goals manageable. You're more likely to stick with a routine that doesn't require superhuman willpower. And if you still find yourself freaking about your figure, just remember that you're about to get hitched to someone who can't get enough of the way you look (really, truly) right now.

You'll want to lose the extra weight before your second trial. Your final fitting should be for last-minute tweaks, not a total overhaul.

YOU TRY ON YOUR SHOES THE DAY OF THE WEDDING

I know you want to keep your bridal shoes in pristine condition, but try wearing them at least around your house for several hours, few days before the wedding, to avoid painful blisters or pinched toes. Even if you're planning on changing after the ceremony, you want to make sure you can comfortably and confidently walk in your heels during your wedding.

YOU DON'T DO ANY HAIR OR MAKE-UP TRIALS

Assembling your look of the day, head-to-toe, prior to the wedding is an absolute must. How else would you know that the magazine hairstyle you've been dreaming of just doesn't look that great after all? Imagine turning around to face the mirror once your hairdresser or make-up artist has worked their magic, only to feel faint at the results. It is imperative to book a make-up and hair trial prior to your big day, unless you totally trust the professional or if you are keeping your hair and beauty simplistic.

You do not want to feel self-conscious on your wedding day; it will distract you from focusing on more important things and also leave you dissatisfied with your wedding photographs later on. So invest in that make-up and hair trial. See it as your insurance to having a gorgeous day and pictures you will cherish for a lifetime. Make it more fun by inviting your best buddy or by having your mom put together her complete look of the day too.

You Pack for the Honeymoon Last-minute

Why wait? The trip is booked and you'll have enough to do in the mornings after the wedding, without also trying to remember if your toothbrush and contacts are in your suitcase. Do yourself a favour and finish your packing before your wedding, especially if you are leaving within a week's time from the wedding. So, all you'll have left are the last-minute items.

Forgetting What It's All About

It's so easy to get caught up in the details and the 'Big Perfect Day' ideal, such that we often lose focus of what a wedding really is: The beginning of a lifelong commitment to another person. If it doesn't go exactly as planned, it doesn't mean the marriage is doomed! It just means you've got something ridiculous to laugh (or, okay, cry) about for years to come...together.

Losing Your Sense of Humour

One way to keep your sense of humour is to work mostly with people you like—hire wedding vendors who are not just talented but also congenial. This occasion is too important and stressful anyway, why spend time with those who are difficult!

Having a sense of humour is really an asset in wedding planning. On your wedding day, if something goes wrong, remember you are probably the only one who will notice. Relax and let it go! Even if your brother-in-law is a big jerk, give him a hug anyway.

Your marriage will be a lifelong memory. So cherish every moment of it minus the hassles!

BRIDAL MISTAKES

Do wedding albums of your parents, cousins or friends make you wonder 'For god's sake, what were they thinking!' Oh yes, in an effort to create the perfect wedding, brides sometimes end up committing serious blunders. For the benefit of all brides, I have compiled the most common bridal beauty mistakes so that you take every care to avoid them.

Oops, I forgot to carry my lipstick! The long hours, the constant greetings and the countless smiles at your wedding mean your picture-perfect make-up would need touch-ups from time to time. Despite tall claims by your make-up artist that it will last for the entire length of the evening, make-up tends to lose its sheen after few hours. Carry with you a little blush and lipstick to avoid giving the washed-out look on photographs. Ask a friend or cousin to carry around the emergency bridal beauty make-up kit.

My head hurts already! Severe updo, side-swept hair, French braid, puffy curls…a girl who isn't comfortable with any of these hairstyles may still go for it on her wedding day. To get the desired look, brides sometimes tend to overlook the discomfort. The numerous pins, sprays and gels to keep the hairstyle in place can make the long hours of your wedding extremely strenuous. If you want to have fun at your wedding, choose a stylish but comfortable hairstyle.

Black tears running down my cheek? Oh no! Weddings are an emotional affair. Teardrops would be an on-and-off visitor. But don't let them play spoilsport. Waterproof make-up is a must for brides. Be it the foundation, concealer, eyeliner or mascara, whatever brand/s you choose, make sure you invest in a good kit of water-resistant make-up items. And as a precaution, always keep wet tissues and blotting paper handy.

Why red and patchy skin? Every bride likes to look fresh and radiant on her big day. Any last-minute cleansing, peeling and facial, just before the wedding, followed with heavy bridal make-up right after can leave the skin irritated and patchy. It is a well-known fact that the afterglow of facials take few days to show. So finish your facial cleansing three-five days prior to your wedding.

Why did I wear those six-inch heels? Heels make a lady look sexy. A pair of elegant golden heels is almost a necessity for every Indian bride. But the long hours at the wedding can be hard on a bride. Instead of a six-inch heel, opt for a more comfortable height that would look just as good on you. And keep a pair of flats handy, just in case—especially when you step on the dance floor to actually enjoy the wedding. You don't want to end up looking for Band-Aids and cotton.

Chapter 15

Stress Manager

Stress comes secretly hidden in the wedding planning kit. So let's deal the devil out of your beautiful wedding!

Bridezillas are made, not born. It's supposed to be the happiest time of your life—and you want it to be—yet planning a wedding is like working a second job. You have to find the time to tend to a multitude of details. Besides your already busy schedule, you must now manage vendors, family anxieties and demands, your groom, your emotions and an array of tricky wedding dynamics. True, some brides are downright demanding but most are nice people, sucked into the vortex of wedding planning stress and overwhelmed by the stress, pressure and expectations of those around her.

If you have been experiencing an increased sense of stress lately, congratulate yourself. It probably shows that you are in touch with your feelings. However, if you feel bad or somehow inadequate because you feel stressed, think again. No one escapes stress because getting married is a major life change and one of the biggest stress inducers of all time.

This little five-letter word often wreaks havoc in the lives of brides

and grooms everywhere. Just exactly what is stress? Simply put, it's
that unpleasant state experienced by people when they feel they can't
cope with a situation. It's that heart-thumping sound in your chest
sometimes accompanied by the urge to pound on the wall with your
fists and scream, 'I can't take it anymore!' Even though getting married
is viewed as a positive experience in itself, all the details associated
with it can have negative effects and lead to stress.

It's not realistic to think you can totally avoid stress, so let's find
ways to handle it. Managing stress and anxiety effectively can be
crucial to making this time a positive one for you and your partner.
You want your wedding planning process to bring you closer and build
your intimacy. Stress can interfere with this important goal.

A major difference between those who feel overwhelmed by stress
and those who do not is not the presence or absence of stress but the
ability to recognise stress when it occurs and to manage it.

Stress management involves four tasks:

- Recognise and understand the signs of stress
- Identify and understand the sources of stress
- Learn to manage controllable sources of stress
- Learn to support yourself and cope with stress reactions to
  situations beyond your control

Signs of Stress

Over-stress reactions include a wide range of symptoms—stomach
aches, headaches, sleep problems, poor concentration, moodiness,
irritability and racing thoughts. It's important to recognise that
these are all signs of stress overload, probably not of a more
serious condition.

Sources of Stress and Taking Control

During the pre-wedding period, there are so many stressful decisions,
expenses, expectations and new roles. Many people do not realise
how great an impact this stress can have on their happiness and
relationships. Perhaps one of the most difficult aspects of the pre-
wedding period can be the disparity between its inherent stress, on
one hand and expectations that it will be a time of happiness and

fulfilment, on the other. Perfectionism about wedding arrangements is very common and can be a big source of stress.

MONEY STRESS

You begin with plans for a simple yet elegant affair and before you know it, your wedding budget begins to approach the national debt. Don't let this happen to you. One of the major causes of wedding stress is money. If you start spending more than you budgeted for (and this is very easy to do), you are rolling out the welcome mat for stress. If your goals exceed what you can really afford, this will create a high level of stress. People create wonderful weddings, with great meaning and memories on small budgets. Make sure you don't set expectations for yourself that can't happen. Wedding vendors (caterers, florist, photographers, etc.) want to make money and will pressure you into getting the more expensive option.

Antidote: Since money is such an easy thing to fight about:

- Make sure you sit down at the beginning of the process and agree on how much money each of you or your family will spend! And stick to it.
- Before meeting a potential vendor, educate yourself on the prices in your area and carry a list of questions with you to the appointments. Some vendors may be willing to negotiate the cost of package deals, if you're willing to sacrifice components that aren't high on your priority list.
- If you're tempted by what they offer but it is more expensive, say firmly, 'That's not in my budget, I'll have to go home and see if I can move some things around and get back to you.' At home, it will be easier to decide if that extra option is really necessary or just an expensive add-on.
- If you realise later on that your budget isn't realistic or that you want to add new details you didn't budget for, then you need to sit down together and renegotiate.
- I also recommend building your budget to 90 per cent of what you're truly comfortable spending. You'll be able to splurge on that unforeseen can't-live-without addition and cover last-minute incidentals without breaking the bank.

HIGH EXPECTATIONS STRESS

One of the largest causes of wedding stress is trying to keep up with social and personal expectations. The problem is more apparent when your ideal wedding doesn't follow the rules and doesn't fit in with the vision that friends or family members have. No matter who you are or what age...everyone has something to say about your wedding. You may be showered with congratulations and gifts but you are simultaneously bombarded with unsolicited advice, wedding horror stories you don't want to hear and negative vibes from well-meaning friends and relatives, who are too lost in their own experience to realise they are imposing on you. People tend to see your wedding as a chance to fulfil their own needs and family dynamics erupt in every direction. As the clan prepares to gather, they begin to act out what it's all about for them—not you! The issues are classic—mom wants it to be the wedding she never had, sister or best friend wishes it were her, your groom is afraid to stand up to his family. Or the experience may be fraught with more modern challenges such as questions about mixing faiths, opting for a non-religious wedding or planning an alternative kind of affair.

Antidote: Listen to what they have to say but with a grain of salt. Repeat this mantra: They are not the ones getting married, we are. If you listened to what everyone thought, you would have a mishmash wedding that would not reflect who you are in the slightest. You're not getting married to please them, after all. A bride has to clarify the wedding she truly wants, try to stay centred and set clear boundaries that no one can penetrate with words or attitudes. If all else fails, consider this: The reality is that weddings tend to be for other people but marriage is for you two. Focus on what your marriage will mean to you.

PARENTAL STRESS

Whether its complaining about the money you're spending, wanting to have a hand in everything, doubting if the wedding is ideal by their standards or disapproving of your marriage totally, parents can stress you a lot too.

Antidote: While the idea that 'it's your day' is a great one, it doesn't mean that you discard the opinions of parents to get what you want. A wedding is an event that unites two families, especially for us, Indians. It's not just you and your partner anymore. Your parents and in-laws, have a stake in the game and an expectation here and there.

- Sit down with your parents early in the wedding planning process to learn what sort of wedding they have in mind.
- Get them to agree on a set number of people they'll be inviting.
- Discuss your initial ideas including when/where/style. Then try to avoid the pitfalls.
- Don't promise your mother something if you haven't talked to your fiancé about it first.
- Don't lose sight of your vision for your wedding—write it on a big sheet of paper and tape next to the phone, if necessary.
- It's the time to get to know your future in-laws too. Family rituals may look unfamiliar but take care not to judge or dismiss 'suggestions' that are important to your fiancé's family. Maybe your parents are divorced, your mother-in-law isn't your biggest fan or your partner has an uncle with a penchant for showing up drunk at family events—whatever the situation, talk with your family, (both yours and your fiancé) about any issues that may cause problems at the wedding, so that the two of you can devise a solution to minimise chaos on your big day.

EMOTIONAL STRESS

Getting married can stir up a lot of emotions. The process itself sets forth a period of growth and change that can be very confusing and nerve-wracking. Once you decide to marry, the process to get ready for marriage begins, pushing to the surface many unresolved emotions—about parents and family, past loves and concerns about the person you have chosen. This doesn't mean you shouldn't marry, it just means inner work is called for, along with all the outer preparations.

Antidote: A bride can embrace the awareness that she is embarking on a journey of evolution, going from one part of life to another. She must honour and address the emotions and fears that arise.

Trust them to be natural and attend any issues that require support or counselling. It is important to stay on top of your emotions and be honest with yourself during this time. Don't sweep things under the rug. Schedule a weekly rant session with girls in your inner circle.

WEDDING PLANNING STRESS

There is so much focus on the external experience that a bride can become mired in details and demands and lose track of herself and the reason she is getting married in the first place. When she finds that planning her dream wedding means battling—parents, family, friends, groom and almost anyone involved—she becomes hostile and reactive. What began as a joyful experience turns into a fight...a fight for having the perfect wedding! It is exhausting and can turn even sweet-tempered people mean and cranky.

Antidote: First, control those negative thoughts. If you think plans will go wrong, they probably will. And if you think plans will go well, you will most likely succeed.

- Practise positive self-talk. Look in the mirror every morning and repeat, 'I am in control of my wedding and it will be beautiful.' This is your mantra.
- Build no unrealistic expectations and you won't be disappointed.
- Remember that the true meaning of marriage is to bring two individuals and families together in sacred union—the party is meant to be a celebration, not something that will kill your spirit in the planning. When two people commit themselves to one another in matrimony, they have the opportunity to unite not just their hearts, lives and families but their very beings. And it is not just the couple that benefits from the ceremony—anyone who witnesses a wedding can be empowered and inspired by the love in the room. Focus on the love and remember that's always been your aim.

PERFECT WEDDING STRESS

Your happiness in life does not hinge on your wedding alone (it really doesn't...so lighten up!) Some brides believe that they must have a perfect wedding in order to have a perfect marriage and a perfect life.

They give the wedding day too much power—treating the wedding as something to be worshipped and served. They're scared that if something goes wrong with the wedding, it will affect the marriage. Our culture places tremendous emphasis on having a great wedding and not enough focus on having an awesome marriage. It's okay to be temporarily obsessed and yearn for the perfect wedding—we all get there at some point—but you have to keep your eye on what's truly important.

Antidote: Step back and realise, the most important part of the day is not the celebration but the fact you are getting married to the person, you look forward to building your life with.

- You will have a lifetime in which you can create more memories. The wedding day, while important, is only one of the many experiences and memories you will share!
- Remember, no wedding is perfect but it can be close to perfect if you start out by thinking positively. Your day will be beautiful, romantic and personal but it won't be perfect. Nothing is! Accept that there are limits to your control over the wedding.
- Any event involving so many other people will have a few imperfections.
- Go into the process with a plan B (vendors or locations you'd be just as happy with, in case your first choices don't work out), and accept that it's the best you can do. Ultimately, if something small goes wrong—your make-up artist falls sick, your shoes go missing or your photographer turns up late—it's not going to ruin your day. Those are the moments that make your wedding unique and memorable.
- Don't try to wear too many hats. Your role in the wedding is to be the bride—not the caterer, the florist or the photographer. **Antidote**: Interview your vendors carefully. If possible, get references from people you know. And once you've hired them, let them do their job. Communicate clearly via emails and keep records of your arrangements but don't micromanage. Trust them to deliver what you're paying them for. You can't handle everything by yourself as super as you may be. Weddings are

major endeavours, so enlist friends and family to help run errands. It's down to the wire and you find yourself pulling out your hair because the florist is slow at returning your calls, the tailor is taking too long to alter your gown and you can't decide which dish to serve at the reception. It's enough to make anyone go crazy but surviving wedding stress is possible.

SPOUSE STRESS

It's true; no one can stress you out during wedding planning as much as your future spouse. Of all the people involved in the planning, he's probably the one whom you'll most frequently need to consult over decisions. It's probably also the biggest project you've worked on together, and so differences in issues like budgeting, organisation styles and even taste can crop up. The most common complaints however, are 'He's not doing anything to help with the wedding' and 'She never talks about anything other than the wedding.' Avoid this with some simple planning.

Antidote: Talk with your partner about who will lead the wedding efforts. Will it be the bride, a wedding planner, the mother-of-the-bride or will you share the responsibility? There's no right or wrong choice. The important thing is to agree on who is doing what and communicate that to everyone involved.

- You may decide to let one person plan the wedding, still it's important for both parties to discuss their requirements. Even the most laid-back groom is likely to have one or two things he is keen about for his own wedding. Write down what you each want, attach a priority to each item and then discuss your expectations. Don't worry, if you don't agree on all the points right away. Set those items to the side and revisit them after you have a chance to think about them. Learning to share your expectations will be valuable later in life.

- Sit down with a wedding planner or a wedding checklist and divide the listed tasks into three categories—bride's, groom's and 'together'. Each will have creative control for what's on your list and what you are responsible for. Post the list in prominent locations in your houses and agree to have regular check-in meetings to review progress.

- Go on a no-wedding date, every week. This is perhaps the most important thing to stop you both from stressing each other out. One night a week, neither of you is allowed to mention the word wedding or anything wedding related. This can be a date night or just anything that you both like doing together, just to remind you why you're going through all this craziness in the first place!

Keep in mind that all change is stressful, including good change (And isn't getting married a huge good change?). Other sources of stress don't go away just because you are getting married. These additional stressors can compound pre-wedding stress. The common factors that can contribute to stress include work, overcommitment, moving, travel, illness and loss of a family member, friend or pet. For those embarking on a second marriage and single parents, the demands of child-rearing and financial complications can be stress factors.

Some of these stressors are controllable. You can control how perfect you expect your wedding to be and whether to accept many social invitations. Other stressors are beyond your control. For example, no one can prevent personal losses and illnesses. To deal with overstress, you must first recognise and manage sources that are within your control.

Support Yourself During Stress
MEDITATE
With so much to do and stay on top (not to mention the life-changing event to come), it's easy to feel overwhelmed. Clear your head of worries. Start focusing on the in-and-out cycle of your breath—do it just a few minutes a day or when you're lying in bed at night. It will slow down your heart rate and relax your muscles too.

CONSIDER SOFTENING SCENTS
Lavender is well-known for its soul-soothing capabilities but others like jasmine, chamomile and basil have proven relaxing benefits

as well. Dab some lavender or rose essential oil onto your wrists to shift your mood quickly. Or light a perfumed candle; brew a cup of floral tea for a little sweet-smelling repose.

Adopt a Mantra
Is your future mother-in-law getting on your nerves? It's pretty natural for two strong women to have their own opinions. Find a solitary spot and close your eyes. Breathe in thinking, I feel good and breathe out thinking, I am peaceful.

Exercise
If you haven't already upped your pre-wedding workout routine, here's good reason to. Exercise has positive emotional and psychological effects. Take a walk, go for a run or hit the gym. Any type of physical movement will help produce more uplifting and stress-stabilising endorphins.

Allow Yourself to be Nervous
It's okay to feel a little jittery. Our culture and society believe that engagement is supposed to be only a happy time but that's just not reality. In fact, fear often accompanies pre-wedding excitement and joy. It's normal, healthy even, to question this lifetime commitment. Just because you're concerned, doesn't mean you don't want to get married. Acknowledge your nerves, discuss it with a trusted confidant and move on. A close friend can help you traverse the tricky transition from fiancé to wife.

Jot Down Your Feelings
Journaling is a safe and accessible way for you to express those bottled up emotions. It'll help them from festering into anxiety. Identify what's bothering you and address that topic solely. For example, if you're upset that your late father won't be there for the wedding (especially the *kanyadaan*), title the entry 'Missing Dad'. Avoid flooding yourself with too many emotions at once.

Pamper Yourself
A massage, a facial or even a manicure and pedicure in a spa setting can do wonders for your stress levels. Don't think of these

as indulgences. Rather treat them as necessary for staying well balanced and on task. If you can't spring a spa, settle into the tub from time to time. A nice bath can melt stress away.

DANCE

Dance focuses the mind, drawing you away from stressful life circumstances and prevailing worries. You can vent your frustration and find an avenue for creative expression and imaginative exploration.

Some more ways to handle and recover from stress

- Get adequate sleep.
- Eat regular, balanced and moderate meals.
- Avoid excess sugar, caffeine, nicotine, alcohol, drugs, etc. All of these cause your system to 'crash' after the temporary stimulating or relaxing effect.
- Make time for fun and other pleasure activities.
- Make time to connect with your partner and spend positive time together.
- Stay within your comfort zone

Many stressed brides experiment with new 'relaxing' activities. Instead, do whatever relaxes you ordinarily: If you're not a person who's into yoga, the week or the day before the wedding isn't the time for some elaborate yoga class.

Include stress management, self-nurturing and time to chill out in your wedding planning process and see how things get a lot easier. You have to love, honour and cherish yourself, if you want to be loved, honoured and cherished by someone else!

Chapter 16

Beauty Diaries

Fitness for the Bride

It is true that every bride looks beautiful on her wedding day. Nobody denies that it's the bride's day to shine. But the only way to truly look your best is to begin a health regime months before your wedding. You might even surprise yourself! Unfortunately, there are no shortcuts.

There's nothing like an engagement ring to motivate a woman to get serious about weight loss. The dress! The photos! The honeymoon! A wedding has a deadline that can inspire you to spring into action.

The problem is many brides-to-be resort to extreme measures and quick fixes to drop weight quickly. Some of those methods may work a little (even if they're not so safe or healthy) but often they fail miserably. That's because quick fixes, diet pills and extreme exercise plans don't usually deliver, especially in the long-term. When countless studies show that marriage itself tends to pack on the fats, wouldn't you rather make smart, reasonable and sustainable changes to your current diet and fitness plan to help prevent the 'inevitable' weight gain of wedded bliss? This way, you'll look great by the time of your wedding and also stay fit and svelte as you celebrate your first, second and twenty-second anniversaries.

Amid all the stress of wedding planning, is a healthy diet and fitness programme possible? Yes, just stay committed to your plan—choose to stay in control, one day at a time.

The simplest advice is often the most effective and this is true in the case of your health. A nourishing diet and plenty of solid rest will do you a world of good.

Track your food: That means all of it, from the spoonful of soup you sampled for your reception menu to the little bites of desserts you taste. These 'hidden' calories are easy to gloss over but can really add up. Plus, research shows that the simple act of tracking your food can help you lose twice as much weight than if you don't track at all (mental tracking does not count). Keep a food diary and log every single morsel that enters your mouth. You'll be amazed at how much you haven't considered before.

Sample smart: If you're meeting caterers for a tasting session, sample small portions. And if you sample a variety of sweets one day, cut back on sugary foods for the next few days.

Eat breakfast: Eat a healthy breakfast to get your metabolism fired up and you'll be more likely to make healthy choices throughout the day like ordering a smart lunch and swinging by the gym after work.

Make fitness a priority: Don't let your workouts go by the wayside. Rather, workout more than before if you really want to drop a few kilos. With a hectic schedule, how will you fit it in? That's what this next tip is for.

Treat your workouts like an appointment: You wouldn't miss your event-planning meeting, pre-marriage counselling session or dress fitting, would you? Add your workouts to your calendar so that other obligations don't get in the way of your gym time. Why not discuss wedding plans with your fiancé and family while you enjoy a walk? Or pace around the room, if you're on the phone. Multitasking can help.

Get support: Get someone to cheer you on towards your fitness goals. Make friends at the gym/aerobics/fitness class. Connect with people having similar goals to get tips, motivation and your own personal cheerleading squad.

Limit alcohol: It lowers inhibitions, you're more likely to forget about your nutrition plan and overindulge. Plus, alcohol alone is pretty high in calories. Try to relax and de-stress without drinking. If you must drink, nurse your glass slowly, choose diet-friendly drinks and limit the number of servings. Add every drink to your Nutrition Tracker.

Pick healthy venues for pre-wedding festivities: As your wedding draws near, there will be showers, parties and outings galore. Pick a restaurant known to serve nutritious meals. Focus on your friends and family while you're there, enjoying those conversations and activities instead of hovering around the appetisers.

Catch your 'zzzs': Your mind and calendar may be full of to-dos, but is 'plenty of sleep' on your agenda each day? It should be. Too little shut-eye can hinder your weight-loss efforts—increased cravings leading to poor choices. Sleep at least seven-eight hours every day.

Don't make mountains out of molehills: Exceeding your calories one day does not mean you failed. It takes more than one day of overeating to thwart your progress. Accept your slip-ups, learn from them and move on.

Steer clear of fads: Don't fall for fad diets or fitness gimmicks. How do you spot them? By their too-good-to-be-true claims. Fad diets don't work and their results are fleeting.

No crash dieting: The repercussions include bad skin, bowel problems, tummy upsets and even bad breath. No bride wants to feel puffy and bloated on her wedding day. Also, having to make frequent trips to the bathroom as a result of eating too many eggs and grapefruits the week before can be a big nuisance.

Maintain an active lifestyle: Running errands as you plan your wedding isn't the same as actually running or exercising for that matter. Don't confuse being busy with being fit. The more physical activity you can add to your days (in addition to planned fitness), the better off you'll be. Try short workouts and find simple ways to turn downtime into active time.

Eat smaller, healthier amounts, more frequently: Aim to eat, on an average, four-five times per day. Meals don't have to be huge and can consist of half a banana, an apple, cottage cheese on crackers or fish and salads. This will, in turn, increase your metabolic rate as your body sees you fuelling it, not starving it of calories.

Keep an emergency snack on hand: Stashing some healthy and portable food in your car, purse and desk drawer can help satisfy your cravings and prevent you from going overboard on all the wrong foods. This is a good idea when you're hungry at work and cookies sound tempting or when you're out all day and see the glowing fast food signs beckoning you.

Don't let yourself get too hungry: Between smart snacking and balanced meals, keeping your body properly fuelled can help you keep hunger at bay. Eating too little, on the other hand, creates monstrous cravings that are too hard to ignore. When ravenous, you're likely to grab anything and usually a lot of it, to quell your discomfort. Keep hunger at bay with proper planning.

Manage stress: Every bride worries over tiny details, schedules, budget and even fit of her dress. Life doesn't stop just because you're planning a wedding. But all that stress can wreak havoc to your mental health and your waistline, especially if you're prone to emotional eating. Try some relaxation and rejuvenation techniques, even if it's as simple as a one-minute breathing exercise or an extra couple of minutes in a hot shower.

Drink your water: Recent studies found that when people drink more water throughout the day, they end up eating fewer total calories. Another study found that drinking water before each meal resulted in greater weight loss. Water and water-rich foods can help fill you up longer. At parties, keep sipping water between bites to prevent overeating.

Wake up with exercise: People who exercise first thing in the morning are more likely to exercise regularly than those exercising later in the day. Morning workouts might be the best way to squeeze fitness into your days before other things come up. Plus, when you exercise first, you're less likely to overindulge with food later.

Add some exercise here and there: I am being repetitive here just to get my point across. Add some small exercise moves into your daily routine. Do bum clenches while sitting at your desk. Avoid using elevators and escalators.

Slow down: Savour your food and the experience of eating. You'll tend to eat less and feel more satisfied.

Keep your eye on the prize: Before you take a bite or hit snooze to avoid the gym, remember your goals. Ask yourself, 'Will this help me achieve my goal by my wedding day?' If not, make another decision. And remember that you are in control of your life and your choices.

Build muscle and burn calories: A muscular body burns more calories. Exercise regularly at least three (ideally five) times a week—do forty-five minutes of cardio workout and fifteen minutes of weight bearing exercise, at the very least. Change your routine regularly to keep it fun and challenging.

Make exercise fun: Choose an activity that you enjoy like swimming, dancing or yoga. Take some couple dancing lessons—get fit and spend quality time together. Also, if you have plans of dancing in your sangeet/bachelor party, hold a lot of practice sessions.

Set long-term goals: Whether it be five or twenty kgs before the wedding or a slimmer waistline for the lehenga, break your long-term goal down into mini steps—two kgs in one month, one inch off the waistline, etc. Reward yourself at each mini step achievement point with a massage, a pedicure, a pair of skinny jeans—whatever rocks your boat!

No time to get to the gym? Try dancing while getting dressed in the morning. You can burn an extra 50-100 calories as you get ready, just by adding a little two-step or the twist. Or for quick toning, while you're sitting at your desk or standing in line, alternate between contracting your abs and glutes for sixty seconds, then release.

Wedding Diet

Whether it is the build-up during the weeks before your wedding day or on the actual day, every bride and groom must carefully consider what they are eating.

Weeks before your wedding, start a regime to eat better. This will help you feel healthy and refreshed.

Enjoy the diet changes you make, they will benefit you in the long run. And do not be afraid to try something new, be it a fruit you never had or an exercise you did not think you would be good at, such as hiking or cycling.

What Not to Eat the Day Before

What you eat the day before your wedding is of great importance as certain foods can make you weak and lethargic. So avoid:

- Spicy or rich foods
- Too much alcohol
- Heavy meals—steak and potatoes, for instance
- Garlic and onions
- Anything that you haven't had before—you may have an allergic reaction
- Going overboard on vegetables or baked beans
- Having too much salt the day before as this can cause bloating as well as water retention
- Late night snacks

Go for a healthy dinner such as stir-fry or salad.

On the Big Day

- Be sure to eat a little something before you leave your room/ parlour, you don't want your stomach rumbling during the ceremonies or feel dehydrated.
- By all means, drink coffee but don't go overboard.
- Make sure you have a good breakfast, nothing too big or heavy.
- Take a few snacks along to nibble on but avoid anything crumbly or sticky.
- Drink plenty of water during the day, stop an hour before you start getting ready—using the restroom with the wedding dress would be a tough job.
- You may be nervous and feel you cannot stomach anything. Drink water and try having a banana or a power bar.

Make Sure You Consume These Daily

- Asparagus, cantaloupe, cucumber and watermelon—these are great anti-bloating agents
- Avocados—these give you great young looking skin
- Grapes—claim to prevent wrinkles and sagging of skin
- Pomegranates—help to improve your skin tone

Snack Options Which are Not As Sinful

- Slice up one medium-sized apple and dip slices into 1 tbsp all-natural peanut butter.
- Mix together 100 gms low-fat cottage cheese and half-a-cup fresh pineapple chunks.
- Combine one medium-sized pear (sliced) with 25 gms cheddar or gouda cheese for a sweet and savoury snack.
- In a small bowl, mix together 1 cup melon chunks, 2 tbsp low-fat plain yogurt and 1 tsp honey.
- Sprinkle 3 cups all-natural popcorn with garlic salt and 1 tbsp grated Parmesan cheese.
- Make a gourmet snack out of low-fat Greek yogurt, mixed with 2 tsp honey and topped with 2 tsp chopped pistachios or walnuts.
- Spread or dip ten whole-grain pita chips with a quarter cup roasted eggplant dip or hummus.
- Want to get your chocolate fix without the guilt? Snack on ten almonds and one to two squares of dark chocolate (look for 70 per cent cocoa or higher).
- Yes, you can still have your morning or afternoon latte! Just order a smaller size with skim or soymilk and a sprinkling of cocoa powder or cinnamon on top.
- My favourite—drizzle one cup fresh berries with chocolate syrup (or try balsamic vinegar) and top it with two tablespoons whipped cream—now that's a dessert!
- Top half-a-cup all-natural ice cream or chocolate sorbet with half-a-cup fresh berries.

This is possibly the most important day of your life, so it's no surprise that most brides hit the gym and the diets in the months leading up to the day.

If you find your diet/exercise routine slipping, just picture yourself in your wedding dress and the photographs that will be taken on the day, they are going to be a constant reminder of how you looked.

With a bit of planning, little hard work and a dash of discipline, you'll be looking your best, feeling your best and without doubt, be the well-deserved centre of attention on your wedding day.

Beauty Countdown

The First Thing to Do: Take Stock of Your Skin

If you are prone to breakouts or want to address issues like dark spots, redness or fine lines, you could consult a dermatologist, ideally nine months before your wedding. Most products require months for results to show. Set that first appointment early to give yourself ample time to learn what works best for you.

Several Months Before: Consider How You Want Your Hair

- Sure, you don't have to commit right away. But if you love a style and need to grow your hair out or get the right cut for it, it pays to plan ahead.
- Ideally, carry magazine pictures of styles you like or photos of yourself at formal occasions as well as a snapshot of your dress to a stylist, six to eight months before your wedding.
- Be open to your stylist's suggestions—she may know how best to flatter your face shape or your dress's neckline. After testing a range of styles (up, down and half-up), settle on two looks. Then discuss your colour, cut and any necessary conditioning treatments.
- Remember, your stylist needs time to perfect your wedding-day look, from adding highlights to coating strands with a shine-enhancing gloss.

Leave the salon with one goal—to narrow down your options before your next appointment.

One to Three Months Before: Think About Brightening Your Smile

To reduce darker staining, visit a dentist for professional whitening treatments. If you just want to brighten up a shade or two, enlist an over-the-counter product. Apply after a professional teeth cleaning for best result.

Two to Three Months Before: Get Serious About Finalising Your Hairstyle
Once you've decided which style you prefer, head back to the salon for a dress rehearsal. This time, carry your dupatta and jewellery along, so that you and your stylist can determine exactly what you'll look like on the big day.

One to Two Months Before: Go for a Make-up Trial
- Arrive wearing make-up similar to what you would like for your wedding. Your make-up artist will then know your colour preferences and also how much product you're comfortable wearing for a special occasion.
- Carry photos from magazines to show her your desired look. Everyone's version of a smoky eye is different.
- And don't forget your brows. Well-shaped ones can help frame your make-up look but sometimes you need to let hair grow into sparse spots.

Two to Five Days Before: Have Your Brows Done
Most professionals recommend threading or plucking over waxing because it's gentler on the skin and lets the groomer precisely target individual hair for a better shape overall.
- If you've threaded or tweezed before, shaping them two days prior to the wedding can take care of redness, if any.
- First time? Book at least three days in advance. Swipe just-tweezed or threaded areas with astringent to prevent breakouts and apply moisturiser to help soothe redness and swelling.

One Day Before: Get a Manicure and Pedicure
You won't be rushed this way and your nails will have adequate time to dry and harden and they'll look great. On the big day, keep an extra bottle of polish and a file handy for last-minute chip repairs.

Looking for a Magical Make-up Artist
We all know the horror story—the make-up artist wordlessly picks up a brush and starts to paint, occasionally pausing to say, 'Trust me,

I'm going to make you look fabulous!' You wait, nervously, as layers upon layers of product are applied to your face. 'Voila!' he exclaims, turning you to face the mirror. You stare in horror at your reflection, completely unrecognisable. And with no time to wash it off...that is the face your groom will see on this very special day of yours.

Okay, so I'm being a little dramatic. But I know this story lurks in the back of your mind too. I wish to free brides from fear, so that they can confidently choose the bridal make-up artist who is right for them. Thankfully, there is no shortage of great wedding make-up artists. These professionals are experienced enough to realise that you want to still look like 'you' when your groom sees his bride. So where do you find them?

First and foremost, do your research. Don't simply get up and go to your neighbourhood parlour. They will not charge a great deal (some are willing to do it for as little as ₹2,000). But imagine what they will turn you into...

WHERE TO FIND THEM?

Do some Facebook stalking: Click through the wedding photos of friends, friends of friends, and heck, even old frenemies from high school. See whose make-up you absolutely love and then find out who did it. Also, put the word out among your acquaintances. It's best to locate one in your network rather than blindly search for someone through listings.

Ask around and get referrals: Seek recommendations from friends, family, colleagues and hairdressers and if possible, look up the recommended make-up artist's portfolio to see if you like her work.

Check with your wedding planner: As she is constantly in contact with other brides and wedding vendors, your consultant should be able to suggest many names.

Visit bridal shows and wedding expos: Meet stylists at an expo and see how they work, before committing to an appointment. Sometimes, vendors offer discounts at these exhibitions.

Go to the mall: Over the course of a few weekends, get makeovers done from different beauty counters. If you are pleased with the results you got in a department store, check if the stylist is available to do your make-up on your wedding day—having the full selection of the make-up counter to try out different looks will be an added benefit.

Review several make-up artist websites from your chosen area: Check the portfolio images for things like skin tone matching and attention to detail. See if any current bridal make-up trend pictures have been included.

Decide whether you wish to have your bridal make-up done at your home/venue or prefer going to a salon/mall on your wedding day: Seek out freelance artists if you want the convenience of having someone come home to you on your wedding day.

Both choices have their pros and cons.

If you have to go to the make-up artist's studio:

- Make sure you keep a buffer as the wedding season is notorious for huge traffic jams. You don't want to reach late for your own wedding.
- You may not be the only bride there. Therefore, you may not get a personalised service. I have heard people say that in such places they feel like they are in a factory assembly line and all brides come out looking similar.

The good part is that once you reach the studio, you are taken care of and needn't worry about relatives and the surrounding chaos anymore.

If the artist comes home to you—you get a personalised service in the comfort of your home/hotel room.

The downside can be that you are smack in the middle of the whole chaotic atmosphere which can be a little stressful. You can however escape that by getting ready at a friend's/neighbour's place, where you will not have as many interruptions.

Decide if you want both your wedding day make-up and hair arranged at the same location: Most bridal make-up artists also provide hair styling services. They can accommodate draping of the wedding lehenga or sari too.

Make an appointment for a bridal make-up trial with your favourite make-up artist and be specific about how you would

like to look on your big day: Carry magazine clippings that reflect your preferred style and make sure that your make-up artist clearly understands what you want. If you aren't that sure, sit before a mirror so that you can keep checking on your make-up even as it's done.

Know what you want: A good make-up artist can give you a flattering look. But to get the best results, share your preferences closely with your artist during a trial—tell her how you wear your make-up daily, what colours you're attracted to, colours that you never wear or dislike, products/finishes that are uncomfortable. Your artist can't read your mind, so don't hesitate to inform her.

Top Trial Tips:

- If you are unhappy with the first attempt, speak up. It is normal practice to make adjustments to achieve the required look. An experienced artist will not feel offended but will appreciate your input.

- Try to match the colours with your wedding dress. Wearing strong colours that reflect on the face may affect the look of your make-up. On your wedding day, remember to wear a top that can easily be removed without damaging your hair or make-up.

- Ensure your hair and skin is cleansed and free from products. A good facial scrub or exfoliator the night before will remove dead skin cells and leave you with refreshed, soft skin. A final rinse in cool water will add shine to the hair.

- **Get hairstyling too**: Make sure the artist gives you a hairstyling trial too! If you want to wear any hair accessories on your wedding day, carry them to the trial without fail. Most artists charge a fee for giving trials but it's totally worth it.

- **Don't go alone**: Take a friend or family member along for feedback. Click a photograph of yourself after the trial, you can refer to it during your wedding day make-up.

- Avoid scheduling your beauty appointments too close to the wedding day. If you are dissatisfied with the results, you'll have no time then to change your look.

How to Choose?

Every make-up application, bridal especially, should begin with a consultation and not a short one. She should ask you to describe your current make-up routine: Products, colours, how and where you apply them. Extra points, if she asks you to come to the trial in your everyday make-up instead with a clean face. Think about it: Every bride wants to look 'like myself but better'. So how is someone going to make you look like yourself if they don't know what you usually look like?

Your make-up artist should ask you what you want to look like on your wedding day and really listen to your response before making suggestions. She should then quiz you on wedding details like the location (indoor/outdoor) and time of day which affect the lighting in which you'll be seen. The colours, flowers, decor and mood of the wedding will help shape the make-up look (romantic, natural, vintage or modern). Finally, she must consider your wedding dress—see its colour (warm versus cool) and style. The neckline, jewellery and hairstyle will influence the application as well.

The more questions she asks, the more you will like it. Beware of anyone following her 'creative vision', disregarding your opinion. At the end of the day, the only person who needs to like the make-up is you, the bride!

How to Book?

- Understand what the artist requires to secure your date on her book. Sometimes, the deposit will be nominal, but most ask for 25-50 per cent of the total package of services.
- Be sure to get it all in writing, with receipts for each payment. A well-written contract will list the services being provided to each member of your bridal party, with a schedule of appointment times.
- Check for cancellation terms.
- Check if the artist who did your trial run or preview session will be the one doing your make-up on your wedding day. You've built a rapport and discussed your wishes in detail with this person. Some larger studios and salons may not give you that promise, so be sure to ask.

In all your planning and efforts to make this day of your life perfect, looking your best definitely ranks at the top. That is why it is so important to find your perfect make-up artist. Brandishing their brushes with creative flair, they can give you the look you always dreamed of.

Few Things to Keep in Mind

EVEN THE 'NO MAKE-UP LOOK' NEEDS MAKE-UP

Make-up does not have to look 'cakey' nor does it have to look overdone. For bridal make-up, the most important thing is making the skin look soft, dewy and radiant. I love highlighted cheekbones and soft, glossy lips. Creating the perfect canvas, perfect skin calls for a little bit of concealing and colour correction but not a whole tube of make-up.

BEING CAMERA READY

A professional make-up artist will know which products are appropriate for flash photography. Many products these days contain SPF which is great for everyday make-up. But when it comes to flash photography, it will make your face look white and ashy. Also, glitter differs from shimmer. If you apply glitter on your face for your wedding day, it will reflect light and can ruin your wedding photos. Also, the camera tends to diffuse the make-up. Your blush has to be applied heavier than usual to show up on camera. You don't want to look washed-out in your pictures.

LASTING POWER

Whether your make-up artist uses airbrush make-up or traditional make-up, she will know which products to use so that your make-up lasts all day and night—products that can withstand the hot July heat and will not sweat off before the reception is over! It is not an easy task but with the right products, it is definitely possible.

WHAT DOES IT COST?

Find out what the make-up artists in your area are charging.
- Good products are expensive, so if they are not charging enough, they are probably not using them.
- There are different rates for what you need and for the hours you hire.

- It's important to remember that there is no standard rate card for make-up artists. For professional quality bridal make-up, ₹10,000 is a solid starting point.
- Decide how many make-up looks you need, then enquire if you can get a package deal. Most artists work only on a per look rate.
- Also, check for pre-wedding pampering packages.
- For a destination wedding, the cost will change. Also discuss cost for travel, accommodation, assistants and miscellaneous services such as touch-up, drape change and make-up for close family members like mother and sister.
- Make sure you have everything in writing to avoid miscommunication.

Please don't try to squeeze in your mother's make-up and sister's make-up in the amount the artist is asking for. Besides being unethical, it might even compromise the work of the artist as she might have to hurry to get all of you ready. Often, the artist's charges include hairstyling and sari or dupatta draping too.

Experience in Creating 'Bridal' Looks

You may have met several make-up artists who do amazing work but creating a bridal look is altogether a different genre. So enquire about your artist's experience in bridal looks. An experienced bridal make-up artist knows how to handle all types of brides, the nervous ones to those who throw a lot of tantrums. Also, your artist should be good at deciding your look as per the lighting set-up at the venue.

Watch Out for It!

Avoid make-up artists who have a 'know-it-all' attitude. Yes, a make-up artist should be confident in what she is doing but she should be listening to what you want for your wedding day.

Products and Their Brands

Most make-up artists use products from established brands. Yet, it is better to confirm the brand she uses. If you are not fond of a particular product or are allergic to it, you can always ask your make-up artist to use another. Some brides prefer to provide their own products.

A Few Pointers to Make Your Job Easier

START EARLY

You could start six-eight months before your wedding. This trial is mostly about skincare and to determine if you really need to see a dermatologist. You also discuss long-term fixes like should you grow in your eyebrows over time; what skincare and haircare routine must you follow leading up to your wedding.

BOOK EARLY

Considering how far in advance brides consider details like flowers and fonts, it's surprising how long many wait to book a make-up artist. The best artists are booked months in advance.

MAKE YOURSELF CLEAR

Once you've found someone you like, ask plenty of questions. How much does she charge? Will she bring her own make-up and brushes or use yours? Make sure you're entirely clear on the costs and your expectations. Clarify anything she did during the test run that wasn't perfect—'The eyes are heavier than I wanted' or 'That lipstick washes me out'—so she has a chance to correct it. And mention clearly that you need hairstyling as well as draping.

CHARGES AND TAXES

Most make-up artists charge you for every event but some provide packages as well. If you are opting for a package, ask what all it includes—trials, services, taxes, etc. Also, be upfront about your wedding timings. Many make-up artists charge extra for staying back till late.

MAKE SURE TO GET THE TIMING RIGHT

Schedule your appointment about three hours before the event; you won't feel rushed then and the make-up will have a chance to settle. Don't let her use a mix of lipstick shades, it makes touching up more difficult. (Plan to buy the lip colour from the make-up artist, carry it to reapply.)

I strongly recommend hiring a professional make-up artist for your wedding day. You don't want your foundation sliding down your face by the time you get to the *pheras*! Professional make-up will also make you look so much better in your wedding photos. Cameras are quick to pick on any sort of make-up disaster—badly applied foundation, misapplied lipstick! An experienced and creative make-up artist will make you look glamorous as well as natural at the same time. Once finalised, trust your artist and keep a positive attitude towards her work. Don't spoil your mood; it will increase your body temperature, thereby making your make-up look dull. Top your make-up with a sparkling smile instead.

Bridal Bag

Before heading towards the make-up studio, make sure you pack your bridal bag with all the things you need to take to the parlour to get ready. Check for the following:

- Jewellery
- Lehenga (skirt, blouse and dupatta)/sari (skirt, blouse)
- Shoes/sandals
- Hair pins
- Double-sided tape (for those wearing slightly low-cut blouses)
- Safety pins
- Cotton buds (optional—they help in make-up removal)
- Tick tock clips—these help to put your hair out of your face
- Your bridal accessories—*haath phool, pajeb,* nose pin, *maangtika*
- Straws (yes, straws—when there is lipstick on your face and you want water, this will help)
- Mini mineral water bottle or some energy drink
- Reference picture you want to show to your make-up artist
- Snack—chocolate bars, energy bars, nuts, *khakra*—anything you can munch on
- Tissues
- Umbrella—it could rain on the way to the parlour!
- Money (You should always carry some money!)/credit card/ debit card
- Phone and charger (The last thing you want is your battery dying when you have to coordinate stuff)
- Perfume bottle
- Mints

Chapter 17

Bonding at Your Hen Party

Also known as bachelorette party or bridal shower, a hen party is
again a western tradition. There, the bridesmaid (best friend/sibling)
arranges the bridal shower for the bride-to-be. It is a special event to
celebrate the bride's transition from the single life to married bliss.
In India, however, the bride throws the hen party for all her girlfriends
and close cousins. It's a typical girls' night out. The bachelorette party
is modelled after the bachelor party, which itself is a dinner given by
the groom to his friends shortly before his wedding. Planning the
perfect bridal shower is exciting! You can make it as elaborate or as
simple as you choose. You could find ways to make the day special,
without spending every dime you have. It's also a good idea to involve
one or two close friends in the planning.

A bachelorette party is widely seen as an opportunity for female
bonding. Whatever entertainment is planned, it should not embarrass,
humiliate or endanger the bride-to-be or any of the guests. It's held in
the evening, usually about a week (or at least a few days) before the
wedding, and usually includes dinner, although alternative approaches
are not uncommon. Drinking games are common in such parties.

Few Add-ons Can Make the Party a Huge Success

- Have an unusual invitation that is sure to make each guest keel over, send over a singing and dancing telegram. You can arrange for a great looking guy, clad scantily, show up at your guest's house to personally invite them to the bride's shower. There may not be a way for them to say 'no' to the invite.
- Get a hot bartender who can engage in flair bartending. Flair can include juggling, flipping (bottles, shakers), manipulating flaming liquors or even performing close-up magic tricks.
- Arrange for a tiara and sash with a different title for each of the guests.
- Arrange a few games.
- Small favour bags containing tidbits, either complementing the theme of the party or sweet nothings.

If you have a good budget or if all your friends are ready to contribute, you can even plan a 'hen weekend'. Hen weekend is another name for a destination hen party. Going to a place like Goa promises a perfect hen weekend. You can visit sites like http://in.gobananasworld.com/to plan this.

Hen party in a private venue is also a great idea. Depending on the budget and preference of the group, you can plan one of the following:

Spa Party

Also known as a sparty, it is a good option as the bride-to-be and her friends get some well-deserved pampering after all those shopping trips. It also relaxes and prepares them for the wedding. The spa party generally provides express spa treatments including manicures, pedicures, massages and mini-facials. The easiest, but most expensive way to throw a spa party is to find a company that specialises in mobile spa services. A spa party company creates a stylish and comfortable spa atmosphere including candles, spa music with spa robes and slippers for your guests. They send experienced spa professionals who set up various spa stations with proper equipment. Rates are based on the number of guests, the number of treatments and how long the spa party runs. If you want to make it less expensive, you can hire professionals to come and give mini-services without all the extras like robes and slippers. A nail tech gives manicures and pedicures, a massage therapist gives massages and a beautician can give mini-facials and do make-up. Light dinner with salads and cocktails would gel well with the theme.

Cooking Party or Kitchen Tea Party

It can be a good way of having fun in the kitchen and trying hands-on cooking. A professional chef can be called for the party who teaches the bride-to-be and her friends interesting recipes. Cooking parties truly bring people together in a unique way—slicing, dicing and sautéing. Include a blank recipe card in the party invitation and ask guests to fill it in with one of their favourite recipes. The day of the party, the cards can be assembled into a small album or recipe box and gifted to the future bride. Suggest guests bring a gift related to the kitchen party theme. A cooking party would be very light on budget as the food cooked by all can be served. Few games can definitely add some fun to the party.

Bartending Party

It is a more relaxed, non-traditional party in the evening that's set up more like a classy cocktail party. Hire a local flair bartender to come and teach your guests how to make some fun cocktails. You can even try out some signature concoctions to serve at the wedding. This is again a modified version of the cooking party. The venue can be turned into a bar and if the budget permits, hire a DJ.

Dance Party

You can hire a hot dance instructor to teach some sexy moves to all your gals. Be sure to film this, as it would be fun seeing your friends trying out new moves.

Naughty Party

If you want to let the party guests know just what you have in store for them, begin with an outrageous invitation. Send out classic paper invites and write a naughty saying inside or wrap the note around a banana for the perfect mood setter. For decor, use condoms as balloons, lace for tablecloth and to drape on chairs, hang neckties and silk ropes as streamers. Create 'naughty plants' by placing upright bananas and cucumbers in small planters filled with dirt. Some male dancers would be perfect for the theme and can provide great entertainment. Play some naughty drinking games and send your friends back home with naughty favour bags.

Nice and Naughty Party

A perfect blend of naughtiness and sophistication. For the decorations, stick with black and hot pink or even red for the 'naughty' side of the room. Choose a graceful white for the nicer side. Divide the room into two halves by draping black velvet fabric on one side and white faux silk on the other to symbolise being 'nice'. Decorate the 'naughty' table and chairs with black lace, feathers and devil-horn headbands for the guests to wear. The 'nice' table should be all white, covered in glitter and halo headbands. You can brainstorm games to complement your theme. Favours could include both naughty and nice things.

Pyjama Party

You can go with the traditional pyjama party with lots of alcohol, some naughty drinking games and music. If you like things low-key, then an evening spent in the company of close friends would be the best option. Plan a simple slumber party at a private place with lots of fun-filled games and good food. Talk about all those mischievous days till the early hours of the morning. Alcohol and good music has the ability to transform any girls' night into a dance party. The venue can be decorated in a theme and the bride-to-be can give out some party favours to all her guests.

Road Trip

Take your adventurous self out with your girl gang on a short road trip. Choose a place close to your city. It's a big step in your life, so you can even consider taking a couple of days off and go on a short trip to a nearby hill station (Shimla, Nainital, Dharamsala, Lonavla, Lavassa, Darjeeling, Gangtok, Aizawl, Coorg, Kodaikanal, Ooty, Munnar, Waynad or Thekadi—and indulge in some amazing Ayurvedic massages). Or you might prefer to go to a beach resort (Chennai, Goa, Gokarna, Pondicherry, Fort Kochi, Kovalam) and relax before the big day. Another option is to go camping in the woods and bond around the campfire. Or go on a catamaran ride with all your friends. You can also indulge in some water sports at Goa or Gokarna or even Chennai.

KARAOKE CLUB HOPPING

This might be your last night out as a single woman. Spend it a bit responsibly and at the same time get a little silly: Indulge in some mock self-humiliation! Check out the best places in the city for karaoke nights and hit them. You can also jazz it up a bit by wearing some cheesy, coordinated outfits. Do make sure that you book a cab to get back home safe.

Pick out things you like from any of the above and blend it in your theme. Dinners and cocktail parties, which provide guests comfortable opportunities to converse or to give intimate advice to the bride-to-be, are also popular in India.

If on tight budget, and planning the standard pub-crawl, draw up the itinerary. Start out with dinner at a local restaurant/dhaba (you don't want to drink on an empty stomach), and map out all the establishments you want to hit, plus what time you'll be popping in. Planning it out this way will help you book your transportation for the proper length of time and it limits the carousing so that you don't overdo it or spend too much cash. Make all necessary reservations, even at bars. Ask about special drinks and bachelorette freebies. On a very tight budget? Plan your party on a ladies night to avail free drinks.

Even if you and your fiancé plan to have a combined bachelor party, you should not completely do away with your hen party. In this case, have just a small affair at home, a pyjama party or a tea party. Have all the girlie fun by playing some really interesting games.

Giving out unique party favours at the end of your event is like punctuating a great sentence. Your guests had a great time enjoying the food and playing the games, so be sure to send them home with a chic and unique favour!

Ideas for Favours

GET CREATIVE

Consider buying small pots, spray painting them and planting some herbs or flowers in each one. Attach a small tag and you get a party favour that is unique. Each guest can take it home and watch it grow!

Just think about your talents—are you a whiz in the kitchen? Give out sugar cookies shaped like brides! Love music? Put together a mix CD full of songs that have special meaning for the bride-to-be. Know your way around a sewing machine? Why not make a funky scarf for each guest to take home? You can choose inexpensive items such as sachets, tea packets or fun stationery at local craft shops and dress it up with a bit of fancy ribbon.

LOCAL POWER

You can find multiple options online but for a truly unique guest favour, consider what's available locally. Visit some local artisans—the great rate you get for purchasing in bulk may surprise you. Stained glass, pottery, unique jewellery or local gourmet preserves are really one-of-a-kind items that your guests are sure to cherish. They will make great gifts especially if you have a lot of guests coming from out-of-town! Don't hesitate to ask an artisan to make a special item, personalise a batch of something or create a unique label just for you. Chances are, they'll be happy to work with you to create the perfect favour!

GET NAUGHTY

Edible body lotion, bags of liquorice whips, bottles of chocolate syrup, heart-shaped long stemmed lollipops, chocolate-coated condoms, G-strings and jokes or small games from an adult store are just a few favour ideas for naughty gift bags.

Hen Party Checklists
AT LEAST THREE MONTHS OR MORE BEFORE

- Set your budget—always set it little lower than what you would want to spend on it. As you plan, you would come across things you want to add on.
- Decide on what you want in terms of a bachelorette party. Will it be a night of terror on the town, complete with Jell-O shots, a scavenger hunt and dancers? A quiet weekend getaway? Martinis at a mod cocktail lounge? A living room lingerie exchange? Pizza and pool at a local dive? Karaoke? Girls' night out? Girls' night in? If you want to walk on the wild side,

get your friends involved in the planning. Remember, while you want to cut loose, you don't want to mortally embarrass yourself and your friends.

- Set the date—shoot for a weekend night, about one to two weeks before the wedding day. (If members of the party are travelling from all over and can only convene a few days before, that timing works too.)
- Create the guest list.
- If the party will be at a hot spot (the only happening club in town, a popular disc, a concert, someone's farmhouse) or out-of-town, make reservations, order tickets and deal with lodging and bachelorette party transportation details.
- Send out a casual 'save-the-date' email immediately. If you're partying far away, include specific details.
- Research and book any talent that might make an appearance at the party.
- Brainstorm and decide on a theme in case you want one.
- Place orders for invites or start making them in case you want to send special invitation cards.

At Least a Month Before

- Brainstorm possible game plans and party stunts with your friends and research online.
- No matter what the format, alcohol and bachelorette revelry usually go hand in hand. Be responsible. Arrange for transportation—getting drunken ladies home would be quite a task, you'll need some responsible people in charge.
- Send out invitations. Emailing and calling is okay, too. If you have a theme, politely state it in the invite.
- Make a list of the games you want to play, with rules and how-tos, lest you forget after too many margaritas. Keep it handy.
- Make a shopping list. Divide the to-dos among friends and family—games, decorations, booze buying, stereo and/or karaoke set-up, CD duty, etc.
- Buy or make bachelorette party accessories such as the novelty

veil or tiara, bite-me candy necklaces, sash and other naughty props needed for the games.

- Arrange for party favours as per the theme.

One Week Before

- Confirm your guests.
- Confirm transportation arrangements.
- Confirm the at-home entertainment.
- Confirm your bookings.
- Check if all the above checklists are complete.

One Day Before

- Reconfirm all reservations.
- Get plenty of sleep.

Hen Party Games

Who is the teetotaller in the group? Hand out a sheet printed with letters a-z and ask all guests to write down dirty names of cocktails, starting with each alphabet. Give them five minutes and the one who gets the maximum, is the winner. Let the bride/each guest read out the names. To make the game even more interesting, one can let the guests create probable names or even give them a compulsory word to use.

Guess the goodies: Fill socks/a thin cloth bag with different items such as condoms, sunscreen, sunglasses, keys, tiny drink umbrellas, tubes of lipstick, lingerie and other smaller articles. If you are following some theme, you can use related items. Use a black permanent marker to write a number on each of the socks. Give each player sheets of paper as per the socks and pass the socks around, allowing each player to feel the items in the socks, using only her feet. They must write down what they think is in each sock. The player who guesses the most items correctly wins the game. You can make the game simpler by using a single paper bag instead and let the participants feel it with their hand.

Pop-a-gum: This game is a test for the bride-to-be, to learn how much she actually knows the groom. One of the bride's friends can volunteer to prepare for this game. She needs to list out questions about the groom and get his answers. Then make small cards with each question and hand it over to the guests. Now each guest questions the bride and for each wrong answer, the bride-to-be pops a gum (make sure the size of the gum is huge, if not then make her pop two-four gums at a time) It's fun when the bride-to-be's mouth gets full and her answers are incomprehensible.

Getting the bride-to-be drunk! It's her last day as a bachelorette, so what can be more fun than getting her drunk. It's a variation of the Pop-a-gum game listed above. Here, instead of gum, use shot glasses. Every time the bride answers the question right, everyone except the bride gulp down a shot. For every wrong answer, the bride must have a shot. Get the groom to tell you things about him the bride would not know, only then would you have a drunken bride-to-be.

Who bought it? Again, this is for the bride-to-be, so must be arranged by one of her friends. Each guests need to buy the bride a pair of underwear and give it to the friend at the party. (The friend hosting the game should inform all the guests about this and tell them the bride-to-be's size). Now, this friend should remove all the tags from the underwear and hang it nicely on a string. The string is then displayed in front of the bride-to-be. The bride-to-be has to guess who picked up which pair and elaborate on why she thinks so. It's fun listening to the bride-to-be's explanations.

Handbag game: It's a great game for your party because every girl carries a handbag. All you need is three lists of items that can be in a ladies handbag. The first list has commonly found items like comb, pen, mirror, lip gloss and sunglasses. The second list has items that sometimes find place in a woman handbag like hand sanitiser, hand cream, foot cream, used tissue, etc. And the third, list features very rare or obscure items like a little black book, condoms, pepper spray, and rape whistle. Ask all the guests to sit in a circle and place their purse/handbags on their lap. Start calling out names from the list. Items found from the first list get five points each, second gets ten each and the items on the third list gets fifteen. At the end of the game, ask everyone to pull out the most obscure item from their bags. The one with the most obscure item gets a bonus twenty. The winner is the one with maximum points. A real fun game to see who has what!

The drinking game (my favourite): Want to get all your girls drunk? Assemble them in a circle and have shot glasses lined up in front of them, filled with their favourite alcohol. Place at least five glasses for each girl. Now, each girl starts a sentence with 'I Never', for example, 'I never kissed my friend's boyfriend.' Anyone who has done the deed must drink while the rest of the crowd whoops and demands to know the gory details. You can have single or multiple rounds, depending on the amount of alcohol you want to consume.

Play **a variation of the drinking game** at the party. Each guest is handed a blank numbered card and a pen. The bride-to-be leaves the room while each guest writes down a juicy tidbit about her on a strip of paper. The host of the game collects the card and writes down the guest's name with the number in her sheet. She then jumbles them up in a bowl and calls the bride back into the room. Then the bride-to-be reads out each piece of gossip and guesses who said what. If the bride-to-be can correctly identify the trash-talker, the guilty culprit and all the guests must have a shot. If the bride is wrong, she has to drink.

Tissue roll and the stick: This is a partner game, so split up all the girls in teams of two. Give each team tissue rolls and a broom/mop stick. One person holds a roll of toilet paper between her knees. The other person holds a broomstick or a mop stick between her knees while her eyes are covered or blindfolded. The person with the toilet paper grasps her partner's hands (they are only allowed to touch hands) and guides them in getting the stick into the hole of the toilet paper. The partners who do it the fastest win. This can be done one pair at a time, or two pairs can go head-to-head to see who inserts first. Make sure your handycam is ready, as you would not want to miss the opportunity to film such a hilarious event. To complicate the game, both the partners can be blindfolded.

Bridal bingo (traditional game): Print several blank bingo cards (5x5 blank square boxes) and give one to each guest. In the blank squares, the guests must write down gifts they think the bride-to-be will receive such as a lip gloss, gift certificate, towels, crystal, lingerie, purse, chocolates and massage oils. Give the guests a bowl of bingo markers. When the bride-to-be starts opening her gifts, guests mark off the items on their bingo cards. The first three players to bingo vertically, horizontally or diagonally win a prize.

First night game: This is a game your guests won't really understand until later on, when you explain it to them but that's the fun! Have a friend host this game. Keep construction papers and markers ready, instruct guests to place the paper on the floor and trace their hand with the marker—they can't bend their knees. The host should write down everything the guests say as they try to bend over and draw their hand. Later, the host explains that the point of the game was to find out what the bride-to-be will say on her first night. You'll get classic sound bites like, 'Gosh, this is harder than it looks!' and 'Oh! This hurts!' You probably won't be able to get through the list of quotes without dissolving into laughter.

This is another **variation of the first night game**. While the bride-to-be opens her gifts, a friend secretly takes note of the bride's exclamations. For example, 'Oooohh it's so beautiful!' or 'You'll have to show me how this works, okay?' Or 'I am totally loving it.' When all the gifts have been opened, the mischievous friend comes forward and reads out the bride's comments to the group as the (sexy) things she'll be shouting out on her first night.

Needle and the thread: Yet another one of those **first night games**! Ask the bride to leave the room. Explain to all the guests that the comments the bride shall make during the game represent her feelings on the first night. Call the bride back into the room. Tell her the game is to thread the needle. You can hold the needle and give the thread to the bride. When the bride tries to thread the needle, move it around a bit so that she is unable do so. Soon the bride will start exclaiming, 'Stay still, I can't get it in' or 'Darn, missed again,' and the guests will be rolling on the floor laughing. Make sure you let the bride in on the joke after five-seven minutes.

Dress designers: This is a good game to play if you have a theme party. Divide the guests into teams of three or four. Give each team some coloured sheets, stapler, scissors and some accessory, according to the theme. Allow them fifteen minutes to design a wedding dress on one teammate, in line with the theme of the party. After fifteen minutes, the teams show their wedding dresses to the bride-to-be, who determines the winner of the contest. If you have several teams, award a small prize to the best, funniest and scariest paper wedding dresses.

What if! This outrageous game is a great way to start the party. Each player is handed a list of 'What if' questions. The order of question will not be the same for any of the players. Players fill out answers to different 'what if' questions in a separate sheet. After writing down the answers, they pass the sheet to the player on their right, keeping with them their original question sheet. Now each player reads out questions from her own sheet but answers from the sheet she received from another player. The twist is that when a question is read, its answer will be a randomly chosen one. You just never know what answer might pair up with the question 'What would the bride do if she caught the groom checking her text messages?' Maybe, the answer was originally for the question 'What would the bride do, if she found the groom had his best man write his wedding vows for him?' You can add the groom-to-be and bride-to-be names into the game!

Guess who am I? Prior to the party, get about twenty to thirty (depending on number of expected guests) index cards and write the name of a celebrity on each. As guests arrive, stick a card on their back, and don't tell them who it is. It's their job during the party to ask other guests 'yes or no' questions about their celebrity, trying to figure out who they are. The first person to do so wins a prize. You can also offer prizes to those finishing second and third. Again, if it's a theme party, the celebrity names could be chosen accordingly.

Great for entertaining guests: On a long sheet of paper, write a sentence referring to the bride as if you were beginning a poem (example: 'Pragati and Sunil met at a coffee shop'). Attach the paper to a clipboard and pass it over to the guests, turn by turn, instructing each to compose a line right below the first, to continue the verse ('She was pretty and he fell for her'). The guest should then fold the paper so that only the newest line shows, and pass on the clipboard to the next player, and so on. The lines of the poem needn't rhyme. Also, try to theme the game around the bride and her upcoming marriage. When the paper has circulated to every guest, the host should retrieve it, to unfold and read the zany, haphazard poem dedicated to the bride-to-be.

Date in a Balloon! If you're having a combined party and want to fix all your friends up with a date, then this is a simple and fun party game. Start by listing all the guys present at the event. Now write down these names on slips of paper. Each slip of paper gets one name. If there aren't enough number of guys, use the names of celebrities. Now drop a slip of paper into each party balloon and blow them up! Blow up enough balloons and then pass them around. One balloon for each girl. Ask each guest to pop her balloon: The name on the slip of paper is the girl's date for the evening.

Aladdin's lamp: Grant three wishes—pass the 'Aladdin's lamp' around and ask the bride to make three wishes in secret. The rest then try to figure out the three wishes by writing down questions they will put to the bride. Each person gets only one chance. If that person guesses the wishes correctly, she wins a prize; if no one gets all three right, the one who comes closest wins a prize.

Scavenger hunt with a twist: Play this if you are at a disc partying with your girls. Make a list of things do-able at a disc like dancing on table top, bartending for a drink, get a photo of a guy with a tattoo saying 'mom', get a guy to remove his shirt, likewise. Make teams of two to three girls each and the one who finishes all listed acts first is the winner. For proof, ask them to click photos.

Worst kiss ever: The bride-to-be should start by telling the story of the first time she and her fiancé kissed. The guests would 'ooh' and 'ahh' about how romantic it sounds. Enough with the good stuff, now have each guest tell her own story of her absolute worst kiss. Tell about the time you got a really sloppy one and were left with drool on your lip or the time a guy with really bad breath leaned over for a smooch. Together, you can decide which kiss was the worst and the bride-to-be will be left thinking her first kiss was 'so romantic'.

String squirt game: This game simulates guys peeing in the snow. The object of the game is to get as much strings as possible onto the target, a paper plate. The catch is—you have to do it by holding the can of snow string between your knees as if it were your extra girth.

You are only allowed to touch the top of the can with one finger to push the spray button. Each person has ten seconds to spray the plate with as much string as possible. You can even try to write your name after some practice! The game works best if you place the paper plate about eight feet away from each participant. Each player takes a turn or set them all loose at the same time. If you play one at a time, lift up the person's plate and have them hold onto it, until the 'judging'. The bride-to-be can judge who has the most strings on their plate.

Talented girl! Give each party guest one candy necklace to place over the wrist of her weak hand (if she is right-handed, put it on her left wrist). When someone yells, 'Go', everyone tries to eat their necklace the fastest. They can't remove the necklace from their wrist or use the other hand, else they get disqualified. Have someone click pictures: It will be messy and priceless! See which friend has the most talented tongue. Reward the talented girl with drinks and gifts.

These games promise to make your party a huge success. Adapt them as per your expected guest list and theme for a good fit.

Chapter 18

Make Your Mehendi Memorable

The mehendi ceremony held before a marriage is a statement of the beauty and elegance underlining Indian traditions. The mehendi or henna motif not only adorns the bride but epitomises her transformation from a virgin girl to a temptress for her husband.

From simple home-made designs to intricate professional art, each has its own charm. The motive, however, is common—to enhance the bride's beauty and make her glow. In some parts of India, even the groom applies mehendi on his hands.

Different regions of the country celebrate the rituals differently. The celebrations also depend on the wealth and status of the wedding couple. Usually, it's the females in both the families that take part in this fun-filled pre-wedding ritual. The bride's family generally celebrates mehendi by gathering the bride's friends and relatives to come bless the bride and have some fun.

Preparing the Mehendi
Mehendi that is applied during Indian weddings is not just a plain paste of mehendi powder and water. Eucalyptus oil, a bit of clove oil and a few drops of lemon are added. These oils not only help in

darkening the colour of mehendi on the body but also enhance the benefits of mehendi and make the paste highly medicinal.

The colour and smell of the mehendi lingers on for days, boosting the romance in the initial days of the wedding. It is a common belief that darker the colour the mehendi leaves on the hands on a bride, the more will she be loved by her husband and mother-in-law.

Heating about eight-ten cloves in a pan and gently turning the hands with henna over it, thus absorbing the warmth, deepens the colour. Also, the bride can apply some balm over the mehendi once the dried henna is taken off and sleep wearing a pair of gloves, this would also induce heat and darken the colour of the mehendi.

Applying the Mehendi

A family member or mehendi expert applies mehendi on the palms and feet of the bride. Elaborate designs are made using a cone filled with mehendi. Popular motifs for the bridal mehendi are: Conch shell, flowers, *kalash*—urn, peacock, *doli*—palanquin, bride, groom and *baraat*—wedding procession patterns. While the mehendi is being applied, other members of the family play the traditional dhol and dance to its beats. Generally, all female members of the family get mehendi put on their hands and feet. The mood is extremely festive.

Celebrations

The mehendi ceremony is usually held at the bride's place a couple of days prior to the wedding. It is a night ceremony, where guests sing, dance and laugh to the accompaniment of dhol or live music. The mehendi ceremony for the groom takes place separately at his home. Once the mehendi for the bride is done, in some cultures the female relatives of the bride, especially her sisters, visit the groom's ceremony. It is fun to see the would-be sister-in-laws play pranks on their future brother-in-law and try to wangle some money from him—it's a tradition!

The bride and groom do not usually deck up elaborately for mehendi application. However, the scale of the ceremony depends upon individual choice. It is also common for the bride to wear flower jewellery for such an event.

Mehendi ceremonies are highlighted by song and dance performances by the bride's female friends. Over time, the mehendi ceremony has grown in stature. Today, families bring in DJs to play songs and celebrations go on till late in the night.

Another thing that has changed are the designs and patterns. While only intricate Indian designs were applied in the past, brides, today, are experimenting with Arabic and Indo-Arabic designs, even mixing shimmer pastes with the traditional mehendi paste. Semi-precious stones are also embedded in the design. It is traditional to write the name of the groom on the bride's palm.

Mehendi Styles

- The **Arabic style** of mehendi art consists of spacious floral designs, very similar to the paintings and textiles in the Middle East.
- The patterns used in the **Indian style** of mehendi art are more suggestive and symbolic, for example, the outline of the national bird peacock, images of a bride and a groom. It is more detailed and narrates a story.
- The **African style** of mehendi art involves a lot of geometrical patterns. This style is not very popular among Indian brides but can nevertheless be flaunted as a very modern style by brides who like to set trends.
- **Pakistani style** of mehendi art is very intricate and pretty but extremely time-consuming.

Nowadays, brides even have the option of adding colours like metallic silver and gold. A bride usually selects a mehendi style for its design or because the patterns complement her bridal outfit.

The mehendi ceremony is a reflection of the rich Indian culture, sentiments and beliefs. Filled with fun and joy, the ceremony is the perfect precursor to the auspicious wedding day.

Choosing Your Mehendi Artist

If you already know who and what you want then perfect. Else just follow these steps to help you along.

- **Look for artists in your area**. If you know a mehendi artist in another area, she can perhaps recommend one in your area. You can also find some mehendi artists online—see photos of their work and note down contact details from their website. If the artist has a Facebook or Flickr page, read the comments. It is very easy for someone to create a portfolio of stolen images; this practice is rampant in the mehendi community, so take care. Look for watermarks and check with the artist if all the images on her site are her individual work.
- **Schedule a consultation** with the artist(s) you are considering for your mehendi. Discuss your needs, see your comfort factor and learn if she can accommodate your ceremony in her schedule.

As You Do Your Research, Here is What You Should be Looking for

Quality of work and style: Your mehendi day is an important part of your celebration. Your designs will attract the attention of not just your friends and family but also your photographer! You'll only have your mehendi done like this once in your life, so it should be something special. Look at the details. Look at the balance in the overall design. Take a note of the different styles in the artist's portfolio to gauge the breadth of her experience. You want an artist who can do the style you want or can mix styles. Ask her what style is her favourite or if she specialises in any particular style.

The quality of the stain is also important. Request a sample design to see the results for yourself. A good mehendi artist will mix her own paste fresh for each bride and produce a dark stain. Everyone's body chemistry is different, so you may get a darker or lighter stain than another. But when you meet multiple artists, you can compare the stains.

- The artist should use high quality, natural ingredients, avoiding premade cones or black henna. We've all heard horror stories about brides breaking out in hives or blisters from unknown ingredients in the henna or worse, scarring from black henna.
- You have the right to know what is in the henna paste that will

be used on your skin; if your mehendi artist is using safe and natural ingredients she has nothing to fear from your questions.

- Let her know if you are allergic to anything, especially any essential oils.
- Beware of artists who don't make their own henna paste; store-bought paste sometimes contains mystery ingredients or is too stale to leave a good stain. Don't risk this for your wedding.
- It should smell nice. Black henna and some other premixed cones have an unpleasant chemical odour.

What are their booking policies? Do they book more than one bride on the same day? Your artist should be rested and fresh for your mehendi and not in a rush to go to the next bride.

Do you get along with your artist? Don't forget that you'll be spending quite a few important hours leading up to your wedding with this person, while they do your mehendi. You should feel comfortable.

Are they professional? Once you've discussed what you need for your mehendi, as well as any extras (such as a henna party for your guests), you'll probably have to give a deposit to secure your date(s). Once this is done, your artist should provide an agreement or contract that outlines the details and gives the final cost.

Do Not Forget!

- If you have any special requests (hennaing your mother-in-law, dress code, early arrival, etc.) be sure to state it to avoid last-minute surprises. Ask the artist if she has any requirements like seating or lighting (especially important if the mehendi is happening at the sangeet/mehendi party). Check with the artist if you need to do anything to prepare your skin for the mehendi.
- Ask your mehendi artist for suggestions on post application care to ensure the darkest possible stain. She may give you printed information or verbal instructions. She is an expert and knows her henna paste very well, she can tell how it stains, so listen up!

- Keep in mind that the stain takes two days to darken, so plan your appointment accordingly. You might decide to do your mehendi the day before the party, in the comfort of your home. You can then enjoy the party instead of sitting around for hours with wet paste on your hands.

Find the right artist and your mehendi will be gorgeous and the experience will be relaxing and fun. Choose the wrong one, and you'll add an unnecessary headache to a full schedule of pre-wedding activities.

Mehendi Favours for Your Guests

The most common mehendi giveaways are bangles and bindis. You can however make it different by keeping a live bangle maker instead of ready bangle sets. The bangle vendor can make live lac bangles to match your guests' outfits. This one is a big hit especially when you have many outstation guests.

Similarly, instead of gifting similar bindis to every guest, set up a stall with a bindi vendor displaying different types of bindis—from the very simple to ornate colourful bindis.

Pre-packed gifts could include small Indian pouches or jewellery boxes with lac earrings or fancy Indian rings, anklets and bracelets. Cones filled with sweets or *churan*: You may choose to add all the above mentioned things or maybe a few, depending on your budget.

Another good option is mehendi-inspired cookies. These are just simple sugar cookies with icing and frosting designed in mehendi-like patterns.

Another good giveaway would be colourful *bandhni* or *leheriya* dupattas—traditional stoles. These can be easily paired with a plain white or black kurta. One more thing that guests will love—a little floral jewellery like a floral bracelet, *haath phool* or a ring. The bride usually wears floral jewellery for the mehendi function, so doing something similar for the guests will surely leave them speechless.

Chapter 19

Sing and Dance at the Sangeet

An Indian wedding is incomplete without some *naach gaana* and *band baaja*!

For generations, wedding dancing has brought families closer. Be it group performances or competition between families, Indians have always taken their dance very seriously.

What Makes It So Popular?

Dulha-dulhan—couple, their parents, *chacha-chachi, mama-mami*— uncles and aunts and several other couples in the family wait with a flurry of excitement for that one night when they can all let their hair down. For the eligible singles, sangeet is the chance to win a heart or two! Hum the right tune and swing a brisk *thumka*, and who knows, cupid may strike. The festivities may include some good-natured ribbing of the couple's soon-to-be in-laws. It's the perfect occasion for wedding guests to meet and get to know each other.

There was a time when sangeet was a 'ladies only' affair, with females on the bride's side gathering to herald her happiness and bless her. There would be music and dance and a little party that went on for three to four hours. Earlier, only the North Indian families celebrated the sangeet ceremony, but today, sangeet is an essential aspect of desi weddings anywhere.

For almost a decade, sangeet has assumed an altogether new avatar in context of Indian wedding ceremonies. Almost all weddings are now preceded by a sangeet, where people on the bride as well as the groom's side perform on traditional, folk or peppy Bollywood numbers.

In most families, the sangeet party is a grand affair and celebrated on an elaborate scale. But some combine it with the mehendi function to save time and money.

While sangeet nights are packed with fun galore, making preparations for an electrifying evening is a serious affair. Choosing a venue, selecting apt song-dance numbers, roping in a choreographer and gastronomic arrangements...the list is exhaustive. But it's all worth it, for sangeet is the only pre-wedding event of merriment that brings the families and friends of bride and groom together.

The Concept

Today, the concept of performing at a wedding has been elevated to a different level altogether. From impromptu performances to self-choreographed dance numbers, people, today, have graduated to hiring professional wedding choreographers and taking classes. The good thing about it however, is that besides a trained performance at the functions, these wedding choreography classes offer many a chance to learn a new form of art.

Professionals are hired to learn a particular style of dance, it could be salsa, hip hop, Bollywood or even belly dancing. Classes begin early so that participants have enough time to perfect their moves.

Hiring choreographers has become a trend these days—copying moves from television or dance videos is not enough.

Cost

There are no fixed rates for wedding choreography. It totally depends upon the number of songs, students, classes and also the client's budget and chosen dance style. Experienced choreographers are much in demand and charge more.

Number of Classes

This depends on how much time you have before the wedding functions. If you contact the choreographer a month or two before the performance day, once or twice a week is enough. Approaching them at the last moment gets tricky, especially if you are a non-dancer. Starting ten to fifteen days before means you would need regular classes.

Venue for the Classes

Normally, people are more comfortable taking classes at their own place. But choreographers also hold classes at their studio. They charge accordingly.

Age Group

The participating age group is mostly between fifteen and fifty-five years. But often four-to-twelve-year olds are also seen dancing enthusiastically to the latest numbers. Even elders are frequently roped in to give the ceremony a very personal touch. They mostly prefer dancing to the tune of couple songs like *Ae meri zohra jabi*.

The Theme

Most of the times, participants know what kind of choreography they want. At times, if they are familiar with the choreographer's work, they may let her decide the format. Some people ask the choreographer to suggest a sequence according to a theme—the 1970s or 1980s—the choreographer then uses music of that time. People often theme it around the person who is getting married—choreography is then done with siblings, childhood friends, cousins, college friends, work mates and the finale being a couple dance.

Imaginative Themes

Get creative with your event. Choose cuisine that goes with your theme. I had organised a Bollywood themed sangeet where we had a red carpet entry for every guest. The food was Mumbai street food like pani puri counters, *pav bhaji* stalls and of course, the ever-popular chai stall. Your event should leave a mark. It is a personal signature that reflects the personality and taste of the couple.

A lot goes into making this evening as special as it can be—hours of dance practice ensures coordination of steps but most of all, it is the selection of great songs that captivates your guests. Even though trends in song selections and performances have changed vastly over the years, the basic idea is still to have a great time organising the dance show. With all your friends and family bopping to fantastic desi beats, the sangeet night is bound to be an electrifying evening!

Planning the Sangeet Night

DETERMINE YOUR BUDGET

It can be a pretty expensive affair. Like any other event, you need to decide how much you can spend without breaking the bank. At the same time, you don't want to skimp on the quality of food, venue or equipment involved. So first estimate these costs and set aside a percentage of the wedding budget well in advance. Your budget should include snacks and drinks (alcohol is a good idea at these events), music systems and speakers, charges for booking a venue, band and caterers, as well as extras like lighting and decor.

CHOOSE THE VENUE WELL

Depending on the number of people you have invited as well as vendors, performers and necessary equipment, locate a venue that includes a dance floor, stage or an open area. Book it as early as you can, as the 'wedding season' approaches, the best venues may slip out of reach. Visit the location in person and ask the venue provider for details about services and extras. These include parking space, accessibility of toilets, electrical outlets for equipment, kitchens (for the caterers to set up), tables and chairs. While choosing the venue, also keep in mind the convenience of friends and families of the bride and the groom. No one's willing to drive three hours just to reach the venue. Guests would rather save their energy for crooning and *thumka*s.

KEEP IT A DAY OR TWO BEFORE THE WEDDING

As both sides need to participate, the sangeet *sandhya*—evening is ideally held a day or two before the nuptial.

DECIDE THE CHOREOGRAPHER

The ones who dance well on either side often end up planning the performances, selecting the participants and the songs. But professional choreographers are increasingly being hired to lend an expert touch to the overall ceremony.

DECIDE THE PERFORMERS

Start planning for it at least a month or two in advance and make a list of all those who would be performing.

THE BRIDE'S SIDE

The sangeet ceremony is generally hosted by the groom's family. Thus, the main person in charge of the performances must coordinate with his counterpart in the bride's family.

CHOOSE THE SONGS WELL!

Since you're celebrating an upcoming union, pick songs that fit the mood. Romantic ballads as well as dance-worthy numbers are traditional choices that will never go out of style. Popular Bollywood music is however the perfect choice for most people, for it blends the two genres with ease. Do not choose songs that would not go down well with a section of the gathering. The selection could perhaps represent your love story in an entertaining and romantic fashion.

DIVIDE THE TIME JUDICIOUSLY

When both sides have performances to present, divide the time such that both get a fair chance. No one should feel left out or at a disadvantage.

MUSIC SYSTEM

The music system should be in good shape and the DJ must be booked at least three-six months in advance or else you may have to make do with your home theatre system.

SWEET AND SHORT

However grand and entertaining an affair is, it must come to an end. The festivities and merriment of the sangeet can turn into boredom and fatigue if it drags for too long. Break the monotony by alternating dance performances with short sketches (skits) that tease the couple by recounting hilarious incidents from their courtship. Set a time limit for each performance such that the entire event winds up in a couple of hours. Allow a break between performances for guests to indulge in snacks or drinks. Make sure food and beverages counters are nearby. As people start to tire, the tone of the celebration changes, so you need to wrap it up before guests begin to leave.

Some Ideas to Make the Sangeet More Exciting
THE SKIT
Letting an array of songs tell the story of how you two met or how as a couple you both are meant to be, makes for an adorable stage performance. Sometimes, the two families join forces and perform together in a bid to get better acquainted. Often, couples have a two-sided performance, where the competition adds to the excitement. Songs can range from the latest Bollywood numbers to classics or even international hits, wherein the lyrics represent steps of your life. At times, even witty snippets of commentary or impersonation are tucked between the songs to add to the entertainment and laughter!

A SLIDE SHOW
Both pictures and music have the power to say what words can't, so imagine how powerful a performance it will be when both aspects come together. Share some of your most special moments with your guests by putting together a slide show of your favourite photos. While the slide show goes on in the background, a song-and-dance sequence enacting the pictures can be staged.

CHOOSE A THEME
Go with a theme, use lots of props and create fun photo ops. Keep the whole event very colourful and lively. For example, you can choose a theme like a 'puppet show'. Instead of a typical MC, the puppets can narrate the story of the couple's journey together. This little element can change the feel of the entire show.

A DESI THEMED SONG AND DANCE
If the bride and groom are from culturally different backdrops—the song selection could be a fusion of beats from both cultures. On a

folk-like Punjabi song *Baari-Barsi* or *Gur Nalo Ishq Mitha,* you could stage a Gujarati garba dance. This blending would represent the union of two families and can be a fun and creative way to celebrate!

An Act or Professional Performance

Perhaps you want to go all out for your sangeet! If your budget allows, consider hiring professional dancers or entertainers. They add an extra edge to the event and the 'oomph' factor. If you are hosting it outdoors, you can have fire-eaters or fire dancers performing in the background, enthralling everyone.

Antakshari

Show-off your songs' gyaan! This is one game, which is evergreen. Begin singing a new song, starting from the last letter of the previous song.

Rapid-fire

Asking several questions within a minute, from a relative or a friend can be real fun.

Family Awards

The laziest award of the house goes to 'Pinki'! You can think of many such witty and funny awards and invite cheers.

Fashion Show

Set the ramp on fire! Who does not want to look like those size zero models? Fulfil your wishes in the wedding fun and have your very own ramp walk show.

Sach ka Saamna—Confronting the Truth

It's time to prove yourself in the court of love! The bride and groom are quizzed about each other from a prepared set of questions. The one who answers better and knows more is the obvious winner!

Karaoke

Trust me nothing can be more fun than having a karaoke system. Everyone gets a chance to perform and has a really good time together.

Games

Special games can be played with different props. Play 'pass-the-pillow' game to the accompaniment of music and every time one gets out, she can dance on the song chosen by the bride/groom. 'Musical chairs' is another game that's always a hit and brings out the child in everybody.

Indian weddings are not only about serious rituals and customs—there are several fun and frothy moments.

Activities for Pre-wedding Functions: Make It Much More Interesting

To make your wedding party memorable, you must keep your wedding guests entertained.

Days or weeks before the wedding, your guests start arriving to participate in the many ceremonies. Engagement, *nallangu*, mehendi, haldi, *baraat*, sangeet, etc.—the events are so many and you want everything to take place perfectly.

PLAN A SURPRISE

Surprising your guests with a little extra entertainment is sure to be a crowd pleaser. If your friends and family enjoy a good laugh then a comedian is a great choice for entertainment. A magician could perform a few acts on stage or have him wander through the reception, performing at individual tables.

BRIDAL PERFORMANCE

Prepare and perform together as a wedding couple. Be it a song, dance, mimicry, playing a musical instrument or any other interesting act; you will definitely create a sentimental moment which will touch the hearts of all your guests.

DANCE BEATS/DJ

Dance is one of the best ways to have an enjoyable time when together. Dance acts may also be rehearsed a few days prior to the wedding party. The wedding couple and other family members can then put up their best performances on the stage or hire some dance professionals to put up their acts. And at the end of the event, leave the stage open for everyone.

DON'T FORGET THE KIDS

A simple and cost-effective arrangement is to provide colouring books and crayons for them. And if the budget permits, a designated kids area with some games and activity.

Have a Caricaturist/Cartoonist

Bring in a cartoonist/caricaturist, he can draw pictures of the guests so they have something fun and memorable to take back home. This can however get a little messy if the gathering is large. So plan to have more than one activity or two-to-three artists.

Fashion Shows

A family fashion show where not only youngsters but also the elders can take to the stage can be very entertaining for all.

Hire a Fortune-Teller

This is sure to be a crowd-puller. Most people enjoy 'learning of their future', even if they don't believe in it. Your fortune-teller could employ a crystal ball, tarot cards, a parrot or all three.

Guest box

A video booth where guests can record a message on video for the newly-wed couple. Give them ideas on what to record. It could be anything: 'How you met the couple', 'some marriage advice' or some heartfelt wishes.

Mini Contests/Lucky Draws

People love the idea of getting a chance to win something. Purchase several gifts and run a mini contest, opening up the contest to your audience. Get the participants to act out on stage and ask your audience to judge the winners or have several lucky draws in which you pick out names of your guests from a container.

Emotional and Popular Indian Dramas

Most of the popular Indian dramas can be enacted with help from family members and friends. For example, you can connect the concepts of the Ramayana with our daily lives and present it on stage. Another option is to present a play surrounding the bride/groom and their families.

Turn Your Guests into Photographers

Challenge your guests to capture a list of photos and just provide a hashtag for them to use. This ensures you get copies of all the moments you missed out on while spinning around the dance floor.

Not only is this fun for kids and adults alike but it is a wonderful way to get extra photos of your wedding. Ask your guests to use their digital cameras or smartphones to capture moments, which even the best photographer may miss. Let them share the pictures on your wedding website. Give away prizes for the best pictures.

TRADITIONAL DANCE
Hire a professional dance group to perform famous traditional dances. There are plenty of choices—Bharatanatyam, Odissi, Kathakali, *Mayilattam*, etc.

PHOTO BOOTH
Renting photo booths where guests can have pictures taken is becoming quite the rage. Guests can take home memories and/or leave the photos for the bride and groom to create a photo book, with all their friends and family. Spice up your photos with the creative use of props.

PLAN AN END-OF-THE-NIGHT TREAT FOR YOUR GUESTS
Nothing stops a party in its tracks faster than guests heading towards the gate early. Take out an insurance policy against a skimpy crowd by planning a treat for the end-of-the-night: Prepare and perform a dance together or plan a reception getaway that'll get guests excited like a fireworks show or lighting up sky lanterns.

Apart from these you can add the following:

- Nail art
- Live bangle maker
- Tender coconut stall
- Panwala
- Ice *golawala*
- Foot masseurs
- Hair beading
- Face painter
- Tattoo artist

Be it haldi, mehendi or sangeet, all the pre-wedding ceremonies are full of light and amusing moments.

Chapter 20

For a Stunning Bride Entry

Gone are the days when the demure Indian bride sat at the mandap and waited for the groom to arrive on a bedecked horse or when the groom waits as the bride walks towards him all shy and coy, surrounded by her family and friends. Things have changed, with more and more brides opting to make stunning entries at their weddings.

So, dear brides-to-be, how about you ditch the monotony of a traditional entry and make your way towards your groom in a different and stylish way?

Brides, and very often both the bride and the groom, want to make spectacular entries, one that is unexpected and will not be easily forgotten. Many brides prefer traditional entrances like in a *doli* (palanquin) or on an elephant but there are couples that explore options like entering through a snowfall or even a spaceship replica!

Just Like a Princess

Conventionally, the brothers escort a bride to the ceremony. They hold a *chunari* or dupatta above her head, treating her like a princess who must be protected from the dust, rain and anything else that might harm her on her special day. Instead of the dupatta, it's trendier now to hold a specially designed sheet of rose petals, carnations or other flowers over the bride's head as she makes her grand entrance.

Dance Your Way

It is said that a wedding is as jubilant as its guests. The guests or some close relatives could participate in a group dance that marks the entrance of the bride. Even the bride can join them and dance her way to the mandap.

Theme Entry

Yet another striking idea would be to use a crane to descend at the venue. A gorgeous vessel, designed in line with the theme of the wedding can be attached to the crane. The bride will then look truly angelic—descending from the heavens to be with her Prince Charming.

Be the Spotlight

One bedazzling idea that will involve all guests present at the ceremony is to light paper lanterns, in honour of the bride as she enters the venue. Not only will the lanterns look ethereal but also guests can make wishes for the celebrated couple. It sure is a great way to collect blessings.

An Embellished *Doli*—Traditional but My Favourite

Another way of getting the eyeballs is to seat the bride in a beautifully embellished *doli* and make an elegant and grand entrance. For greater effect, the bride can also ride a palki, carried by her brothers.

Light the Lamps

The opulent is not necessarily exclusive. Sometimes, something as simple as an earthen lamp can do the trick, especially if the wedding ceremonies are held in the evening. The bride's sisters and friends can carry decorative earthen lamps in their hands as they usher her in. Lights can be dimmed for a more exquisite look.

Flash Mob

That's another popular entrance idea. The couple makes a grand entrance while performing to a song and a couple of minutes later, their friends join in and break into an impromptu performance.

Like entries, even the exit or the *vidaai* ceremony is getting more special than usual. Actor Gul Panag, for instance, turned traditional on its head, when she exited her wedding in a motorcycle with a sidecar, wearing aviators.

Your entrance should create a zesty atmosphere. So, chose your entry song carefully. It should gel with the mood and theme of your wedding. You can also club a few of your favourite songs together and dance on them. Adding English songs to a traditional ceremony, where everyone is not comfortable with the language might not work, especially with elder guests. Your entry or your act is one thing that your guests will remember for long, so decide carefully.

While planning your entry, make sure you are comfortable with it. Just don't follow any style blindly or do it because someone else thinks it is cool. If you are not enjoying it, it will show in your expressions. And you definitely don't want your pictures and video to capture your disinterest or hesitation. So, chalk out your entry carefully and nicely.

Chapter 21

How to Involve Your Groom?

Here is the answer to the most annoying question, 'How to involve your groom in wedding planning?'

Many grooms want to be involved but they don't know where to start and they're scared to step on your toes or your mom's. Your guy probably hasn't thought much about it and has no idea what a wedding entails whereas you've probably been picturing your big day for years. It's up to you to pull him in on the decision-making. Let him know there's room for everyone to participate and that you want to hear his opinions, gut reactions and preferences. Specific questions—'Do we want a band or a DJ,' usually yield better responses than open-ended ones, which cultivate non-committal answers: 'Whatever. You decide'.

Ask your fiancé what he remembers about weddings he's attended. What did he love or hate? Which wedding stands out the most, and why? At which wedding did he have the most fun? The answers to these questions will give you both a better idea of what is important to him. Attend few weddings together if possible and discuss what you liked and what you did not. It is lot of fun and learning each other's preferences will bring you closer.

Truth is he probably doesn't care about the colour of the envelope liner on your invitations. A good habit to practise: Before you bombard him with a million little decisions, step back and recognise when to reach out versus when to just go ahead and handle things yourself. Rather than feeling bummed over his 'invitation indifference', bring up details you think he may be more interested in like the food, music or the signature cocktails.

It's a common misconception that the bride plans the wedding and it is the role of the groom to just show up wearing a sherwani. If your guy hasn't participated in the planning yet, it could be that he has no idea that he's even allowed to! So the first step is to come right out and say, 'I'd like us to plan our wedding together.' If you're lucky, that'll be all it takes to get him to jump aboard the crazy wedding planning train!

A lot of the time, weddings showcase the bride's favourite colours, flowers, themes, etc. Giving your guy a chance to showcase a hobby or interest is one of the best ways of personalising your wedding plans. Give him special projects that cater to his interests:

Is he creative? Ask him to design a save-the-date card online to be sent out to family and friends.

If he never failed a math test, managing the wedding budget is the perfect task for him. Software programmes like Quicken and wedding-planning programmes that include a budget tool might make this task even more appealing.

Is he a good negotiator? Ask him to work out the prices with vendors and see what kinds of 'extras' he can get included in your packages.

Does he have a musical ear? Remember those exciting nights out on the town when you first started dating? Have him research bands and DJs and arrange for the two of you to go out on dates to take notes and compare. He can choose songs apt for the occasion like when you are walking under the *phoolon ki chadar*, when your *doli* is departing or when you two have your first couple dance! He can coordinate with the DJ and have the special songs queued up for the perfect moment!

Has he mastered Photoshop? Design your own stationery

instead of paying for pricey invites. Your groom could also set up and maintain the wedding website.

The bar menu for the wedding is a very big deal for a lot of grooms. Ask him to give his inputs and decide which spirits need to be served at the wedding functions. If he has a special trademark drink, he can pass on the recipe to the staff, few days prior to the function.

If your guy's a 'foodie,' let him determine the menu. Even if he isn't an expert, it's pretty hard to find a guy who doesn't like to eat. Good food is not only a sure way of winning over your guests but is also a great part of wedding planning that you two can work on together.

What groom wouldn't jump at the chance to pick the big-day transportation? Exotic car rentals are huge right now. The Rolls-Royce, the Bentley, the Lotus Esprit, the Hummer, stretch limousines—guys get to test-drive all these exotic cars.

Is he a secret fashionista? He will enjoy choosing his own big-day ensemble, whether it's a linen tux for a beach wedding or a black tux paired with a colourful vest for a more traditional affair.

A lot more grooms are taking charge of the diplomatic issues that come up during all that wedding planning. Can he mediate effectively between you and your respective families, if disagreements arise and discussions heat up? If so, then by all means let him be the official peacekeeper!

Make him the unofficial tour guide for your out-of-town guests. Ask him to create a list of sightseeing spots, restaurants and bars in your area, so your guests can enjoy your wedding location.

More and more men want to take dance lessons because they don't want to make a fool out of themselves during the sangeet. Have him research local instructors and studios.

Ask him to put on a show to wow your guests by creating a PowerPoint presentation that includes childhood photos of each of you as well as ones that document your dating relationship and your courtship.

In regular 'wedding update' meetings, get his input on decisions. As time flies and the big day gets closer, he'll become more and more involved with the details of the day—and that's just as it should be. After all, the wedding belongs to both of you!

Combine wedding errands with an activity your fiancé enjoys. If you'd like your fiancé to spend a Saturday morning with you visiting reception venues or interviewing photographers, offer to have lunch at his favourite restaurant or catch a movie together that afternoon.

'Honeymoon planning' Let him take charge of your honeymoon planning. If he knows you as well as you believe, anywhere he picks is sure to put a smile on your face.

Guys aren't the only ones who complain about brides-to-be talking of nothing but upcoming nuptials. Sometimes, even girlfriends get overwhelmed by all the wedding chatter.

Spend some time alone chatting about anything but the wedding. See a silly movie, split a hot fudge sundae or watch a cricket match. Do something spontaneous that reminds you both of why you decided to marry in the first place.

You can't ask him to be involved and then shoot down all his ideas. He's going to get frustrated with that pretty quickly and you would have blown your chance to have him as your partner in planning. Be supportive of your groom's ideas and willing to go along with them even if they don't exactly fit your overall wedding concept.

Chapter 22

Plan that Special Honeymoon

Honeymoon is a special trip for a newly-wed couple. It is not just a vacation for the couple to de-stress after the wedding hustle-bustle but a chance to bond with each other. Honeymoon gives them some alone time together, to understand each other better. A lot of planning goes into this trip as everything from location to travel arrangements have to be finalised before the wedding. You spent hours planning your wedding, so spend a little time planning for your honeymoon too.

Too often, honeymoons are an afterthought to wedding planning. But a honeymoon is an investment in memories that stay with you the rest of your life. So don't take chances with it. Sit down and talk about the level of luxury and privacy you want, what activities you want to do every day, and the type of nightlife you desire. Honeymoons are a state of mind. Your dreams as well as a host of practical elements must combine to make it perfect.

Remember, your honeymoon isn't only a romantic trip. In fact, this is the time when your new life together really begins.

So, here are a few things to keep in mind while planning your honeymoon.

Decide When to Go and for How Long

First, figure out how many vacation days you have accrued and how many of them you'll need before the wedding for last-minute planning. (It's not uncommon for brides to take a week off, and grooms to take a couple of days.) Do you want to leave the morning after your wedding? Or do you want to have some time after the wedding to unwind and pack, when you can focus more on it? Perhaps, then you'd like to take your honeymoon a few days or even a few weeks later. Another option, for those who don't have a lot of vacation days, is to take a weekend 'mini-moon' after the wedding. You can then follow it up with a long second honeymoon on your first anniversary.

Know Your Geography

Yes, Seychelles, Bora Bora and Fiji are amazing honeymoon destinations but not if you have less than one week for your honeymoon. An exotic location is ideal only if you have enough travel time and don't mind long flights. Some locations require over a day of travel and you also need to adjust to the time difference.

Check for the Weather

Unless you intend to spend all your time indoors, you need to check the weather conditions in the place you have in mind. Google weather details of the place for the month you intend to travel. No one wants their trip to be a washout (despite the fact you'll happily spend a fair amount of time inside your room).

Plan It Well

Set a budget, so that you do not go overboard. Look at different packages before finalising. Search for reviews of different hotels and tour operators. Research online for information on different locations and draw up a small personalised itinerary. Airline fares will play a significant role in your planning.

Start Early

The sooner, the better. Planning ahead gives you time to budget accordingly and to secure all necessary documents. You might also be able to confirm that 'one of a kind room' many resorts offer to make your honeymoon even more special. To avoid last-minute booking hassles and refusals, it is best to plan your honeymoon much in advance. Families should leave the planning part to the couple, since it is their special trip. Also, guys, if you are making the honeymoon arrangements, it is important to consider your partner's preferences as well.

Communicate

Discuss where you would like to go and how long you are willing to travel to get there. Just don't dream about going 'somewhere different'. Consider the reasons that make a place less visited. Such places are always harder to reach from where you live and may require additional travelling time to get there. Are you committed enough to take a connecting flight to your dream destination? Are you willing to spend half-a-day, or maybe even a day getting to this place? With all the cutbacks in flights, the number of non-stop schedules has dwindled, making it even harder to get to 'some place different'. Discuss with your fiancé what you wish to experience on your honeymoon: Adventure, relaxation, touring, a little of everything? Communication is the key!

Homework

Doing your honeymoon homework really pays off. First, discuss your honeymoon dreams and fantasies with your partner. One of you loves the sun, luxury swimming pools and relaxing massages; the other enjoys diving, fine foods and exclusive bars and clubs. Remember, your honeymoon destination needs to work for both of you. Luxury and exclusivity can take many different forms but what is most important is that you choose together.

Don't despair if you reach an impasse. List out your dream destinations separately and then see if any of your ideas match.

If you still can't decide, make it fun! Choose out of a hat or pin-up all the locations you both like, then throw a dart over your back to see which one it lands on! Or simply go to a place that has more of the things that mean something to both of you!

In the following list write [b] for bride and [g] for groom. Select the ones with b and g and then select a few [b]'s and few [g]'s

Honeymoon Style

[　] Beachy and Secluded
[　] Safari and Beyond
[　] Rustic and Romantic
[　] Five Star and Luxury
[　] No TV, Internet or Phones needed in our Room!
[　] Bring on the Beach
[　] Treat us like a King and Queen
[　] Adventurous, and Then Some!
[　] Attractions and Tours, and MORE
[　] Honeyteering (Combining your honeymoon with volunteering)
[　] Go Green
[　] Country Hoppers (The more we see, the happier we are!)
[　] All About the Food (We pick the place because of the food, we are true FOODIES)
[　] Not Leaving the Room Till We Check Out!
[　] All Inclusive and Well-known_____ (insert your own here)

Honeymoon Duration

[　] Overnight
[　] Weekend/long weekend
[　] A Week
[　] Two weeks
[　] Longer_____(insert your own here)

Locations

[　] Oceanfront Sunsets
[　] Quaint Historic Streets
[　] Wilderness and Mountains
[　] Casinos
[　] Local Bars and Restaurants
[　] Sand and Beaches
[　] History and Culture
[　] Weather Conducive to Outdoor Activities

[   ] Large Metropolitan Areas
[   ] Foreign Lands
[   ] Safari (Africa)
[   ] By Land (Driving Cross Country, Camping, Hiking)
[   ] By Sea (Cruising, Private Yachts, Sailing)
[   ] By Rail (Orient Express, Rail Adventures)
[   ] The More Snow the Better! (Skiing, Tubing, Snow Boarding)
[   ] Adults Only Please
[   ] Clothing Optional Please
[   ] Cottages and/or Cabins
[   ] _____(Insert your own here)

Accommodation

[   ] Large Luxurious Resorts
[   ] Quaint and Intimate Villas
[   ] Mountain Lodges
[   ] Ocean/Water Views
[   ] Butler Service
[   ] Chic Decor
[   ] Jacuzzi in Room
[   ] Swim Up Bars
[   ] Balconies or Terraces
[   ] Large Plush Rooms
[   ] Private Plunge Pool
[   ] Boutique Properties Only (fifty rooms or less)
[   ] Bed and Breakfast
[   ] Chain Hotels (I want to get or use my points)
[   ] All inclusive Properties
[   ] Castles and Mansions
[   ] Relais and Chateaux
[   ] Top Spa Properties
[   ] Adventure Properties (hotels based on adventures and outdoor activities)
[   ] _____(Insert your own here)

Meals

[   ] Casual Dining

[   ] Formal Dining

[   ] Street Food

[   ] Midnight Buffets

[   ] Diners and Fast Food Franchise

[   ] Inexpensive Local Restaurants

[   ] Ethnic Cuisine

[   ] Local Cuisine

[   ] Picnics

[   ] Entertainment While Dining

[   ] Dining Based on Your Own Schedule

[   ] Special Diet Meals: Spa Style/vegetarian/Gluten Free

[   ] Our hotel. I want a honeymoon where food is included in the price

[   ] We Want To Cook For Ourselves

[   ] _____(Inset your own here)

Activities

[   ] Adventure Travel

[   ] Golf

[   ] Spa Treatments

[   ] Fishing

[   ] Sun Bathing

[   ] Snorkelling Scuba Diving

[   ] Reading and Relaxing

[   ] Water Sports

[   ] Snow Skiing/Boarding

[   ] Hiking/Rock Climbing

[   ] Nightlife—Wild and Crazy Clubs

[   ] Nightlife—Cosy and Relaxing Lounges

[   ] Nightlife—Shows and Entertainment

[   ] Nightlife—Casinos

[   ] Listen to Live Music

[   ] Experience the Local Culture
[   ] Tennis
[   ] Pool Games and Entertainment
[   ] Quiet Pool with NO KIDS
[   ] Sightseeing
[   ] Planned/Guided Tours
[   ] Art Museums and Theatre
[   ] Daytime Adventures (ATV Tours, Bike Tours, Parasailing, Zip-lines)
[   ] Dolphin Swims
[   ] Antiquing
[   ] Bicycling
[   ] Birding
[   ] Cruising
[   ] Hiking
[   ] Horseback Riding
[   ] Motor Sports
[   ] Mountain Biking
[   ] Sailing
[   ] Yachting
[   ] Educational programmes (Cooking Lessons, Art Lessons, Surf Lessons)
[   ] Wine Tasting
[   ] Swimming up to the Bar is the Only Activity I Will Do
[   ] _____ (Insert your own here)

Travel Accommodation
[   ] First Class Only
[   ] Use My Mileage
[   ] Who Cares About Service, Just Get Us There!
[   ] We Can Only Drive
[   ] We Will Train It There!
[   ] _____(Insert your own here)

Choose the one that matches your dreams. All-inclusive resorts are an easy way to go. Most meals, sports equipment, tips and some drinks are part of the price. Honeymoon packages, available from hotels, airlines and tour operators are designed with romance in mind. They often include special perks that other stays do not. When booking a hotel, ask if they have special packages. If you choose to cruise, the ship is your home away from home and most on board meals and activities are included in the cost. Book early to get a table for two in the dining room. If you have a special place in mind and want a custom trip, work with a travel agent.

STAY ORGANISED

If you're planning your honeymoon with your fiancé, then whoever is more organised should keep track of the bookings.

Use Multiple Resources When Researching Your Destination

So many times, the information you get about hotels, airports, restaurants, excursions and other activities happens to be outdated. Use multiple, frequently updated sources before making those reservations.

Let an Expert Help You

Coordinating flight and hotel bookings with excursions and honeymoon activities can be quite a struggle. Get professional advice to take some of the pressure off. The internet has made finding and booking that luxury honeymoon a lot easier and you might want to do it all yourself. But it's always worth remembering that there are experts out there who can help. It's a once in a lifetime holiday you're planning, so using a travel agent or a consultant from a luxury resort might make it worthwhile.

A Travel Consultant Helps to Save Money and Avoid Mistakes

You only want to plan one honeymoon, so make sure you do it right. A good travel consultant will seldom cost more than if you 'do-it-yourself'. Often, he can save you money too. They have an insider's knowledge about fares and deals that are circulating around and can get you 'wholesale' prices for your honeymoon. Also, they know the places to avoid and the places that are the best in their category.

Most important: If something goes wrong, you'll have someone you can call. They have a network of contacts for problem resolution. This can be a big blessing in a foreign country.

Travel Documents

Book the Bride's Ticket in her Maiden Name to Avoid Confusion. Women are advised to make reservations under their maiden name and wait until returning to legally change their name after marriage. It's important that your names match your ID. This is particularly true if you're travelling out of the country—your airline tickets and hotel room names will need to match the name on your passport.

Always check your passport for its expiry date. Also, make sure that other travel documents like visa and identity cards are in place, at least two weeks to a month before you leave for your trip.

If you already have a passport, note that some countries require that it be valid for at least six months or longer, beyond the dates of your trip.

Most visas must be procured before you leave; some can be obtained upon arrival. Call the country's embassy or consulate for details.

When travelling to an exotic destination, confirm with your doctor whether you need to take any vaccinations.

For each country's entry requirements, visa instructions, and contact information, do some googling. Your travel professional can advise you on visa requirements and even assist in obtaining them, should you need.

Inform Hotel/Resort

At the time of reservation, be sure to let the hotel know that it is a honeymoon trip. You can avail the many courtesies reserved for honeymoon guests. You may get upgraded to a better room at no charge, receive a welcome bottle of champagne and who knows what else. Many resorts offer amazing honeymoon packages that can be purchased for a certain amount or are complimentary when booking a certain room category, with minimum nights. These packages can include anything from a romantic dinner on a beach, complimentary massages and breakfast in bed, to free anniversary stays and many more.

Plan for Downtime and Active Time

You probably don't want to plan too much—it is your honeymoon, after all. But scheduling some key activities in advance can take the stress out of things. You're on your honeymoon, you'll want to spend every breathing moment together, right? Actually, it's a great idea to plan a little time apart, too. Having a massage while your husband or wife enjoys some 'me time' with a book will give you both a bit of relaxing space and something to look forward to—your reunion.

Schedule time to do nothing at all. While it's great to know you have plenty of options, in terms of things to see and do, this is, after all, a honeymoon.

Plan Some Surprises

Check with your tour operators and on the internet for ways to make your honeymoon trip even more special. An escapade to a lonely island or a night spent in a makeshift tent by a serene lake can be a very romantic gesture indeed. Surprise your other half with a special treat like a romantic dinner on the beach, a treasured piece of black pearl jewellery, a spa treatment or even a sunset cruise.

Money Matters

Money is the last thing you want to worry about on a romantic getaway, so it's important to do four things before you leave—set a budget; know your limits (checking account balance, limits on your credit cards); carefully consider the mix of cash, traveller's cheques and credit cards you should take; and assemble emergency contact numbers, should your wallet go missing. Arming yourselves in advance will ease your mind regarding money and let you shop at outdoor flea markets and chichi shops with equal ease.

Take More Money Than You Think You'll Need

If it's possible, allow a few days to readjust when you get back from your honeymoon. If you have to rush back to work straightaway, your luxury break might seem like a distant memory, all too soon. Block a couple of extra days to enjoy being home together, relax and unpack, before the real world can barge in again.

Relax Your Expectations

Yes, your honeymoon is supposed to be special and romantic but don't set expectations that may not be achievable. If you've already vacationed with your future spouse, you may be wondering how you can top all the great times you've had together. The truth is that it doesn't have to. Your honeymoon is about spending romantic time together and enjoying one another's company. You'll have many more vacations in time; so don't expect your honeymoon to be the perfect vacation of a lifetime.

In the end, keep in mind that the wedding is a stressful affair for the couple. So, plan your honeymoon two to three days after the wedding. This will help you calm your 'wedding nerves', before you leave for the trip.

Checklist for Planning Honeymoon

Eight Months to a Year Before

- Set a budget.

Five to Six Months Before

- Obtain or renew passport for honeymoon.
- Decide whether to use a travel agent.
- Make a list of preferred travel agents.
- Investigate destinations.
- Shortlist preferred destination.
- Get quotes and itinerary of the destinations from preferred travel agencies.

Three to Four Months Before

- Finalise honeymoon plans/itinerary.
- Finalise all the reservations.
- Purchase travel insurance.
- Apply for required visa or any other documentation according to the destination.
- Make a list of the things/clothes required for your honeymoon and shop accordingly.
- Purchase honeymoon clothing, luggage and accessories.

Two Months Before

- Start packing for your honeymoon.
- Get any required vaccinations.
- Plan your activities.

One Month Before

- Finish packing and set aside your honeymoon luggage.
- Confirm honeymoon travel arrangements (flight, hotel, rental car and so on).
- Book any special trips.
- Arrange for transportation from home or hotel to airport for honeymoon.
- Get traveller's cheques and/or foreign currency.
- Make arrangements for the caring of pets and plants while on honeymoon.
- Write down important phone numbers.
- Learn how and where to exchange currency and find an ATM in your destination.
- Make photocopies of passports, airline tickets, traveller's cheque numbers and credit cards.

One Week Before

- Get your honeymoon bags to wherever you need them to be—your hotel room or the trunk of your car, for example.
- Reconfirm all flight and hotel bookings.
- Leave a copy of your itinerary with relatives.

Congratulations…and bon voyage! Your honeymoon is just the starting point as you venture out to explore the world together.

Chapter 23

Post Wedding

Register Your Marriage

While women spend a lot of time and energy planning the perfect wedding, they ignore an important detail that is aimed at their own protection. They forget about the paperwork formalising the union— the marriage certificate. Sometime around 2005-06, the Supreme Court made it mandatory for couples to register their marriages.

A marriage certificate is not just 'another licence' that one must obtain. It is, in fact, a very essential document that couples generally tend to overlook in the euphoria and fanfare surrounding their marriage. Many people even believe it to be a waste of time, 'Who needs a marriage certificate?' But the reality is that every couple entering a marriage needs this legal authorisation.

- You may want to travel abroad, in such cases, a marriage certificate is taken as proof of a marriage—photographs or anything else depicting ceremonial marriages don't count. No certificate means no spouse visas—that is the rule.
- Today, it is common for people to marry outside their caste/ religion, which may not be accepted by all. A marriage

certificate will help couples overcome all these and solemnise a marriage. They will not be subjected to any force/coercion whatsoever.

- If a party is being forced into marrying someone, she can easily deny and record this in front of the registrar and the marriage will not be registered.
- Marriage registration helps the authorities keep a check on child marriages. If you are legally underage, your marriage will not be registered, irrespective of the amount of love, feelings et al.
- A marriage certificate acts as a deterrent to any abandonment. It helps you establish your rights in a marriage, in a court of law.
- In case of death of either partner, a marriage certificate facilitates the inheritance of property.

Registration of marriages is not as tedious as many think. Submit the necessary documents/certificates (document checklist given below) and your marriage could be registered within a day.

In India, there are two acts under which a marriage can be registered. One is the Hindu Marriage Act of 1955 which is applicable only to Hindus. The other is the Special Marriage Act of 1954, applicable to all the citizens of India. The Hindu Marriage Act provides for registration of an already solemnised marriage. It does not provide for solemnisation of a marriage by the Registrar. The Special Marriage Act provides for solemnisation of a marriage as well as registration by a Marriage Officer. The Hindu Marriage Act sets a minimum age limit of twenty-one years for the groom and eighteen years for the bride, while the latter places a minimum age limit of twenty-one years for both the partners.

Steps to Register a Marriage Under the Hindu Marriage Act, 1955
To register under this Act, both the partners need to be Hindus.

- The first step is to apply to the sub-registrar under whose jurisdiction the marriage took place. Alternatively, you can apply to the registrar of the place where either spouse stayed for at least six months before marriage.
- The couple will have to appear before the registrar along with witnesses, they could be the parents, guardians or friends.

- Both partners need to fill the relevant application form, sign it, and submit it, along with photocopies of the necessary documents. Don't forget to carry a copy of your wedding invitation card.
- Keep in mind that both parties will need to disclose their previous marital status, if any.
- Lastly, you will have to deposit a fee with the cashier and attach the receipt with the form.
- Once the application has been submitted and the documents verified, the concerned officer will assign a date for registration, when the marriage certificate will be issued.
- The people who have converted to Hinduism will have to provide a certificate of conversion from the priest who solemnised the marriage along with relevant documents.
- A provision for delay up to five years is available by the registrar and after that by the district registrar concerned.

DOCUMENTS CHECKLIST

- Address proof: Passport, driving licence, gas bill, ration card, voter ID, proof of residence must be of the city in which the marriage is being registered.
- Age proof of both bride and groom.
- Two joint photographs of the bride and groom in marriage dress taken while the marriage ceremony was in progress and which shows them taking part in the ceremony, with signatures over such photo.
- Wedding invites: Both of the bride and the groom, in case separate invites where sent from each side.
- Application of marriage form filled and signed by husband and wife. And signatures of two attesting witnesses present at the time of marriage, along with their names and addresses.
- Certificate of conversion (if either party is a convert), from the priest who solemnised the marriage.
- Affirmation that the parties are not related to each other within the prohibited degree of relationship.

- Attested copy of the divorce decree, if applicable and death certificate of spouse if a partner is a widow or a widower.
- If one of the partners is a foreigner, then No Impediment Certificate/NOC from the concerned embassy and valid visa is required.

All original documents, along with photocopies attested by a gazetted officer will be required. Note: Carry a pair of scissors, a fine felt-tip pen (for signing on photos), a gel pen, a ballpoint pen, a stapler and a glue stick along.

STEPS TO REGISTER A MARRIAGE UNDER THE SPECIAL MARRIAGE ACT, 1954

This Act covers both marriage solemnising and registration and requires the same documents as prescribed under the Hindu Marriage Act. However, the procedure is complex. To begin with, both the parties have to give a thirty-day notice to the marriage officer, in whose jurisdiction at least one spouse has resided. If you are marrying under this Act, you won't need to submit a wedding card and the priest's certificate and the registration will take place after the wedding. If you are married, include the wedding card, if possible.

- The couple has to give a notice to the marriage officer in whose jurisdiction at least one of the parties has resided for not less than thirty days prior to the date of notice. It should be affixed at some conspicuous place in his office.
- If either of the two is residing in the area of another marriage officer, a copy of the above mentioned notice should be sent to him for similar publication.
- The marriage may be legally sanctified after one month from the date of publication of the notice, if no objections are received.
- In case of receipt of objections, the marriage officer will have to enquire into them and decide whether to solemnise the marriage or to refuse it.
- The marriage officer will administer the oath in the prescribed form and solemnise the marriage.

- Groom and bride and three witnesses shall sign the declaration and the certificates of marriage.
- Registration will be done after solemnisation of the marriage.

Non-registration of marriage affects women the most. Women, most prominently victims of bigamous relationships and property disputes, face enormous hardship in establishing their marriage as they have no proof of marriage. In many cases of bigamy, the wives lose their cases due to their failure to prove the first or second marriage of their husbands.

For women, registration of marriages is a critical issue and will help:
- Prevent child marriages and ensure minimum age of marriage.
- Prevent polygamy, unless the same is permitted under any law or custom.
- Ensure that prior wives get notice of intended marriage.
- Enable the married women, including the women married to NRI/foreigners to claim her right to shelter and maintenance.
- Prevent the practice where men desert women after performing the marriage, including act as a deterrent to the practice of selling daughters to any person including a foreigner, under the garb of marriage.

Changing Your Surname

Life sure changes for a girl post marriage. It starts with her very identity—her name. Though not a mandatory practice, changing one's maiden surname with the husband's name is a common practice amongst Indian women. Nowadays, most women prefer to keep both surnames (Aishwarya Rai Bachchan is a case in point). In any case, there are some legal formalities to be kept in mind.

STEP BY STEP PROCEDURE
- Having a marriage certificate is mandatory.
- Visit the local authorities with your marriage certificate, along with the proof of your husband's identity like his passport or voter's card. Present the documents and your surname will be officially changed.

- Once your surname is officially changed, all appropriate bodies must be notified immediately. Get a joint notarised affidavit from a notary public, which will list your maiden surname, your changed surname, your signature and pictures of you and your husband. The affidavit along with your marriage certificate should then be used to change your surname on your bank records, driving licence, tax documents, passport, etc.
- Instead of getting the notarised affidavit, you may also take your marriage certificate to the government gazette office. For a nominal amount of money, the office will publish an announcement of your surname change and provide multiple copies of it. The marriage certificate combined with the copy of the gazette will serve as proof and official notice of your surname change. The advantage of the gazette over the affidavit is the cost factor; the services of the notary can be quite expensive compared to the government gazette office.

Update all necessary papers with your new name and ensure there is uniformity in all your financial documents.

Permanent Account Number (PAN)

Ensure that you get a change of surname on your PAN card. These days it's almost impossible to do any financial transactions without giving a copy of the PAN card.

The process is similar to applying for a new card; the only difference is that you will need to provide your old card number. Your new PAN card will carry the old number but with a new name.

Keep in mind that you will have to submit your marriage certificate or a copy of the official government gazette while applying for name change in the PAN card. Even a copy of a joint (with spouse) notarised affidavit will do, to get the PAN updated. After that, ensure that your income tax papers also get updated.

Banking Relationships

The next step is to get all your banking relationships updated with your new surname. Generally, the marriage certificate and the joint notarised affidavit can get the job done. Remember also to update the change of address along with the name change request. Here, the bank may ask you for your husband's address proof as well such as a copy of his passport.

CREDIT REPORT

Do ensure that you get the new surname on your deposit accounts as well as loan accounts. As far as credit report goes, you need not worry. Any changes in customer database for all loan customers, including name and address, gets refreshed every month by the bank to Credit Information Bureau (India) Ltd.

PASSPORT

If you already have a passport and need to update your post marriage new surname, you will have to apply for a reissue. Along with marriage certificate, you will have to submit the old passport in original, with a self-attested photocopy and a copy of the husband's passport.

OTHER DOCUMENTS

Other documents where you will need to update your new surname are driving licence, voter's identity card, etc. As far as insurance policies go, if you are a nominee, ensure that the correct name is mentioned.

Also, you will need to get your know-your-client information updated; name change across other financial investments such as mutual funds and shares will follow.

Being financially smart is very important and everyone knows the significance of a name on any property-related document, be it as an owner or a nominee. Be a smart woman, take care that all things related to the property you own or are nominated in are updated with proper plans. For property-related matters, contact your legal adviser; for name change, go to the local registrar's office.

Of course, it's not as easy as it sounds and you probably will have to spend a month or so to get all this done. But it's best done sooner than later to avoid problems in the future.

Chapter 24

Get Organised Before You Get Married

Checklist—Twelve Months to Go

AS SOON AS POSSIBLE—TWELVE MONTHS OR MORE (ONCE THE WEDDING IS FINALISED)

- What's your wedding day vision? Start deciding now on the formality, style and theme (if you're having one).
- Set wedding priorities—make a list of the elements most important to you. This will help you decide on a date, budget your expenses and delegate tasks.
- Get organised! Find a system that works for you (binder, folder, book, etc.) to keep notes, brochures, checklists, menus and other printed material.
- The B-word already? Yes, it's time to talk budgets. Talk about it together first, then if your parents (or other generous souls) wish to contribute, discuss with them who's paying for what.
- Establish how the expenses would be divided between groom and bride.
- Consult a priest/pandit and discuss a wedding date. Get more

than one option for the date, if possible. In the next month or so, you should determine who your most important vendors will be and finalise the wedding date with them and with your close family members before confirming it.

- Research and make a list of wedding planners; also start thinking about how your friends, family and wedding party can help out. If people offer their services, don't be afraid to delegate, nicely.
- If your parents haven't met yet, plan to get them together for the first time.

Ten–eleven Months

- Think about the events and the number of days you want to spread it to.
- Meet shortlisted wedding planners.
- Draw up a preliminary guest list with input from both sides. Think of it as a wish list and then narrow it down to a close idea of final number, based on your budget.
- Edit the guest list.
- Draw up a first draft guest list for the various functions.
- Shortlist the venues for wedding and other functions.
- Check on availability of the venues for the required dates.
- Research and make a list of caterers.
- Research and make a list of decorators.
- Research and make a list of photographers.
- Research and make a list of DJs and any other entertainers.
- Figure out unpreventable factors that could impact your chosen wedding calendar day (e.g. weather, elections and so forth).

Nine Months

- Finalise how many functions you need to organise and set their dates and times.
- Consider your budget and decide the size of the wedding.
- Allocate responsibilities between both families.
- Finalise your wedding planner (if you decide to have one)

and ask her to draft a written contract with service and payment terms.

- Thoroughly read the contract with the wedding planner, sign and preserve your copy.
- Visit possible venues to discuss their availability and cost.
- If you see a great reception or ceremony site that's available on your chosen date and within your budget, book it now. (If any one vendor is a higher priority for you than the site, make sure he is free before reserving a location.)
- Meet shortlisted caterers and go for food tasting.
- Meet shortlisted wedding photographers, see their portfolio and list out what they have to offer.
- Meet shortlisted decorators and go through your wedding day vision with them.
- Meet the entertainers or speak with them to understand their services.
- Select or create save-the-date cards.

Six–eight Months

- Book the venue for the wedding and other ceremonies.
- Thoroughly read the contract with the venue manager, sign and preserve your copy.
- Look through books, magazines and websites for wedding lehenga/sari/dress ideas.
- Finalise your guest list; inform family and friends who may need to travel.
- Organise a system to record payments completed as well as the person who made the transaction.
- Finalise your caterer and ask him to draft a written contract with service and payment terms.
- Thoroughly read the contract with the caterer, sign and preserve your copy.
- Finalise your photographer and ask him to draft a written contract with service and payment terms.
- Thoroughly read the contract with the photographer, sign and preserve your copy.

- Finalise your decorator and ask him to draft a written contract with service and payment terms.
- Thoroughly read the contract with the decorator, sign and preserve your copy.
- Finalise your DJ/entertainers and ask them to draft a written contract with service and payment terms.
- Thoroughly read the contract with the DJ/entertainers, sign and preserve your copy.
- Find out about pre-wedding bridal beauty packages and compare the rates and services.
- Start looking out for wedding invites and other stationery.
- Look out for bridal jewellery.
- Buy silverware needed for gifting and trousseau.
- Buy gifts for groom's family.
- Start your trousseau shopping.
- Research and make a list of make-up artists and hair stylists.
- Schedule appointments and meet with shortlisted make-up artists and hair stylists.
- Finalise and book the make-up artist and hair stylist that suits your requirement the most.
- Research and make a list of henna/mehendi artists.
- Go through the work of the mehendi artists and select the one you like.
- Finalise and book the henna/mehendi artist that suits your requirement the most.
- Pick up the engagement rings.
- Start a fitness routine.
- Start a skincare/beauty routine.
- Start looking for or thinking about wedding favours.
- Obtain or renew your passport for the honeymoon, if you plan to travel abroad.

FIVE MONTHS
- Send save-the-date cards, especially required in case of a destination wedding.

- Create your wedding website.
- Create online wedding invites.
- Finalise invitee list and obtain invitation mail addresses.
- Select the wedding invitation cards and related stationery.
- Finalise your wedding invites content.
- Review and approve proofs of wedding invitations and stationery.
- Place an order to get the wedding stationery printed.
- Create hotel information cards and maps to include with your wedding invitations.
- Decide on a probable menu with the caterer for all your functions.
- Book the pandit for the wedding.
- Finalise and start with pre-bridal package (in case you decide to opt for one at a spa)
- Visualise what you want to wear for all your events.
- Visit your favourite designer stores to look at wedding outfits for all the wedding events.
- Begin the search for transportation and other rentals.
- Get your engagement ring insured and consider purchasing wedding insurance.
- If you don't have a wedding consultant, ask a friend or relative (but not your parents) to be 'supervisor' (the person to deal with problems) on your wedding day. If you don't have someone in mind, consider hiring a wedding-day organiser.
- Arrange accommodation for out-of-town wedding guests (do this sooner if your wedding falls in peak wedding season).
- Research things to do in town during their stay.
- Research on your honeymoon options.
- Shortlist preferred destinations.
- Get quotes and itinerary of the destinations from preferred travel agencies.

Four Months
- Secure parking and/or transportation for your guests at the reception location.

- Visit your pandit to finalise details for all the functions.
- Browse through all the possible floral and decor arrangements.
- Book your wedding decor arrangements (confirm your colour theme, flowers, mandaps, etc.).
- Figure out all your music and entertainment needs.
- Meet with the photographer and videographer—advise them on what you want on the day (different photographic styles—give them a run down on what the days will be like so they know what to expect).
- Place an order for your wedding attire.
- Finalise and order outfits for all the occasions.
- Buy your accessories:
  - Shoes
  - Hosiery
  - Jewellery
- Buy any special lingerie required for wedding outfits.
- Decide what style of attire the groom will wear.
- Make sure the groom has the information he needs to buy or reserve his attire.
- Choose attire for your family members if you want to make them feel special.
- Want a new hair colour for the big day? Do a trial run of any new hair colour or highlights now.
- Consider and hire a security escort if guests will wear heavy jewellery at the venue.
- Arrange for a bridal portrait or pre-wedding photo-shoot.
- If you plan to have a prenuptial agreement, meet with your attorney to discuss it.
- Purchase a gift for your spouse-to-be.
- Finalise on what to give as wedding favours.

THREE MONTHS
- Buy or order the groom's wedding attire and accessories.
- Buy all the accessories (shoes/clutches/bangles, etc.) to match each of your outfits to be worn during the wedding events.

- Finalise on welcome baskets/gifts to be given to outstation guests.
- Buy or create welcome gifts for out-of-towners (to be waiting for them in their hotel rooms) and/or wedding favours.
- Appoint a choreographer from your family or hire a professional and discuss the possible ways to perform at the sangeet.
- Start thinking of the songs you want to use for your sangeet.
- Finalise all songs for sangeet dance and start practising.
- Book sweets or mithai for your functions.
- Book any other party rentals you may require for all your functions—for example chairs, tables, etc.
- Order your wedding cake.
- Collect your wedding invites.
- Determine the method of addressing wedding invitations and hire a calligrapher, if applicable.
- Address the invites and get them ready to be mailed.
- Mail out your overseas invites.
- Finish shopping for your trousseau (even if it's just one new nightgown).
- Meet with (or call) vendors to finalise arrangements (caterer, florists, musical performers and so on).
- Compile a list of all your wedding vendors with phone numbers to ensure a stress-free wedding.
- Compile a probable menu for all the events.
- Reserve a room for your wedding night.
- Schedule activities for out-of-town visitors, both before and after the wedding.
- Book an appointment for trial make-up and hairstyling for next month.
- Finalise honeymoon plans/itinerary and apply for the required visa if travelling abroad.
- Make a list of the things/clothes required for your honeymoon and shop accordingly.
- Purchase honeymoon clothing, luggage and accessories.

Two Months

- Assign a friend or family member to be your 'wedding assistant' for the day of your wedding to help with anything and everything. Take this person for all your trials (hair/make-up/dress).
- Bride and groom may buy a gift for each other.
- Choose and purchase presents for wedding helpers.
- Confirm all your floral and decor arrangements.
- Confirm all your music and entertainment needed for your functions.
- Confirm music selections—playlist, with musicians/DJ for all the events.
- Arrange transportation/entry ideas for bride and groom to the venue.
- Book wedding transportation together with decoration for wedding vehicle and wedding party entourage.
- Confirm all final payment amounts with your vendors (including pandit) as well as date, time, location and so on.
- Start rehearsals for your sangeet.
- Think about bleaching or cleansing your teeth.
- Go for a trial of your wedding outfits.
- Go in for a dry run with the professional make-up artist and hair stylist to determine your wedding day look.
- Mail wedding invitations and/or email e-invites (six weeks prior to wedding).
- Start packing for your honeymoon.

One Month

- Keep track of all wedding invites and RSVP. The same list can be used to track gifts obtained and send thank you messages.
- Make appointments for you and your groom to get manicures, pedicures, massages, spa treatments, etc. the week before your wedding (do this even earlier if you're getting married during a busy month).
- Discuss the details of your wedding ceremony with your pandit; procure all the needed puja articles.

- Determine the placement or distribution of programmes at the ceremony venue.
- Arrange for preparation, storage and break areas for musicians/ DJ at the reception venue.
- Determine seating arrangements for guests.
- If you had coloured your hair previously, make an appointment for a touch-up the week before your wedding.
- Go for final wedding attire trial/fitting.
- Have your outfits picked up or delivered to you.
- Have groom's wear fitted and picked up.
- Finalise the menu with the caterers for each event.
- Finalise details with wedding photographer and videographer, determining arrival times at each function.
- Arrange for preparation/storage area for photographer and videographer at each venue.
- Confirm all transportation needs.
- Confirm with family and friends who is doing what on the days (helps if you give them a list so there is no confusion).
- Create day plans for all your functions, informing when and where things are happening.
- Go over song lists and requests with your band or DJ (for sangeet, set a meeting of the DJ with your choreographer).
- Get in touch with invitees who have not replied and finalise staying arrangements.
- Confirm hotel arrangements for out-of-town guests.
- Confirm when final payments need to be made to vendors.
- Sign your prenuptial agreement, if applicable.
- Finish packing and set aside your honeymoon luggage.
- Confirm honeymoon travel arrangements (flight, hotel, rental car and so on).
- Arrange for transportation from home or hotel to the airport for your honeymoon.
- Get traveller's cheques.
- Make arrangements for the care of pets and plants while on honeymoon.

- Start packing for your wedding/wedding week—pack each outfit with all matching accessories separately for each event and put a sticker on it, marking the event so that you have a relaxed wedding week.

Two–three Weeks

- Pre-wedding parties begin (bachelor and bachelorette party).
- Verify wedding ceremony details and exactly what to bring with the marriage official.
- Write out a schedule outlining the order of events (with specified times) for your wedding day. (If you have a consultant, wedding day organiser or delegated 'supervisor', let her do this.) Give a copy to your fiancé and all involved parties.
- Provide your service vendors a version of the comprehensive timeline.
- Confirm all arrival times with vendors.
- Finish and print ceremony programmes.
- Give final count of guests to the caterer.
- Confirm all bookings and check if things are going as per plan.
- Supply your wedding photographer a summary of particular photos you want captured.
- Provide your videographer a summary of special persons or events you would like included in the video clips.
- Make sure everybody knows their roles/performances for the sangeet.
- Get ready your wedding site road-guide boards and gift storage containers.
- Begin breaking in wedding shoes.
- Pack for wedding night.
- Put together a bridal emergency kit for your wedding.

One Week

- Visit your beautician for facials, waxing, etc.
- Get your manicure and pedicure.
- Write any cheques that are required for the wedding day—put them in separate labelled envelopes.
- Confirm everything with vendors again.

Appoint three or four persons (preferably educated and well-mannered security guards) and assign them the following responsibilities:

- Maintain a record of all gifts received during the wedding.
- Make sure that bride and groom's outfit, jewellery, presents, all rented items and other items are safe.
- Look out for suspicious people.
- Make sure that guests do not face any problem.
- Take care of all the kids. Keep them away from electrical appliances, heaters, burners, etc.
- Transport gifts from the ceremony site to the bride's suite or car.
- Make sure that everything is running smoothly and in case of a mishap or any problem contact the event manager.
- Switch on generators during a power failure.
- Use fire extinguishers in case of fire.
- Handle the entire security of the wedding.

Delegate. Decide what each member of the wedding party is responsible for on the wedding day, write it on a note card, and be sure to thank them.

- Arrange for a trustworthy person to help you pay the service providers on the special day.
- Designate someone to return rental materials after the wedding party.
- Designate someone to place wedding site road-guide boards at specific junctions.
- Designate someone to coordinate reception food and beverage layout and receipt with the caterer on the wedding day.
- Designate someone to coordinate reception site and stage performances—to manage MC, DJ, entertainers, site lighting, etc.
- Touch base with the 'supervisor' you asked to be 'the person to deal with problems' on your wedding day (if you don't have a wedding planner).
- Get cash ready for tipping and emergencies and give it to the designated 'payment person'.

- Make arrangements for your wedding gifts to be brought to your 'new' home.
- Revisit the wedding schedule.
- Present the configuration of the wedding reception to your caterer and wedding reception manager.
- Provide the final number of guests to the caterer and reception manager.
- Communicate final changes to your service vendors.
- Make sure all puja items are in place.
- Get 'welcome baskets' for outstation guests to hotels; arrange for them to be delivered to the appropriate rooms before guests arrive.
- Having an outdoor wedding? Check weather forecast (do you have a rain plan?), treat area for ants and other bugs if necessary.
- Familiarise yourself with each other's guest lists—this makes it easier to greet everyone during the reception.
- Prepare final costume fittings to ensure your garment is all set and ideal.
- Have a trial run for your sangeet.
- Leave a copy of your honeymoon itinerary with someone in case of emergency.
- Make sure honeymoon airline tickets, itinerary, passports and so forth are all in one won't-forget-them place.
- Get your honeymoon bags to wherever you need them to be—your hotel room or the trunk of your car, for example.

ONE DAY BEFORE THE START OF WEDDING FUNCTIONS
- Confirm wedding-day transportation.
- Revisit this checklist and record down all objects to be brought for the wedding event.
- Transport everything you need (decorations, guestbook, programmes, text for ceremony readings) to the venue, if you have access to the site early.
- Provide all participants of the wedding party with particulars of event timelines.

- Provide all service providers with details of event timelines.
- Deliver welcome basket.
- Make sure all your outfits are placed in the venue with the help of your wedding day assistant.
- Rehearse for your sangeet.
- Remind yourself to enjoy the day as it's your wedding.
- Make sure you get plenty to eat and drink a lot of water. You don't want to faint.
- Take a bath, drink some warm milk (or whatever works) to get ready for sleep.
- Get to bed at a reasonable hour (if possible).
- Get plenty of rest before the big day!

WEDDING DAY

- Start your day by exercising, get a massage, meditate, pray or do something equally energising yet relaxing.
- Eat a carbohydrate-plus-protein meal but don't overdo the caffeine.
- Show up on time for hair and make-up appointments.
- Get dressed (remember to use the bathroom first).
- Give yourself plenty of time to get ready.
- Take a look at yourself in the mirror and smile.
- Spend a moment alone to calm down before the ceremony.
- Give your parents hugs before everything gets too crazy.
- Relax and enjoy your wedding day.

POST-WEDDING DAY

- Arrange for transport of gifts.
- Make sure all vendor bills have been paid in full (for exceptional service, you may want to send a small gift or send a 'thank you' letter, which vendors can use as a letter of recommendation for future clients).
- Ensure all the rentals have been returned.
- If you haven't already, give gifts to your parents to thank them for their help and support.

After You Come Back from Your Honeymoon
- Arrange for your bridal outfits to be cleaned and preserved.
- Upload pictures and share with family and friends.
- If you choose to do so: Do all the paperwork to change your name and arrange to combine finances, insurance policies, etc.
- Change name and address on credit cards, driving licence, etc.

Checklist—Nine Months to Go
- What's your wedding-day vision? Start deciding now on the formality, style and theme (if you're having one).
- Set wedding priorities—make a list of the elements most important to you. This will help you decide on a date, budget your expenses and delegate tasks.
- Get organised! Find a system that works for you (binder, folder, book, etc.) to keep notes, brochures, checklists, menus and other printed materials.
- The B-word already? Yes, it's time to talk budgets. Talk about it together first, then if your parents (or other generous souls) wish to contribute, discuss with them who's paying for what.
- Establish how the expenses would be divided between groom and bride.
- Consult a priest/pandit and discuss a wedding date. Get more than one option for the date, if possible. In the next month or so, you should determine who your most important vendors will be and finalise the wedding date with them and with your close family members before confirming it.
- Research and make a list of wedding planners; also start thinking about how your friends, family and wedding party can help out. If people offer their services, don't be afraid to delegate, nicely.
- If your parents haven't met yet, plan to get them together for the first time.

Eight Months
- Think about the events and the number of days you want to spread it over.
- Meet the shortlisted wedding planners.

- Finalise your wedding planner (if you decide to have one) and ask her to draft a written contract with service and payment terms.
- Thoroughly read the contract with wedding planner, sign and preserve your copy.
- Draw up a preliminary guest list with input from both sides. Think of it as a wish list and then narrow it down to a close idea of final number based on your budget.
- Edit the guest list.
- Draw up a first draft guest list for the various functions.
- Shortlist the venues for wedding and other functions.
- Check on availability of the venues for the required dates.
- Research and make a list of caterers.
- Research and make a list of decorators.
- Research and make a list of photographers.
- Research and make a list of DJ and any other entertainers.
- Figure out unpreventable factors that could impact your chosen wedding calendar day (e.g. weather, elections and so forth.)

Seven Months

- Finalise how many functions you need to organise and set their dates and times.
- Allocate responsibilities between both families.
- Visit possible venues to discuss their availability and cost.
- If you see a great reception or ceremony site that's available on your chosen date and within your budget, book it now. (If any one vendor is a higher priority for you than the site, make sure he is free before reserving a location.)
- Consider your budget and decide the size of the wedding.
- Meet shortlisted caterers and go for food tasting.
- Meet shortlisted wedding photographers, see their portfolio and list out what they have to offer.
- Meet shortlisted decorators and go through your wedding day vision with them.

- Meet the entertainers or speak with them to understand their services.
- Select or create save-the-date cards.

Six Months

- Book the venue for wedding and other ceremonies.
- Thoroughly read the contract with the venue manager, sign and preserve your copy.
- Look through books, magazines and websites for wedding lehenga/sari/dress ideas.
- Finalise your guest list; inform family and friends who may need to travel.
- Organise a system to record payments completed as well as the person who made the transaction.
- Finalise your caterer and ask him to draft a written contract with service and payment terms.
- Thoroughly read the contract with the caterer, sign and preserve your copy.
- Finalise your photographer and ask him to draft a written contract with service and payment terms.
- Thoroughly read the contract with the photographer, sign and preserve your copy.
- Finalise your decorator and ask him to draft a written contract with service and payment terms.
- Thoroughly read the contract with the decorator, sign and preserve your copy.
- Finalise your DJ/entertainers and ask them to draft a written contract with service and payment terms.
- Thoroughly read the contract with the DJ/entertainers, sign and preserve your copy.
- Find out about pre-wedding bridal beauty packages and compare the rates and services.
- Start looking out for wedding invites and other stationery.
- Look out for bridal jewellery.
- Buy silverware needed for gifting and trousseau.
- Buy gifts for groom's family.

- Start your trousseau shopping.
- Research and make a list of make-up artists and hair stylists.
- Schedule appointments and meet with shortlisted make-up artists and hair stylists.
- Finalise and book the make-up artist and hair stylist that suits your requirement the most.
- Research and make a list of henna/mehendi artists.
- Go through the work of the mehendi artists and select the one you like.
- Finalise and book the henna/mehendi artist that suits your requirement the most.
- Pick up the engagement rings.
- Start a fitness routine.
- Start a skincare/beauty routine.
- Start looking for or thinking about wedding favours.
- Obtain or renew your passport for the honeymoon, if you plan to travel abroad.

FIVE MONTHS
- Finalise invitee list and obtain invitation mail addresses.
- Select the wedding invitation cards and related stationery.
- Finalise your wedding invites content.
- Review and approve proofs of wedding invitations and stationery.
- Place an order to get the wedding stationery printed.
- Create hotel information cards and maps to include with your wedding invitations.
- Decide on a probable menu with the caterer for all your functions.
- Book the pandit for the wedding.
- Finalise and start with pre-bridal package (In case you decide to opt for one at a spa).
- Visualise what you want to wear for all your events.
- Visit your favourite designer stores to look at wedding outfits for all the wedding events.
- Begin the search for transportation and other rentals.

- Get engagement ring insured and consider purchasing wedding insurance.
- If you don't have a wedding consultant, ask a friend or relative (but not your parents) to be the 'supervisor' (the person to deal with problems) on your wedding day. If you don't have someone in mind, consider hiring a wedding-day organiser.
- Arrange accommodation for out-of-town wedding guests (do this sooner if your wedding falls in peak wedding season).
- Research things to do in town during their stay.
- Research on your honeymoon options.
- Shortlist preferred destinations.
- Get quotes and itinerary of the destinations from preferred travel agencies.

Four Months

- Send save-the-date cards, especially required in case of a destination wedding.
- Create your wedding website.
- Create online wedding invites.
- Secure parking and/or transportation for your guests at the reception location.
- Visit your pandit to finalise details for all the functions.
- Browse through all the possible floral and decor arrangements.
- Book your wedding decor arrangements (confirm your colour theme, flowers, mandaps, etc.).
- Figure out all your music and entertainment needs.
- Meet with the photographer and videographer—advise them on what you want on the day (different photographic styles—give them a run down on what the days will be like so they know what to expect).
- Place an order for your wedding attire.
- Finalise and order outfits for all the occasions.
- Buy your accessories:
  - Shoes
  - Hosiery
  - Jewellery

- Buy any special lingerie required for wedding outfits.
- Decide what style of attire the groom will wear.
- Make sure the groom has the information he needs to buy or reserve his attire.
- Choose attire for your family members as you want to make them feel special.
- Want a new hair colour for the big day? Do a trial run of any new hair colour or highlights now.
- Consider and hire a security escort if guests will wear heavy jewellery at the venue.
- Arrange for a bridal portrait or pre-wedding photo shoot.
- If you plan to have a prenuptial agreement, meet with your attorney to discuss it.
- Purchase a gift for your spouse-to-be.
- Finalise on what to give as wedding favours.

THREE MONTHS
- Buy or order the groom's wedding attire and accessories.
- Buy all the accessories (shoes/clutches/bangles, etc.) to match each of your outfits to be worn during the wedding events.
- Finalise on welcome baskets/gifts to be given to outstation guests.
- Buy or create 'welcome gifts' for outstation guests (to be waiting for them in their hotel rooms) and/or wedding favours.
- Appoint a choreographer from your family or hire a professional and discuss the possible ways to perform at the sangeet.
- Start thinking of the songs you want to use for your sangeet.
- Finalise all songs for sangeet dance and start practising.
- Book sweets or mithai for your functions.
- Book any other party rentals you may require for all your functions—for example chairs, tables, etc.
- Order your wedding cake.
- Collect your wedding invites.
- Determine the method of addressing wedding invitations and hire a calligrapher, if applicable.

- Address the invites and get them ready to be mailed.
- Mail out your overseas invites.
- Finish shopping for your trousseau (even if it's just one new nightgown).
- Meet with (or call) vendors to finalise arrangements (caterer, florist, musical performers and so on).
- Compile a list of all your wedding vendors (with phone numbers) to ensure a stress-free wedding.
- Compile a probable menu for all the events.
- Reserve a room for your wedding night.
- Schedule activities for out-of-town visitors, both before and after the wedding.
- Book an appointment for trial make-up and hairstyling for next month.
- Finalise honeymoon plans/itinerary and apply for the required visa if travelling abroad.
- Make a list of the things/clothes required for your honeymoon and shop accordingly.
- Purchase honeymoon clothing, luggage and accessories.

Two Months

- Assign a friend or family member to be your 'wedding assistant' for the day of your wedding to help with anything and everything. Take this person for all your trials (hair/make-up/dress).
- Bride and groom may buy a gift for each other.
- Choose and purchase presents for wedding helpers.
- Confirm all your floral and decor arrangements.
- Confirm all your music and entertainment needed for your functions.
- Confirm music selections—playlist with musicians/DJ for all the events.
- Arrange transportation/entry ideas for bride and groom to the venue.
- Book wedding transportation together with decoration for wedding vehicle and wedding party entourage.

- Confirm all final payment amounts with your vendors (including pandit) as well as date, time, location and so on.
- Start rehearsals for your sangeet.
- Think about bleaching or cleansing your teeth.
- Go for a trial of your wedding outfits.
- Go in for a dry run with the professional make-up artist and hair stylist to determine your wedding day look.
- Mail wedding invitations and/or email e-invites (six weeks prior to wedding).
- Start packing for your honeymoon.

ONE MONTH

- Keep track of all wedding invites and RSVP. The same list can be used to track gifts obtained and send thank you messages.
- Make appointments for you and your groom to get manicures, pedicures, massages, spa treatments, etc. the week before your wedding (do this even earlier if you're getting married during a busy month).
- Discuss the details of your wedding ceremony with your pandit, procure all the needed puja articles.
- Determine the placement or distribution of programmes at the ceremony venue.
- Arrange for preparation, storage and break areas for musicians/ DJ at the reception venue.
- Determine seating arrangements for guests.
- If you had coloured your hair previously, make an appointment for a touch-up the week before your wedding.
- Go for final wedding attire trial/fitting.
- Have your outfits picked up or delivered to you.
- Have groom's wear fitted and picked up.
- Finalise the menu with the caterer for each event.
- Finalise details with wedding photographer and videographer, determining arrival times at each function.
- Arrange for preparation/storage area for photographer and videographer at each venue.

- Confirm all transportation needs.
- Confirm with family and friends who is doing what on the days (helps if you give them a list so there is no confusion).
- Create day plans for all your functions informing when and where things are happening.
- Go over song lists and requests with your band or DJ (for sangeet, set a meeting of the DJ with your choreographer).
- Get in touch with invitees who have not replied and finalise staying arrangements.
- Confirm hotel arrangements for out-of-town guests.
- Confirm when final payments need to be made to vendors.
- Sign your prenuptial agreement, if applicable.
- Finish packing and set aside your honeymoon luggage.
- Confirm honeymoon travel arrangements (flight, hotel, rental car and so on).
- Arrange for transportation from home or hotel to the airport for your honeymoon.
- Get traveller's cheques.
- Make arrangements for the care of pets and plants while on honeymoon.
- Start packing for your wedding/wedding week—pack each outfit with all matching accessories separately for each event and put a sticker on it, marking the event so that you have a relaxed wedding week.

Two–three Weeks

- Pre-wedding parties begin (bachelor and bachelorette party).
- Verify wedding ceremony details and exactly what to bring with the marriage official.
- Write out a schedule outlining the order of events (with specified times) for your wedding day. (If you have a consultant, wedding day organiser or delegated 'supervisor', let her do this.) Give a copy to your fiancé and all involved parties.
- Provide your service vendors a version of the comprehensive timeline.

- Confirm all arrival times with vendors.
- Finish and print ceremony programmes.
- Give final count of guests to the caterer.
- Confirm all bookings and check if things are going as per plan.
- Supply your wedding photographer a summary of particular photos you want captured.
- Provide your videographer a summary of special persons or events you would like included in the video clips.
- Make sure everybody knows their roles/performances for the sangeet.
- Get ready your wedding site road-guide boards and gift storage containers.
- Begin breaking in wedding shoes.
- Pack for wedding night.
- Put together a bridal emergency kit for your wedding.

One Week
- Visit your beautician for facials, waxing, etc.
- Get your manicure and pedicure.
- Write any cheques that are required for the wedding day—put them in separate labelled envelopes.
- Confirm everything with vendors again.

Appoint three or four persons (preferably educated well-mannered security guards) and assign them the following responsibilities:
- Maintain a record of all gifts received during the wedding.
- Make sure that bride and groom's outfit, jewellery, presents, all rented items and other items are safe.
- Look out for suspicious people.
- Make sure that guests do not face any problem.
- Take care of all the kids. Keep them away from electrical appliances, heaters, burners, etc.
- Transport gifts from the ceremony site to the bride's suite or car.
- Make sure that everything is running smoothly and in case of a mishap or any problem contact the event manager.
- Switch on generators during a power failure.

- Use fire extinguishers, in case of fire.
- Handle the entire security of the wedding.

Delegate. Decide what each member of the wedding party is responsible for on the wedding day, write it on a note card, and be sure to thank them.

- Arrange for a trustworthy person to help you pay the service providers on the special day.
- Designate someone to return rental materials after the wedding party.
- Designate someone to place wedding site road-guide boards at specific junctions.
- Designate someone to coordinate reception food and beverage layout and receipt with the caterer on the wedding day.
- Designate someone to coordinate reception site and stage performances—to manage MC, DJ, entertainers, site lighting, etc.
- Touch base with the 'supervisor' you asked to be 'the person to deal with problems' on your wedding day (if you don't have a wedding planner).
- Get cash ready for tipping and emergencies and give it to the designated 'payment person'.
- Make arrangements for your wedding gifts to be brought to your 'new' home.
- Revisit the wedding schedule.
- Present the configuration of the wedding reception to your caterer and wedding reception manager.
- Provide the final number of guests to the caterer and reception manager.
- Communicate final changes to your service vendors.
- Make sure all puja items are in place.
- Get out-of-towner 'welcome baskets' to hotels; arrange for them to be delivered to the appropriate rooms before guests arrive.
- Having an outdoor wedding? Check weather forecast (do you have a rain plan?), treat area for ants and other bugs if necessary.

- Familiarise yourself with each other's guest lists—this makes it easier to greet everyone during the reception.
- Prepare final costume fittings to ensure your garment is all set and ideal.
- Have a trial run for your sangeet.
- Leave a copy of your honeymoon itinerary with someone in case of emergency.
- Make sure honeymoon airline tickets, itinerary, passports and so forth are all in one won't-forget-them place.
- Get your honeymoon bags to wherever you need them to be—your hotel room or the trunk of your car, for example.

ONE DAY BEFORE THE START OF WEDDING FUNCTIONS
- Confirm wedding-day transportation.
- Revisit this checklist and record all objects to be brought for the wedding event.
- Transport everything you need (decorations, guestbook, programmes, text for ceremony readings) to the venue, if you have access to the site early.
- Provide all participants of the wedding party with particulars of event timelines.
- Provide all service providers with details of event timelines.
- Deliver welcome basket.
- Make sure all your outfits are placed in the venue with the help of your wedding day assistant.
- Rehearse for your sangeet.
- Remind yourself to enjoy the day as it's your wedding.
- Make sure you get plenty to eat and drink a lot of water. You don't want to faint.
- Take a bath, drink some warm milk (or whatever works) to get ready for sleep.
- Get to bed at a reasonable hour (if possible).
- Get plenty of rest before the big day!

WEDDING DAY
- Start your day by exercising, get a massage, meditate, pray or do something equally energising yet relaxing.

- Eat a carbohydrate-plus-protein meal but don't overdo the caffeine.
- Show up on time for hair and make-up appointments.
- Get dressed (remember to use the bathroom first).
- Give yourself plenty of time to get ready.
- Take a look at yourself in the mirror and smile.
- Spend a moment alone to calm down before the ceremony.
- Give your parents hugs before everything gets too crazy.
- Relax and enjoy your wedding day.

Post-wedding Day

- Arrange for transport of gifts.
- Make sure all vendor bills have been paid in full (for exceptional service, you may want to send a small gift or send a thank you letter, which vendors can use as a letter of recommendation for future clients).
- Ensure all the rentals have been returned.
- If you haven't already, give gifts to your parents to thank them for their help and support.

After You Come Back from Your Honeymoon

- Arrange for your bridal outfits to be cleaned and preserved.
- Upload pictures and share with family and friends.
- If you choose to do so: Do all the paperwork to change your name and arrange to combine finances, insurance policies, etc.
- Change name and address on credit cards, driving licence, etc.

Checklist—Six Months to Go

- What's your wedding-day vision? Start deciding now on the formality, style and theme (if you're having one).
- Set wedding priorities—make a list of the elements most important to you. This will help you decide on a date, budget your expenses and delegate tasks.
- Get organised! Find a system that works for you (binder, folder, book, etc.) to keep notes, brochures, checklists, menus and other printed materials.

- The B-word already? Yes, it's time to talk budgets. Talk about it together first, then if your parents (or other generous souls) wish to contribute, discuss with them who's paying for what.
- Establish how the expenses would be divided between groom and bride.
- Consult a priest/pandit and discuss a wedding date. Get more than one option for the date, if possible. In the next month or so, you should determine who your most important vendors will be and finalise the wedding date with them and with your close family members before confirming it.
- Research and make a list of wedding planners; also start thinking about how your friends, family and wedding party can help out. If people offer their services, don't be afraid to delegate, nicely.
- If your parents haven't met yet, plan to get them together for the first time.
- Think about the events and the number of days you want to spread it to.
- Meet the shortlisted wedding planners.
- Draw up a preliminary guest list with input from both sides. Think of it as a wish list, and then narrow it down to a close idea of final number based on your budget.
- Edit the guest list.
- Draw up a first draft guest list for the various functions.
- Shortlist the venues for wedding and other functions
- Check on availability of the venues for the required dates.
- Research and make a list of caterers.
- Research and make a list of decorators.
- Research and make a list of photographers.
- Research and make a list of DJs and any other entertainers.
- Figure out unpreventable factors that could impact your chosen wedding calendar day (e.g. weather, elections and so forth).

Five Months

- Finalise how many functions you need to organise and set their dates and time.
- Consider your budget and decide the size of the wedding.
- Allocate responsibilities between both families.
- Finalise your wedding planner (if you decide to have one) and ask her to draft a written contract with service and payment terms.
- Thoroughly read the contract with the wedding planner, sign and preserve your copy.
- Visit possible venues to discuss their availability and cost.
- If you see a great reception or ceremony site that's available on your chosen date and within your budget, book it now. (If any one vendor is a higher priority for you than the site, make sure he is free before reserving a location.)
- Look through books, magazines and websites for wedding lehenga/sari/dress ideas.
- Meet shortlisted caterers and go for food tasting.
- Meet shortlisted wedding photographers, see their portfolio and list out what they have to offer.
- Meet shortlisted decorators and go through your wedding day vision with them.
- Meet the entertainers or speak with them to understand their services.
- Select or create save-the-date cards.
- Obtain or renew your passport for the honeymoon, if you plan to travel abroad.

Four Months

- Finalise your guest list; inform family and friends that may need to travel.
- Send save-the-date cards, especially required in case of a destination wedding.
- Organise a system to record payments completed as well as the person who made the transaction.
- Book the venue for the wedding and other ceremonies.

- Thoroughly read the contract with the venue manager, sign and preserve your copy.
- Finalise your caterer and ask him to draft a written contract with service and payment terms.
- Thoroughly read the contract with the caterer, sign and preserve your copy.
- Finalise your photographer and ask him to draft a written contract with service and payment terms.
- Thoroughly read the contract with the photographer, sign and preserve your copy
- Finalise your decorator and ask him to draft a written contract with service and payment terms.
- Thoroughly read the contract with the decorator, sign and preserve your copy.
- Finalise your DJ/entertainers and ask them to draft a written contract with service and payment terms.
- Thoroughly read the contract with the DJ/entertainers, sign and preserve your copy.
- Find out about pre-wedding bridal beauty packages and compare the rates and services.
- Start looking out for wedding invites and other stationery.
- Look out for bridal jewellery.
- Buy silverware needed for gifting and trousseau.
- Buy gifts for groom's family.
- Start your trousseau shopping.
- Visualise what you want to wear for all your events.
- Visit your favourite designer stores to look at wedding outfits for all the wedding events.
- Research and make a list of make-up artists and hair stylists.
- Schedule appointments and meet with shortlisted make-up artists and hair stylists.
- Finalise and book the make-up artist and hair stylist that suits your requirement the most.
- Research and make a list of henna/mehendi artists.

- Go through the work of the mehendi artists and select the one you like.
- Finalise and book the henna/mehendi artist that suits your requirement the most.
- Pick up the engagement rings.
- Research on your honeymoon options.
- Shortlist preferred destinations.
- Get quotes and itinerary of the destinations from preferred travel agencies.

THREE MONTHS
- Create your wedding website.
- Create online wedding invites.
- Finalise invitee list and obtain invitation mail addresses.
- Select the wedding invitation cards and related stationery.
- Finalise your wedding invites content.
- Review and approve proofs of wedding invitations and stationery.
- Place an order to get the wedding stationery printed.
- Create hotel information cards and maps to include with your wedding invitations.
- Decide on a probable menu with the caterer for all your functions.
- Book the pandit for the wedding.
- Visit your pandit to finalise details for all the functions.
- Browse through all the possible floral and decor arrangements
- Book your wedding decor arrangements (confirm your colour theme, flowers, mandaps, etc.).
- Figure out all your music and entertainment needs.
- Meet with the photographer and videographer—advise them on what you want on the day (different photographic styles— give them a run down on what the days will be like so they know what to expect).
- Place an order for your wedding attire.
- Finalise and order outfits for all the occasions.

- Buy your accessories:
  - Shoes
  - Hosiery
  - Jewellery
- Buy any special lingerie required for wedding outfits.
- Decide what style of attire the groom will wear.
- Make sure the groom has the information he needs to buy or reserve his attire.
- Choose attire for your family members as you want to make them feel special.
- Consider and hire a security escort if guests will wear heavy jewellery at the venue.
- Arrange for a bridal portrait or pre-wedding photo-shoot.
- If you plan to have a prenuptial agreement, meet with your attorney to discuss it.
- Purchase a gift for your spouse-to-be.
- Finalise and start with pre-bridal package (in case you decide to opt for one at a spa).
- Start a fitness routine.
- Start a skincare/beauty routine.
- Start looking for or thinking about wedding favours.
- Begin the search for transportation and other rentals.
- Get your engagement ring insured and consider purchasing wedding insurance.
- If you don't have a wedding consultant, ask a friend or relative (but not your parents) to be 'supervisor' (the person to deal with problems) on your wedding day. If you don't have someone in mind, consider hiring a wedding-day organiser.
- Arrange accommodation for out-of-town wedding guests (do this sooner if your wedding falls in peak wedding season).
- Secure parking and/or transportation for your guests at the reception location
- Research things to do in town during their stay.

TWO MONTHS

- Buy or order the groom's wedding attire and accessories.
- Buy all the accessories (shoes/clutches/bangles, etc.) to match each of your outfit to be worn during the wedding events.
- Finalise on welcome baskets/gifts to be given to outstation guests.
- Finalise on what to give as wedding favours.
- Buy or create welcome gifts for out-of-towners (to be waiting for them in their hotel rooms) and/or wedding favours.
- Appoint a choreographer from your family or hire a professional and discuss the possible ways to perform at the sangeet.
- Finalise all songs for sangeet dance and start practising.
- Book sweets or mithai for your functions.
- Book any other party rentals you may require for all your functions—for example chairs, tables, etc.
- Order your wedding cake.
- Collect your wedding invites.
- Determine the method of addressing wedding invitations and hire a calligrapher, if applicable.
- Address the invites and get them ready to be mailed.
- Mail out your overseas invites.
- Meet with (or call) vendors to finalise arrangements (caterer, florists, musical performers and so on).
- Compile a list of all your wedding vendors (with phone numbers) to ensure a stress-free wedding.
- Compile a probable menu for all the events.
- Reserve a room for your wedding night.
- Schedule activities for out-of-town visitors both before and after the wedding.
- Book an appointment for trial make-up and hairstyling at least eight weeks prior to the wedding.
- Finalise honeymoon plans/itinerary and apply for the required visa, if travelling abroad.

- Make a list of the things/clothes required for your honeymoon and shop accordingly.
- Purchase honeymoon clothing, luggage and accessories.

ONE MONTH

- Assign a friend or family member to be your 'wedding assistant' for the day of your wedding to help with anything and everything. Take this person for all your trials (hair/make-up/dress).
- Finish shopping for your trousseau (even if it's just one new nightgown).
- Choose and purchase presents for wedding helpers.
- Confirm all your floral and decor arrangements.
- Confirm all your music and entertainment needed for your functions.
- Confirm music selections—playlist with musicians/DJ for all the events.
- Arrange transportation/entry ideas for bride and groom to the venue.
- Book wedding transportation together with decoration for wedding vehicle and wedding party entourage.
- Confirm all final payment amounts with your vendors (including pandit), as well as date, time, location and so on.
- Discuss the details of your wedding ceremony with your pandit, procure all the needed puja articles.
- Start rehearsals for your sangeet.
- Think about bleaching or cleansing your teeth.
- Go for a final trial of your wedding outfits.
- Go in for a dry run with the professional make-up artist and hair stylist to determine your wedding day look.
- Mail wedding invitations and/or email e-invites (six weeks prior to wedding).
- Keep track of all wedding invites and RSVP. The same list can be used to track gifts obtained and send thank you messages.
- Finish packing for your honeymoon.
- Sign your prenuptial agreement, if applicable.

- Confirm honeymoon travel arrangements (flight, hotel, rental car and so on).
- Arrange for transportation from home or hotel to the airport for your honeymoon.
- Get traveller's cheques.
- Make arrangements for the care of pets and plants while on honeymoon.

TWO–THREE WEEKS

- Make appointments for you and your groom to get manicures, pedicures, massages, spa treatments, etc. the week before your wedding. (do this even earlier if you're getting married during a busy month)
- Determine the placement or distribution of programmes at the ceremony venue.
- Arrange for preparation, storage and break areas for musicians/ DJ at the reception venue.
- Determine seating arrangements for guests.
- If you had coloured your hair previously, make an appointment for a touch-up the week before your wedding.
- Have your outfits picked up or delivered to you.
- Have groom's wear fitted and picked up.
- Finalise the menu with the caterer for each event.
- Finalise details with wedding photographer and videographer, determining arrival times at each function.
- Arrange for preparation/storage area for photographer and videographer at each venue.
- Confirm all transportation needs.
- Confirm with family and friends who is doing what on the days (helps if you give them a list).
- Create day plans for all your functions informing when and where things are happening.
- Go over song lists and requests with your band or DJ (For sangeet set a meeting of the DJ with your choreographer).
- Get in touch with invitees who have not replied and finalise staying arrangements.

- Confirm hotel arrangements for out-of-town guests.
- Confirm when final payments need to be made to vendors.
- Start packing for your wedding/wedding week—pack each outfit, with all matching accessories separately for each event and put a sticker on it, marking the event so that you have a relaxed wedding week.
- Write out a schedule outlining the order of events (with specified times) for your wedding day. (If you have a consultant, wedding day organiser or delegated 'supervisor', let her do this.) Give a copy to your fiancé and all involved parties.
- Provide your service vendors a version of the comprehensive timeline.
- Confirm all arrival times with vendors.
- Finish and print ceremony programmes.
- Give final count of guests to the caterer.
- Supply your wedding photographer a summary of particular photos you want captured.
- Provide your videographer a summary of special persons or events you would like included in the video clips.
- Make sure everybody knows their roles/performances for the sangeet.
- Get ready your wedding site road-guide boards and gift storage containers.
- Begin breaking in wedding shoes.
- Pack for wedding night.
- Put together a bridal emergency kit for your wedding.

One Week
- Pre-wedding parties begin (bachelor and bachelorette party).
- Visit your beautician for facials, waxing, etc.
- Get your manicure and pedicure.
- Write any cheques that are required for the wedding day—put them in separate labelled envelopes.
- Confirm all bookings and check if things are going as per planned.

Appoint three or four persons (preferably educated and well-mannered security guards) and assign them the following responsibilities:

- Maintain a record of all gifts received during the wedding.
- Make sure that bride and groom's outfit, jewellery, presents, all rented items and other items are safe.
- Look out for suspicious people.
- Make sure that guests do not face any problem.
- Take care of all the kids. Keep them away from electrical appliances, heaters, burners, etc.
- Transport gifts from the ceremony site to the bride's suite or car.
- Make sure that everything is running smoothly, and in case of a mishap or any problem, contact the event manager.
- Switch on generators during a power failure.
- Use fire extinguishers, in case of fire.
- Handle the entire security of the wedding

Delegate. Decide what each member of the wedding party is responsible for on the wedding day, write it on a note card, and be sure to thank them.

- Arrange for a trustworthy person to help you pay the service providers on the special day.
- Designate someone to return rental materials after the wedding party.
- Designate someone to place wedding site road-guide boards at specific junctions.
- Designate someone to coordinate reception food and beverage layout and receipt with the caterer on the wedding day.
- Designate someone to coordinate reception site and stage performances—to manage MC, DJ, entertainers, site lighting, etc.
- Touch base with the 'supervisor' you asked to be 'the person to deal with problems' on your wedding day (if you don't have a wedding planner).
- Get cash ready for tipping and emergencies and give it to the designated 'payment person'.

- Make arrangements for your wedding gifts to be brought to your 'new' home.
- Revisit the wedding schedule.
- Present the configuration of the wedding reception to your caterer and wedding reception manager.
- Provide the final number of guests to the caterer and reception manager.
- Communicate final changes to your service vendors.
- Make sure all puja items are in place.
- Get 'welcome baskets' for outstation guests to hotels; arrange for them to be delivered to the appropriate rooms before guests arrive.
- Having an outdoor wedding? Check weather forecast (do you have a rain plan?), treat area for ants and other bugs if necessary.
- Familiarise yourself with each other's guest lists—this makes it easier to greet everyone during the reception.
- Do final costume fittings to ensure your garment is all set and ideal.
- Have a trial run for your sangeet.
- Leave a copy of your honeymoon itinerary with someone, in case of emergency.
- Make sure honeymoon airline tickets, itinerary, passports and so forth are all in one won't-forget-them place.
- Get your honeymoon bags to wherever you need them to be—your hotel room or the trunk of your car, for example.

ONE DAY BEFORE THE START OF WEDDING FUNCTIONS
- Confirm wedding-day transportation.
- Revisit this checklist and record all objects to be brought for the wedding event.
- Transport everything you need (decorations, guestbook, programmes, text for ceremony readings) to the venue, if you have access to the site early.
- Provide all participants of the wedding party with particulars of event timelines.

- Provide all service providers with details of event timelines.
- Deliver welcome basket.
- Make sure all your outfits are placed in the venue with the help of your wedding day assistant.
- Rehearse for your sangeet.
- Remind yourself to enjoy the day as it's your wedding.
- Make sure you get plenty to eat and drink a lot of water. You don't want to faint.
- Take a bath, drink some warm milk (or whatever works) to get ready for sleep.
- Get to bed at a reasonable hour (if possible).
- Get plenty of rest before the big day!

Wedding Day
- Start your day by exercising, get a massage, meditate, pray or do something equally energising, yet relaxing.
- Eat a carbohydrate-plus-protein meal but don't overdo the caffeine.
- Show up on time for hair and make-up appointments.
- Get dressed (remember to use the bathroom first).
- Give yourself plenty of time to get ready.
- Take a look at yourself in the mirror and smile.
- Spend a moment alone to calm down before the ceremony.
- Give your parents hugs before everything gets too crazy.
- Relax and enjoy your wedding day.

Post-wedding Day
- Arrange for transport of gifts.
- Make sure all vendor bills have been paid in full (for exceptional service, you may want to send a small gift or send a thank-you letter, which vendors can use as a letter of recommendation for future clients).
- Ensure all the rentals have been returned.
- If you haven't already, give gifts to your parents to thank them for their help and support.

After You Come Back from Your Honeymoon

- Arrange for your bridal outfits to be cleaned and preserved.
- Upload pictures and share with family and friends.
- If you choose to do so: Do all the paperwork to change your name and arranging to combine finances, insurance policies, etc.
- Change name and address on credit cards, driving licence, etc.

Your Emergency Bridal Kit Checklist

Stay ahead of any wedding day mishaps by putting together an emergency kit that you can keep close at hand throughout your wedding.

Basic

- Scotch tape
- Pad and pencil
- Scissors
- Earring backs
- Needle and thread (sewing kit)
- Moist towelettes
- Camera
- Extra batteries
- Safety pins
- Stain remover
- Fevikwik
- Tissues
- Wrinkle remover
- Drinking straw (to keep lipstick in place)
- Chocolate/candy bar

Beauty

- Hairpins
- Brush and comb
- Make-up kit (touch-ups for make-up)
- Lip gloss/balm
- Nail glue
- Nail polish (the colour you are wearing)
- Clear nail polish

- Nail polish remover pads
- Nail clipper
- Cotton swabs/buds
- Tweezers
- Pocket mirror

Personal Care

- Toothbrush and toothpaste
- Mouthwash/breath mints
- Tylenol/aspirin
- Contact lens solution (if needed)
- Antacid
- Adhesive bandages
- Tampons/sanitary napkins
- Disposable razor
- Mini body lotion
- Insect repellant
- Oil absorbing sheets
- Water

Bridal Make-up Kit

External ornamentation is necessary but it is equally important (sometimes more important) to indulge in pre-wedding grooming sessions that show their effect only gradually.

You may have hired the best make-up artist in town to do your bridal makeover. You may have also chosen the most celebrated hairstylist for the gorgeous updo at your wedding. But beauty emergencies may strike at any time. Be a smart bride; keep an emergency bridal beauty kit handy with the person assisting you for the day.

Concealer: Your face sure looks impeccable at the beginning of the evening. But as the hours stretch, signs of fatigue, some irritation (god forbid!) or a minor flaw over the neck might appear. A concealer will save all these troubles. A little dab and you are set to go for another long session.

Blush: Probably, the first to wear out, blush adds a tint of rosy colour to your cheeks.

Mascara: Light up your eyes with a generous dose of mascara. For obvious reasons, your choice should be a waterproof one to get you through all the emotional moments. Brush up your beautiful lashes, time and again, to floor the guests and your man.

Eyeliner: A must-have in every beauty kit. Ask your friends to caution you, if they notice any fade in the colour. A coat or two after every few hours will make sure that the hard work by the make-up artist remains intact throughout the wedding.

Lipstick: Keep the lipstick and lip gloss handy so that your dainty lips remain hydrated and you look absolutely perfect. After all, these lips would be the focus of every smiling photograph.

Hair spray: Your hairstylist must have spent hours to get that apt look. But a few hours later, a few tricky strands may go astray. With a hair spray in your kit, there's no need to worry. Just a few sprays during your occasional washroom trips will work it well.

Body spray/perfume: Is there any bride who wouldn't want to smell nice and feel fresh throughout her wedding? Everyone starts out well but a few odd hours later, strains of exhaustion might act as a dampener. In moments like these, your trusted bottle of perfume/body spray is the best bet.

Blotting paper: Often overlooked and ignored, a small pack of blotting paper can go a long way in keeping your wedding look prim and proper. Any kind of make-up blooper can be fixed by this tiny piece. Excess sweat or messy eyeliner, every faux pas can be managed.

Wishing you the very best for a joyful, memorable and well-managed wedding—and a happy married life thereafter!

Bibliography

1. www.beforetheknot.com
2. www.bigindianwedding.com
3. www.bollywoodshaadis.com
4. www.bridalguide.com
5. www.bridalmusings.com
6. www.bridalmusings.com
7. www.brides.com
8. www.indianweddingsite.com
9. www.marthastewartweddings.com
10. www.myshaadi.in
11. www.perfectweddingguide.com
12. www.rediff.com/Occasionz Unlimited and Mary Fernandez, Mumbai
13. www.shaadi.com
14. www.stayhitched.com
15. www.thebigfatindianwedding.com
16. www.theknot.com
17. www.theunrealbride.wordpress.com
18. www.weddingsforaliving.com
19. www.weddingsutra.com
20. www.wedmegood.com